THE COMPLEAT NEVADA TRAVELER

THE COMPLEAT

NEVADA TRAVELER

A GUIDE TO THE STATE
By David W. Toll

UNIVERSITY OF NEVADA PRESS
RENO, NEVADA
1976

Library of Congress Cataloging in Publication Data

Toll, David W
  The compleat Nevada traveler.

  Includes index.
  1. Nevada—Description and travel—1951- —
Guide-books. I. Title.
F839.3.T64   917.93'04'3   76-22647
ISBN 0-87417-045-1

To all the dozens of people
who helped with this book
the author is truly grateful.
Your suggestions with re-
gard to future editions will
be welcomed.

University of Nevada Press, Reno, Nevada 89557
Printed in the United States of America
Book design by William H. Snyder
Cover design by John Patrick Sullivan

This book is for
SAM, SARAH, MASON, AND TINA,
and for all of Nevada's children
in the hope that the Nevada they inherit
will be as splendidly beautiful
and unspoiled as ours.

CONTENTS

SPECIAL INFORMATION

FOREWORD

The Compleat Nevada Traveler is just what the title says. The first-time visitor, the many-times visitor, and even the long-time resident will find here a guide to places he never dreamed existed. From burning deserts to mountain meadows, from the dazzling neon of Las Vegas and Reno to authentic frontier communities and crumbling ghost towns, the traveler will find a fresh itinerary.

Author David Toll has divided the State of Nevada into four roughly-defined regions — mining country, Big Bonanza country, cattle country and Mormon country. In the immense diversity that makes up Nevada, each region has its own particular identity and history. Included in detail are the outdoor recreation possibilities in national and state parks, campgrounds, and ski areas.

The Compleat Nevada Traveler is not the usual guidebook. The author has captured the mood and beauty of the Nevada landscape, the serious and humorous sidelights of history, scandalous moments and great moments — all in a style of writing that will delight the reader.

MINING COUNTRY

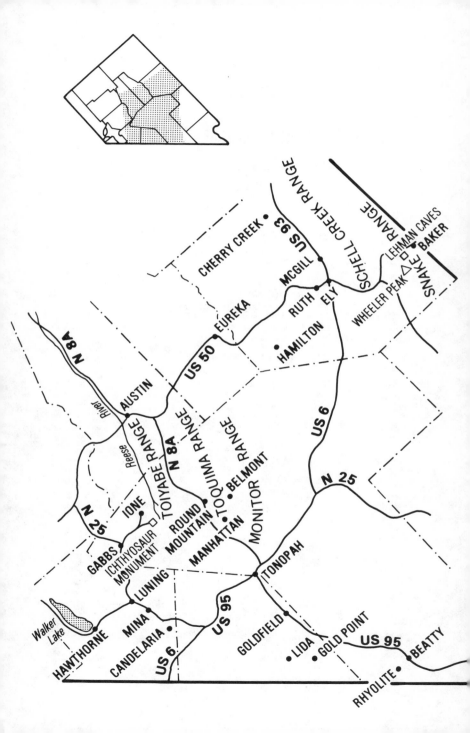

The mountains of central Nevada are like sleeping women, sprawled languorously across every horizon. They are not pretty mountains. They have been scuffed and worn too long by desert winds, and their skirts are stained with the dried mud of long-vanished inland seas. Even the primitive elegance of a forested crest is denied to all but a few of them, and they make do with threadbare patchworks of juniper and piñon pines draped across their summits. And yet the serene, infinitely feminine presence of these rumpled ranges is mysteriously compelling: their smooth, slumbrous forms shade to blue, to purple, to windowglass gray as they recede, rank upon rank, into the distances. In the great central heartland of Nevada, more than fifty thousand square miles, there are only four communities with as many as a thousand citizens each, and the mountains sleep around them undisturbed.

A century ago it was different. Gangs of miners, working in round-the-clock shifts, swarmed into those mountains to tunnel deep into the hips and ribs and rumps of them and plunder them of silver and gold. Those were the glory years, when bustling wagon roads were switchbacks gouged out of mountainsides to connect thriving, rawboned cities near the summits with dusty thoroughfares scratched across the windy flats below. Today only the husks of these cities remain — the few ghosts and almost-ghosts that have not vanished utterly.

Even before the Comstock Lode had been wholly claimed, before Virginia City and Gold Hill were much more than haphazard hillside gatherings of brush-roofed dugouts and unchinked lean-tos, prospectors trailed out across the unexplored vastnesses of Nevada, hurried along by the promise of bigger strikes to come. And they found them. None richer than the Comstock, it is true, but big strikes that made fortunes, though seldom enough for the men who uncovered them.

Some strikes were made by canny men who knew what to look for, and where. But more often prospectors stumbled across their discoveries accidentally, while tracking game or strayed livestock. Occasionally an Indian led an eager prospector to an outcrop of heavy rock in return for the promise of blankets, or a horse, or clothing, and occasionally these promises were kept.

One small party of men, striking south from Virginia City in the summer of 1860, found quartz ledges striped with silver and gold as they sought water for their animals. Thus, the mining camp of Aurora came to be.

A Paiute led two Virginia City men to Buena Vista Canyon on the east flank of the Humboldt Range in the spring of the following year. Samples from the ledge of silver ore assayed as high as $4,000 to the ton. Thus, Unionville.

In 1862 an employee of the Overland Mail Company searching Pony Canyon for strayed horses found himself clambering over exposed veins of silver and gold. When assays demonstrated values as high as $7,000 a ton, Austin burst into being.

From these rich, rough-edged camps prospectors again fanned out into the deserts and mountains, finding precious metals seemingly everywhere. Yankee Blade, Amador, Ravenswood, Canyon City, Clinton, Kingston, Guadalajara — all of them were flourishing camps, if only briefly, and all were within a day's travel from Austin. Star City, Dun Glen, Washington, Talapoosa, La Plata, Como, Trinity, Candelaria, Prince Royal, Eureka, Arabia, Pine Grove — the list of mining camps and milling towns bursting into feverish, fitful existence in the 1860s contains hundreds of names, few of them even dimly remembered today by any except scholars and near neighbors: Dolly Varden, Mineral Hill, Buel, Sprucemont, Rockland, Spring City, Columbia, Torreytown.

Exploration and discovery continued into the seventies: Poker Brown, Vanderbilt, Cornucopia, Queen City — but the seventies were more remarkable as years of consolidation and improvement. Small claims were combined, huge investments made in machinery and technique. Tiny anthill workings plagued by violence and lawlessness grew into respectable towns, scrub towns swelled to become substantial cities. Shafts and tunnels stabbed deep into the guts of the mountains and new foothills were built of the ore dragged out.

And just as there is a certain sameness to the upland desert landscapes of central Nevada, there is a sameness, too, to the histories of settlements established there.

Each began with a few men, or a man alone, breaking rock away from where he found it poking up through the dry skin of the earth, stuffing it into pockets and knapsacks, and piling cairns to mark off claims high in the throat of a nameless canyon. And then he raced to record his claims with the mining district and assay the ore.

If the strike didn't die away to nothing with the assay report, and many did, the men returned to their find to await the rush following close behind them. Every threadbare adventurer, every loosely tethered mining man for a hundred miles around who heard the news struggled to put together a pack and hot-foot it to the "mines," still little more than glorified gopher holes bitten into the brushy hillside. They scrambled in a frenzy to find promising ground as yet unclaimed; failing that, they claimed barren dirt as near as possible to the richest holes. They pitched tents, roofed dugouts with brush, propped up lean-tos, broke out picks, shovels, single jacks, and drills and set to work.

If the camp didn't die of disillusionment after a few weeks of feverish effort, and many did — if some promise of treasure, no matter how false, fleeting, or illusory still remained — small-time entrepreneurs began to make their appearance in the camp. A man unloaded a rump-sprung wagon, tacked together a wooden floor, slapped up rough-sawed wooden sides, covered the framework with a patched and mildewed canvas tarp, and hung a sign hand-painted on the spot: *Groceries*. Another tent enclosed a cast-iron cookstove: *Bakery, Fresh Bread, Pies*. A third tent carried the shaky legend, *Cafe*, and a fourth, a large one erected on a cleared and level patch of ground announced *Lodging*. And saloons. Every second business was a saloon.

If the village didn't die of economic paralysis, and many did, if enough ore was getting, somehow, to a mill, somewhere, to maintain a trickle of cash and a torrent of optimism, a somewhat better-upholstered class of entrepreneurs began to arrive: gamblers and prostitutes scenting a gamy whiff of ready cash across miles of desolate wilderness, real estate promoters, and mining stock speculators. The latter were not deeply interested in the local money, they had their glittering eyes fixed on the pickings far beyond the horizon. They platted townsites well away from any rich ground, and bought up mining claims from paper millionaires for a song. The honest speculators bought rich ground; the others bought whatever they could get. As if by magic teamsters whipped their struggling animals into camp and began unloading a press and racks of type: the camp had a newspaper to trumpet its miraculous richness far and wide. A stage line established a regular schedule to link the camp with established communities nearby. The main street extended a hundred yards from end to end, and several hundred men had settled in with more arriving every day. Each of them had something to sell, if only his labor.

If the settlement didn't die then, if the mines continued to show promise of veins buttered with gold or black with silver, bullwhackers appeared in the low desert distances inching along the valley floor with immense loads of machinery: hoists and stamps and crushers. Permanent buildings of planed lumber, even of brick and dressed stone, began to rise along the business street. If the mines were earnestly in production some of the buildings towered as tall as three stories.

Already the character of the place had changed substantially. It was still a rough town, still had few women and children — who were careful to avoid certain sections of town — but it was no longer a free-for-all. The will-o'-the-wisp prospectors who had first rushed to the place had by now sold their claims and moved on to prowl in other lonesome canyons; those who had no claims to sell moved anyhow, or were transformed reluctantly, usually unsuccessfully, into wage-earning miners working a regular shift under a steady superintendent. Churches were built, a Chamber of Commerce formed, fraternal lodges chartered — formalizing influences of every sort proliferated.

If the town didn't die then, if the miners deep underground continued to drift into rich rock, the combination of self-conscious municipal pride and the desolate social and physical environments prompted the importation of culture. Lecturers, musicians, and repertory troupes followed one another in the halls. A school was built and staffed. A baseball team was formed. If a railroad could be lured by the prospect of a profitable long-term freight business, townspeople contributed to its construction. A telegraph line was stapled to the runty trees and extended over the hilltops to join the main line, streets were illuminated, a movement was drafted among the responsible business leaders to snatch the county seat away from an enfeebled rival, a hotel was built with fireplaces in every room —

And then the town died. Just died.

The veins pinched out six, eight, twelve hundred feet underground, and just as a tree dies when its roots no longer provide nourishment, the city died with the failure of the mines. Slowly at first, and then with a surprising suddenness.

Miners and millworkers were laid off their jobs, and after a few uneasy days or weeks they moved away, leaving their lace window curtains to flutter in the dry desert breeze. With their departure the business district shriveled, and the newspaper, deprived of readership and advertisers, but wheezing optimism to the last, coughed up one small, final edition and was loaded unceremoniously into a wagon to reappear in some new scatter of tents. The whores went, and the gamblers. The mills were dismantled, the railroad pried up its rails and abandoned the roadbed.

A few stayed, a few always did; men who had hurried too often to the next bonanza. They rummaged in leased mines to scrape out a living, and tore down abandoned houses and burned the lumber in their woodstoves in winter.

Despite the presence of these old men the sagebrush grew back in the streets and the buildings along the main street began to sag. And burn. A careless fire, a gust of wind, a single spark on a warping roof, and what was once home to several thousand people became a black patch in a canyon floor, a handful of swooning structures left intact.

Mining ebbed in the eighties. A few new strikes were made, and a few new towns began their doomed lives, but for the most part the eighties in Nevada were a time of petering out. Even the inexhaustible mines of the Comstock Lode, which had produced bonanza after bonanza, were clearly giving out. The nineties were worse. By 1900 only forty thousand people remained in the state.

And then by God if it didn't start all over again. Jim Butler was shanking it across the desert from the county seat at Belmont toward the dwindling camp of Klondyke in May, 1900, when he found some interesting rock. The rock assayed at $50 to $600 to the ton, mostly silver, and a rush brought a population of a thousand, including photographers and reporters for the national press. Their colorful representations of mining camp life — and the continuing discovery of rich deposits in the district — brought thousands more adventurers. The Tonopah strike fanned the enthusiasm of prosectors once again, and soon rich finds were made at Goldfield, Kawich, Rawhide, Pioneer, Rhyolite, Transvaal, Bullfrog, Seven Troughs, Mazuma, Midas, Wonder, and a hundred other remote locations on the Nevada landscape.

At Royston, $20,000 in silver was dragged up from a shaft only twenty-four feet deep. At Weepah, ore was uncovered worth a reported $70,000 to the ton. At Wahmonie, prospectors came jouncing across the desert in a fleet of automobiles and fifteen hundred of them built a town in two months. At Monarch, the Reverend Benjamin Blanchard promoted a valise-full of dubious assay reports into a community of 2,400 lots surrounded by "ranch sites" and "mining claims" before departing with $50,000 of sucker money and leaving $73,000 in unpaid bills behind him. None of these particular communities survived a single season.

Still, a number of these twentieth-century mining camps were founded on solid ground. Tonopah and Goldfield became two of the nation's great gold and silver producers and grew to be the principal cities of the state. Rhyolite had attracted three railroads to itself before it faltered and failed. At Ely, not far from the Utah boundary, a relatively small precious-metals district became an important source of copper, and is still producing. Mining continued on a small scale throughout the state through the dismal Depression years; even the Comstock was still producing small amounts of gold and silver ore on the eve of World War II.

During the war Nevada's gold and silver mines were ordered closed by the War Production Board. Copper assumed extreme importance, and more exotic minerals such as tungsten, barium, and mercury were profitably produced.

Few gold or silver mines could afford to reopen after the war. The years of disuse had made many of them unsafe without extensive (and expensive) retimbering. Labor costs had risen, but the price of gold had not. Mine owners did their annual assessment work and waited. Most of them are waiting still.

Yet Nevada now has the second most productive gold mine in the United States within its borders, and a more recent operation, on the site of a mine first worked in the 1860s, will rank close behind it. No greater contrast can be imagined than that between the modern gold mines and their nineteenth-century ancestors.

No split-seamed, raggedly-elbowed prospectors make the mining strikes these days; it is done by engineers in suits and ties in an air-conditioned corporate headquarters building in New York, or Houston, or Los Angeles. They do it not by studying ore samples, weighty with riches, but the pages of government reports, and sending core-drilling teams to test their conclusions. These teams may drill for more than a year, taking assays as they go, to compile a three-dimensional map of the hidden ore deposits showing width, breadth, thickness, and richness of ore

Copper mining near Ely

beneath great sections of ground. Only after ensuring themselves that a mineral deposit is large enough, rich enough, accessible enough, and workable enough do the executives of a modern major mining corporation commit themselves to development.

The cost of prolonged exploration is high, often ranging into six and seven figures. The cost of development of the Carlin Gold Mine was more than $8 million; and the Du Val copper mines near Battle Mountain required $22.5 million to get into production. With stakes that high, there can be no mistake. Especially since the ore is marginal. At the Carlin Gold Mine there is no gold visible in the ore at all; it is only detectable in the assay. The mill had to be built with equipment husky enough to process thousands of tons of ore daily, yet delicate enough to recover gold particles as small as 0.01 microns, about the equivalent of seventy-five atoms.

No longer does a reduction mill thunder with the beat of giant stamps pulverizing hard rock with smashing hammer blows. No longer does the earth quiver beneath and a pall of dust hang in the air above the building. The mills at Carlin and Cortez are humming factories. From the loading of the ore trucks in the ever-deepening pits through the cleanup of the presses at the other end of the plant, the mills are automated, transistorized, and almost self-regulating.

No tent city sprang up at the Carlin mine, and none will. Company-operated buses bring the nearly 150 employees to work and back from their homes in Elko and Carlin where they live as quietly and unspectacularly as their less glamorously employed neighbors.

Consequently, the new mines have a far greater effect on

Gold mining near Carlin

the economy of the state than they have on its skyline. No brawling new outpost settlements, no burgeoning new cities with brave attempts at elegance to counteract their desolate surroundings. But between 1940 and 1965 there had already been more mineral wealth produced in Nevada than in all the previous years of the state's more romantic history.

The new mines are contributing enormously to the economy of the counties in central Nevada, but they have had little effect, as yet, on the character of the region. There are only a few dozen of them, while the ghosts of the nineteenth century are everywhere. Withered and shabby, these once flourishing cities have survived on a trickle of highway traffic and a dribble of official business as county seats.

And here is one of the ironies about central Nevada: back before the turn of the century, and during the Depression, people were trying everything they could think of to promote that land, to fill it up, get businesses started — anything to bring in a little cash. But they failed. All those square miles stayed as empty as they had always been.

And now, now that California is so overcrowded that a man can't find any solitude there unless he signs up in advance for it, and stands in line to get to it, now these emptinesses of central Nevada are drawing more visitors than they ever did, just because they are so empty.

TOWNS

Austin

171 miles east of Carson City via U.S. 50; 88 miles south of Battle Mountain via Nevada Route 8A. Seat of Lander County. Less than four hundred residents remain in Austin from a peak-year population estimated at more than ten thousand; the mile-long main street has withered to half that length; gaps have appeared in the crowded rows of buildings ascending the steep sides of Pony Canyon. Yet Austin has a dowager's presence:

she may be reduced in circumstances, even raggedy at the elbows, but Austin is still *somebody*.

Founded in 1862 as a consequence of the discovery of silver-bearing quartz ledges showing values as high as $7,000 to the ton, Austin had attracted two thousand residents by the summer of 1863. In its early months, Austin was so isolated and primitive a camp that J. Ross Browne wrote in *Harper's* that "lodgings in a sheep corral had to be paid for at the rate of fifty cents per night in advance," and that "it was a luxury to sit all night by a stove, or to stand against a post behind a six-foot tent. I have heard of men who contrived to get through the coldest part of the season by sleeping when the sun was warm, and running up and down Lander Hill all night; and another man who staved off the pangs of hunger by lying on his back for an hour or so at mealtimes with a quartz-boulder on his stomach."

By 1865 Austin, its population numbering more than five thousand, was Nevada's second largest city, headquarters not only for the prospectors who trekked out in every direction in search of new ore discoveries, but also for the camps which sprang up around the strikes they made. More than sixty mining districts were chartered by Austin-based prospectors in the 1860s and '70s, and more than forty mining camps were settled. In Austin and its immediate environs, more than two thousand mining and milling companies had been incorporated by 1865; many more than there were actual mines or mills. "Of the vast number of mining properties offered for sale in New York," Browne reported, "it is scarcely necessary to say that the great majority are valueless. Every adventurer who possesses the shadow of a claim takes it or sends it east in order that he may realize a fortune." Many of the Austin mining shares were honest offerings, but many were extraordinarily fanciful. Among them was the mine advertised as being within half a mile of a railway, an approximation which stretched the truth nearly a hundred miles, and "within the immediate vicinity" of the rich mines of the Comstock, a two hundred mile exaggeration. The most preposterous fraud in Austin's extensive collection had only indirectly to do with mining.

Austin

The Reese River, which flows north out of the Toiyabe Range to pass the entrance of Pony Canyon on its journey north to the Humboldt River — and the railroad — near Battle Mountain, was one of the few landmarks on the empty map of central Nevada in the 1860s. Shares in the Reese River Navigation Company, formed to freight ore in barges to the railroad, sold briskly to investors who recalled the strategic importance of the Sacramento River traffic to the Mother Lode mines of California fifteen years earlier. Unfortunately for them, the Reese at floodtide has barely the breadth of a man's wrist and the depth of his fingers. Stagecoaches forded it at a full gallop with only the suggestion of a bump, and in the dry season the Reese is even less spectacular.

The Methodist church at Austin, receiving so many mining shares as donations to their building fund, incorporated as the Methodist Mining Company and sold its own shares in other parts of the country. The church building erected with the proceeds was the most opulent in the state.

Austin was the birthplace of what may have been the first national fund-raising campaign when an 1864 municipal election bet was paid off by grocer Reuel Gridley. When Charles Holbrook, the Union candidate, defeated Democrat Dave Buel, Gridley shouldered a fifty-pound sack of self-rising flour decorated with rosettes and small Union flags, and marched the length of Austin's main street, the municipal band right behind him shrieking and thumping its way through a succession of patriotic melodies.

At Clifton, a mile down the canyon, perhaps because of an outpouring of national spirit, perhaps simply to keep a lovely party alive, someone brought out a table and someone else volunteered as auctioneer, and the sack of flour was sold for $350 in gold coin. The purchaser gave the sack back to be auctioned again, and again, and again. By the end of the day, the citizens of Austin had contributed $4,549.80 in gold and silver coin, $24.00 in county scrip, thirty-two city lots, and two-dozen calf-bound ledger books to the Sanitary Fund, which was the Red Cross of its day.

Gridley then took the sack of flour to the Comstock where auctions at Dayton, Silver City, Gold Hill, and Virginia City raised about $25,000 more, Gridley continued on to Sacramento and San Francisco, then took ship for the East with his remarkably productive sack of flour. By the time he returned home to Austin — almost a year after he had carried the sack down the hill from his store — he had auctioned the flour sack to more than ten thousand purchasers and raised more than $100,000 (some authorities say as much as $250,000) for the Sanitary Fund.

Despite Austin's fabulous silver production, and its relative isolation, the town did not attract a railroad until 1879 when construction of the Nevada Central line began at Battle Mountain. A bill had passed the legislature granting Lander County authority to issue bonds in the amount of $200,000 to subsidize the project, but by the time rails were finally being spiked to ties, the deadline for completion of the railroad was only five winter months away. If the railroad failed to reach the Austin city limits within the stipulated time, the subsidy would lapse — and the railroad would fall instantly into bankruptcy. Through blizzards and freezing weather the construction gangs made good progress, but despite every effort they were still a couple of miles short of the entrance to Pony Canyon as the midnight deadline drew near. Unwilling to see the project doomed, the Austin City Council met in emergency session as the work crews labored. A unanimous vote of the Council resulted in a hasty dash out into the desert where a sign reading AUSTIN CITY LIMITS was planted beside the rails with minutes to spare.

But the railroad did not save Austin from the ultimate decline of the mines, and by 1887 Austin had hit bottom. There have been attempts at reviving the mines in subsequent years, and some operations have continued spasmodically and on a small scale, but for most of the past eighty years Austin has been withering quietly away, barely sustained by the driblets of commerce accruing to the county seat and the trickle of traffic afforded by U.S. 50. Most of the mining towns it spawned a century ago have sagged down into the sand, deserted; ranches are its satellites now.

There are good motels in Austin, quiet and clean places, and some not so good; cafes and gas stations, but no doctor. The scarcity of ready cash, the isolation, and the lack of a "Bonanza" television series have combined to deny to Austin the same opportunities for promotion that have made Virginia City so popular a tourist resort. That in itself is one of Austin's principal attractions: it is relatively undiscovered and un-exploited. Some of the principal attractions of the town are listed as follows; plaques have been attached to them by the local chamber of commerce and the Lions Club so that you may take a self-guided tour. Remember, though, that you cannot get the full benefit of a visit to Austin from your car. Townspeople are friendly and willing to help you find your way about.

International Hotel. Near the center of town on the east side of Main Street, the International was originally built in Virginia City. In 1863 the building was dismantled to make room for a successor of larger size and hauled in pieces to Austin where it at once became a favored social center. Its claim to being the oldest hotel in Nevada is a slight exaggeration, but forgiveable if only because it was one of the meeting places of the Sazerac Lying Club, an organization founded in Austin a century ago for the express purpose of swapping tall tales.

Bank of Austin. Operating under a variety of proprietors, banking was conducted continuously in this building from 1861 to 1962, the longest uninterrupted tenancy of its kind in Nevada.

Austin City Hall. Municipal offices were housed on the second floor, police station on the street level, during the seventeen years in which Austin was an incorporated city. The city's official seal (since lost), was embellished with a reproduction of the famous Gridley flour sack and the figure "5,000." It was in this building that the measure was adopted to stretch the city limits north to meet the railroad.

Masonic Lodge & Odd Fellows Building. Built in 1867 to house the solemnities of both fraternal groups, this brick building still serves as their meeting hall.

Reese River Reveille Building. Across the street and a few steps uphill, this was the home of Nevada's oldest newspaper in continuous publication. Founded in 1863, the paper published at least one issue a week from this building until 1968 when it was moved to Tonopah. The paper's longest uninterrupted subscription ran for a record 93.5 years.

Lander County Court House. One street south of Main. Built in 1869 when the original court house had been outgrown, this structure houses the records and offices of county government which are coveted by Battle Mountain to the north. Austin is nothing like the vigorous place she once was, but she is canny enough, so far at any rate, to foil the restless citizens of Battle Mountain in their maneuvering to become the new county seat. The second story balcony once provided local citizens with a convenient place to tether a borrowed riata, the other end of which had been cinched around the neck of a murdering tough.

St. George's Episcopal Church. North side of Main Street. Local legend says St. George's was financed by a single passage of the collection plate after an eloquent Easter sermon in 1877; the church is still used regularly, including the pipe organ brought around the horn and shipped overland from San Francisco. At last notice, open for visitors upon request.

Nevada Central Engine House. Eastern terminal for the "Mules Relief" steam locomotive short line through town from the Nevada Central depot lower down the canyon. So called because mule-drawn cars had operated on the tracks before the introduction of steam.

Gridley Store. East end of town on north side of Main. Located in what was once the separate community of Upper Austin, this small grocery store was the starting point for Gridley's election bet hike with the flour sack. He hefted it downhill a mile and a quarter on the first leg of his journey into fame. Upon his return to Austin in 1865, however, Gridley found that his affairs had been badly managed, and he was bankrupt a few months later. An illness forced him to move to Stockton, California, where he was soon in a destitute condition. A benefit was held for him in Austin and nearly $700 sent to him by his former neighbors. He died in poverty in Paradise, California, in 1870, so completely forgotten that not even the Austin paper mentioned his death.

Methodist Church. On Court Street, a block north of Main. This is the church financed by the sale of Methodist Mining Company shares. Like the mines that formed the basis for its funding, it is padlocked.

Emma Nevada Residence. Two streets north of Main. Born Emma Wixom in a California gold camp in 1859, "Little Wixie" became a citizen of Austin at the age of five. By the time she was eleven the *Reveille* paid tribute to her singing, and upon graduation from high school her father sent her to Mills College in Oakland for voice training. At eighteen she went to Europe for further study, and then began a triumphant concert tour of the Continent. By 1885, when she returned to Austin for a concert during her first U.S. tour, she was an international sensation, singing under the professional name Emma Nevada. She sang at the coronation of King George V of England in 1910.

Stokes Castle. At the lower end of Main take the dirt road south about a quarter of a mile. This architectural curiosity was built in 1897 as the Anson Stokes residence. It is fifty feet square at the base and built three stories high of hand-hewn native granite. First floor housed the kitchen and dining room, second floor an immense living room and bath; bedrooms and another bath were on the third floor, with the roof used as a sun deck. The castle is fenced and locked to prevent injury. From here, arrow signs lead to a scenic overlook of Austin and the Reese River Valley.

Austin's small business district will supply travelers with their basic wants: gasoline, meals, and lodgings. And, yes, there is a historic cemetery, but I'm not going to tell you where it is. Get out of your car and ask someone.

Battle Mountain

88 miles north of Austin via Nevada Route 8A; 53 miles east of Winnemucca, 72 miles west of Elko via Interstate 80. Named to commemorate the 1857 skirmish between a roadbuilding crew

Stokes Castle, near Austin

and a party of Shoshones, the original town of this name was located about ten miles southwest of its present location, at a spot known at that time as Battle Mountain Station. But old Battle Mountain was soon worked out and abandoned, while Battle Mountain Station was augmented by the wholesale migration buildings and all, of the town of Argenta. Faced with the decline of the silver mines at Argenta and the advantageous location of Battle Mountain Station thirteen miles to the west, which served as railhead to the prosperous mines of Austin and the Reese River Valley, Argenta's business community picked itself up in 1870 and reestablished itself as part of Battle Mountain Station.

As the station grew to village size it remained largely dependent upon the trade provided by the railroad and the mines that blossomed and wilted along the slopes and side canyons of the Reese River Valley to the south. Galena, Jersey City, and Lewis were three of Nevada's most promising mining camps in the 1870s and all of them were served from the railhead at the new Battle Mountain, as was Pittsburg in the 1880s and Dean in the 1890s. After the turn of the century the strikes at Hilltop, Bannock, McCoy, and Betty O'Neal all shipped by way of Battle Mountain.

In 1880 the Nevada Central Railroad was completed through the length of the Reese River Valley to the south, connecting Austin with the Central Pacific, and in the following year a short line was built to Lewis. But the Battle Mountain and Lewis lasted less than a year, and the Nevada Central only prospered as long as the mines at Austin operated at full production. By the middle 1930s most of the mines that generated traffic at Battle Mountain had shut down and boarded up, and the NCRR had passed into receivership for the last time.

Battle Mountain's thirty-year snooze by the side of the road ended abruptly in 1967 when the Duval Company invested more than $20 million in the development of large copper ore bodies in the mountains a short distance south. All at once Battle Mountain became a mining boomtown in its own right:

the schools overflowed, the sewer system burst at the seams, the municipal wells began pumping sand, and the cost of policing the town doubled. Things have sorted themselves out since, and the Du Val employees and their families have settled more or less gracefully into the life of the community.

This new economic vigor has renewed long-standing plans to snatch the county seat away from Austin, the almost-ghost far to the south, plans almost certainly forever doomed to failure because of the sentimental affection in which Austin is held in the state legislature, much to the disgust of the Battle Mountaineers.

Most services for travelers are available in the business blocks fronting the highway. Food is adequate and lodgings are fair to good.

Eureka

70 miles east of Austin, 77 miles west of Ely via U.S. 50; 89 miles south of Carlin via Nevada Route 51. Seat of Eureka County. Silver strikes made here in 1864 by prospectors from Austin proved uneconomical to work because of the high lead content of the ores. Reduced profits were realized by shipping the ore to England and Wales for reduction until 1869 when the first of sixteen successful smelters was constructed. Within a decade three mines alone had paid out in dividends more money than had ever been invested in all Eureka County enterprises combined, and Eureka was famous as the "Pittsburgh of the West" because of the black smoke squeezing out of smelter smokestacks to smear the sky and poison the hardy desert vegetation.

Eureka produced more than four times the wealth that Austin did, yet its history is rather prim and staid compared to adventurous Austin. Perhaps it was because the principal product of the mines was lead, rather than silver or gold, and drew a less romantic breed of citizen; perhaps it was because, being richer, Eureka was simply less hysterical.

In any case, Eureka overtook Austin in size and in mining productivity during the middle 1870s when the Eureka &

Palisade Railroad was extended south from the main line of the Central Pacific without the necessity of bulging the city limits to meet it. By 1878, when Austin had already begun its decline, Eureka had a population of about nine thousand and had taken second place among Nevada cities. There were more than a hundred saloons, dozens of gambling houses and bawdy houses, three opera houses, two breweries, five volunteer fire-fighting companies, and two companies of militia as well as the usual complement of doctors, lawyers, merchants, bankers, hotels, newspapers, and other businesses. And fifty mines producing lead, silver, gold, and zinc for the smelters, which were capable of processing more than seven hundred tons of ore a day.

In 1879 the deepest shafts were troubled by water seepage. As flooding became more of a problem, economy measures were taken. One of these was a reduction in the price paid for charcoal at the smelters, a move met by the *carbonari* — members of the predominantly Italian Charcoal Burners' Association — with a boycott. With the smelters shut down for lack of fuel, passions blazed up; threats and counter-threats raged between all parties to the dispute. When the *carbonari* threatened to make charcoal of all of Eureka, a sheriff's posse ambushed a number of them, killing five and wounding more.

Mining production peaked in 1882 and tailed off rapidly after 1885; by 1891 the major mines had been shut down, and production since has been sporadic. Eureka lapsed into the same long snooze that had claimed Austin a decade earlier. Today it is larger than Austin in population — about five hundred — and just as crowded with Victorian buildings and relics of the nineteenth century. The Brown Hotel, formerly the Jackson House, is still taking guests at modest prices in its high-ceilinged rooms.

Visitors to Eureka will have a full day of pleasure wandering through the streets and peering through dusty windows at the vanished glory of the past. Eureka is even farther off the beaten tourist path than Austin, and thus even more ''undiscovered.'' Not much has been formally done to create ''attractions'' for tourists; you will have to scout them out for yourself. Some, like the Farmers and Merchants Bank site, are less remarkable to look at than to know about. When the famous Bank Holiday was declared in 1933, banks were ordered to remain closed at the conclusion of business on a certain day. The Eureka bank obeyed the order by neglecting to conclude its business. It remained open twenty-four hours a day until the Bank Holiday was ended.

Other attractions, like the Eureka tunnels, are utterly unique. Eureka's breweries were located at opposite ends of town. Because the winters here are often heavy with snow and always miserable with cold and winds, tunnels were driven underground from one end of town to the other, to serve the nearly 125 saloons which lay within a block or two of the main street. The breweries made their deliveries through these tunnels, and children used them to get from home to school and back. Nevada governor Reinhold Sadler is said to have had a tunnel connecting his home with his store on the main street.

Much of the old tunneling has collapsed or is unsafe, but if you ask the proprietor of the cafe in the Eureka Hotel, he may get his flashlight and take you back through the kitchen and down into the basement, where the tunnel is still in good condition. Fabulous condition, in fact, complete with an arched-brick chamber reminiscent of a medieval dungeon, which is said to have been used as an opium den in the old days. The fact that Chinatown was located on the slopes behind the hotel near the center of town lends a certain credibility to the story, but it is guaranteed to be the fanciest opium den you are ever likely to visit. When pressed, Eureka folks admit they don't really know why the cavern was built the way it was.

There are nine cemeteries in Eureka, including one that was set aside for smallpox victims. There is an ice cream parlor, a dinner house, several cafes and three hotels, a number of gas stations, seven saloons, a rock and curio shop, and a modern medical clinic. Also note the fine historic architecture.

Eureka's gaunt appearance is doubly misleading. For one thing, many Nevadans consider Eureka the best town in the state, a shade friendlier and easier than the other small communities off the beaten track. For another, there is about $100 million in ore blocked out in sight at the bottom of the shaft of the Ruby Hill Mine west of town. The problem — an ironic problem in this arid land — is water. Early seepage turned into flooding as the shaft was sunk deeper into high-grade ore, and the cost of pumping water out of the deep shaft became prohibitive, since all power is generated locally. The word now, however, is that cheaper power is to be carried by immense transmission lines to Eureka within the foreseeable future, and much of the population is quivering with barely suppressed anticipation.

Already, with tax money derived from the new Carlin gold mine at the far northern end of the county, an $800,000 high school has been built in Eureka. Whether or not the new bonanza materializes, the country around Eureka will continue to provide excellent chukkar hunting, bottle digging, and simply breathing in the cedar-scented air of wide open spaces. Local attitudes pretty much permit camping anywhere you like outside the city limits, but if people continue to leave filth behind them and to loot the occasional empty building, that attitude will certainly change.

By all means ask for the booklet "Eventful Eureka Nevada." It was prepared by someone who knows and loves the old city and who has a fine ear for the folklore of the place. It is free.

Ely
77 miles east of Eureka via U.S. 50; 284 miles north of Las Vegas and 137 miles south of Wells via U.S. 93. Seat of White Pine County. Ely is a bustling town of more than seven thousand (including East Ely), with an abundance of gas stations, motels, cafes, restaurants, grocery stores, and all the necessities of travel. It is also graced by the presence of a chamber of com-

merce of more than ordinary usefulness to the traveler; a stop there will provide excellent and detailed information about every kind of recreation in the area. A small but interesting historical museum is maintained on the premises.

As Nevada towns go, Ely is not old. For several years after its establishment in the late 1870s it existed only as a stagecoach station and post office. By 1888, after Ely had been designated as the seat of White Pine County, it had a population of only two hundred. Most of the region's activity was centered in the surrounding mining towns of Taylor, Ward, Osceola, and Cherry Creek. After the turn of the century, though, the immense copper deposits near Ely began to attract attention away from the district's failed or failing gold and silver mines, and by 1906 a boom had developed in copper.

The Nevada Northern Railway was completed in the fall of that year to connect the copper mines with the Southern Pacific at Cobre. In 1908, when the smelter at McGill went on the line, mineral production leapt to well over $2 million from barely more than $2,000 the year before. By 1917 annual production climbed to nearly $26.5 million. The Kennecott Copper Corporation began acquiring shares of the Ely copper mining companies in 1915; and by 1958 the process of acquisition resulted in control of the region's copper properties.

Today Kennecott employs fifteen hundred persons in the Ely-McGill complex, about half of the total employment in White Pine County. Because U.S. 6, 50, and 93 intersect at Ely, there is a larger than average number of motels and other enterprises serving the traveling public.

The Kennecott influence is felt everywhere. Kennecott's mines are located near Ruth, a company town 8 miles west of Ely, just off U.S. 50. Originally underground mines, the mines are now all open pits, five of them in a six-mile line east and west, from which, each working day, about 80,000 tons of waste dirt and 22,000 tons of ore are taken. The ore goes by rail to the smelter at McGill, 22 miles north, where it is reduced and processed into blister copper. The sixty-pound cakes of metal are freighted north to the main line of the S.P., and the cars return to McGill with coal to fuel the enormous power-generation plant.

Kennecott's headquarters are in Utah, and Ely is more a satrapy of Salt Lake City than of Carson or Reno or Las Vegas. Ely's television comes from Salt Lake City; its wholesalers are located there; the metropolitan paper most often on the news stand is the Salt Lake City *Tribune*.

Highway traffic plays an increasing part in the Ely economy, and the cattle and sheep outfits scattered across miles of open grazing land in every direction are important. But copper is the boss at Ely, and no one forgets it for a minute. Aside from the one-company domination factor, Ely is unexceptional. The Nevada Hotel is the undisputed center of after-dark activity (aside from the brothels near the mouth of Robinson Canyon on the west end of town) offering a routine menu, small gambling casino, and low-budget live entertainment in the cocktail lounge. A small collection of gambling houses is clustered within a few steps of the hotel.

McGill

12 miles north of Ely via U.S. 93. No tourist industry saves McGill from the gothic atmosphere of the company mill town. The enormous smelter on the hillside looms above the town in so brooding a manner that it is positively eerie. The gloom is intensified by a haze of dust raised by the wind from the smelter's waste heaps and by smoke heaving out of two tall chimneys. Despite its almost Transylvanian appearance, McGill is pleasantly treeshaded, offering food, drink, and gasoline to the traveler. A public outdoor pool of majestic proportion is also available during the summer months.

Baker

65 miles east of Ely via U.S. 50 and Nevada Route 73. A tiny settlement at the edge of Lehman Caves National Monument, Baker offers food, gasoline, and lodging to visitors, although the

last time friends visited they fixed their own meals at the small cafe while the proprietors entertained themselves at the bar. Turned out to be a marvelous vacation.

Hawthorne

72 miles south of Fallon, 104 miles northwest of Tonopah via U.S. 95. Founded in 1880 at the south end of Walker Lake as a division point on the now-defunct Carson & Colorado Railroad, Hawthorne became the Mineral County seat in 1910. By the middle twenties Hawthorne was deep in the grip of economic doldrums, but in 1928 a Naval Ammunition Depot was established there, perhaps on the theory that an explosion like the one that had leveled the Lake Denmark, New Jersey, facility in 1926 would take relatively little with it. Hawthorne, if it did not prosper, at least survived the doldrums, and when World War II broke out in Europe, the pace began to quicken. With United States entry into the war, Hawthorne experienced a boom: in 1944 more than seven thousand armed forces and civilian personnel were employed at the arsenal. Hawthorne slowed to a walk after World War II, but was lively during the Korean fighting and the Viet Nam adventure.

Though the ammunition depot continues to provide the town's economic foundation, tourism in recent years has become increasingly important (as everywhere in Nevada). Despite Hawthorne's small supply of historical and architectural distinction, it is a favored recreation destination because of excellent bass and cutthroat trout fishing in Walker Lake, deer and gamebird hunting, and nearby recreational areas in the Sierra Nevada. As for Hawthorne itself, the town offers a full measure of food and lodging, gasoline and groceries, medical and automotive facilities.

Its most interesting landmark is the El Capitan, a hole-in-the-wall that has grown, amoeba-like, to encompass most of two city blocks. A shrewd use of up-to-date promotional techniques, including flights from central and southern California airports in a private fleet of DC-3s, has brought to Hawthorne thousands of happy weekenders who would be hard-pressed to find the place on the map. The "El Cap" has a large restaurant, a medium sized casino with live entertainment, and a small clutch of lesser gambling houses shouldering close around it.

Tonopah

104 miles southeast of Hawthorne, 207 miles northwest of Las Vegas via U.S. 95; 116 miles south of Austin via Nevada Route 8A; 168 miles southwest of Ely via U.S. 6. Nye County seat. Tonopah sprang to life in 1900 following an important silver discovery made by Jim Butler. Butler was an energetic and efficient miner, but he has been described as one of the laziest mining tycoons of all time because of his practice of granting leases to others in order to develop his properties. The lease-holders, working against deadlines, established Tonopah as a major mining bonanza by taking $4 million in ore from Butler's mines and building a substantial city.

Coming as it did when the mining excitement at Nome, Alaska, was tailing off, the Tonopah strike drew a large number of sourdoughs, among them Tex Rickard, Wyatt Earp, and Key Pittman. The Tonopah boom also coincided with the last waning of the Comstock as the center of political and economic influence in Nevada. For more than a generation afterward Tonopah men managed much of the state's affairs. Key Pittman went to the U.S. Senate where he was known as "The Senator from Tonopah" because of his vigorous support of monetary legislation designed to assist the silver mining industry of the West. Tasker Oddie, Jim Butler's attorney, was both a U.S. senator and a Nevada governor. Earp made himself useful as a gambling dealer and "persuader" in local politics; even in his fifties he was not a man to fool with, though the dent he made in Tonopah history is nothing like his previous impact on Tombstone, Arizona.

Two years after its establishment Tonopah was a sprawling city of three thousand people served by stagecoaches, competing newspapers, more than thirty saloons, and a pair of churches. By 1905 it had captured the county seat from failing Belmont; by 1907 Tonopah was a thriving city with five banks, several theaters, luxury hotels offering elevators and steam heat, five newspapers, many of the most impressive residences in Nevada in its extensive residential neighborhoods, and the Big Casino, a dance-hall-and-brothel occupying a square city block in the middle of the sporting district.

Like Austin forty years previously, Tonopah became the headquarters and fitting-out place for hundreds of prospectors whose discoveries helped Tonopah raise Nevada from the economic coma it had been suffering for twenty years and restore the state to its accustomed place on the front pages of the nation's newspapers. Tonopah peaked out in the years leading up to World War I, when the mines averaged $8.5 million a year in production; after that, production continued at a steady but reduced rate until the Depression, and sporadically since. The total production is estimated at something near $150 million, mostly silver.

Tonopah today presents the awkward appearance of a town suspended between destinies. Silver mining has given way to tourism and ranching as the principal economic mainstay, as it has in most of Nevada's surviving boom cities. Still the vision of mines restored to production will not fade from the municipal consciousness. Tonopah was given added vigor in recent years when Howard Hughes based his mining headquarters there. Two dozen mining men did assessment work on claims Hughes bought throughout Nevada. They worked out of an office in Tonopah, and their presence revived the prospecting spirit that sees a bonanza just over the next hill.

There are gas stations and garages, up-to-date motels as well as the historic old Mizpah Hotel, and a surprising number of excellent restaurants. Tonopah's relative distinction in these matters of lodging and food stems from the regular highway traffic along U.S. 95 and from the fact that it is a convenient meeting place for a variety of state fraternal, professional, and business associations. A small but adequate convention center has been constructed.

But as satisfying as this commerce is to Tonopah, it is silver that the old town wants, with three shifts a day in the shafts and half a hundred hammering mills crushing rock all day and all night. Until then, Tonopah will continue to be an amiable, friendly town, but with a distracted, only half-awake air.

Goldfield

25 miles south of Tonopah, 182 miles northwest of Las Vegas via U.S. 95. Esmeralda County seat. Briefly named Grandpa by its enthusiastic founders in 1902, Goldfield was producing $10,000 a day by 1904, and by 1906 was a bigger city than Tonopah. On Labor Day in that year Tex Rickard promoted a prize fight for the lightweight championship of the world between Battling Nelson and Joe Gans. He offered the biggest purses in the history of prize fighting, $20,000 to the champion Nelson and $10,000 to Gans, the black challenger.

It was hailed as the "Fight of the Century" in the national press, and reporters from the East joined writers from the Pacific Coast at ringside. The fighters battered each other for forty-two punishing rounds before Nelson, sagging and bloodied, fouled Gans in a clinch, "as dirty a foul," the Goldfield *Sun* reported, "as was ever witnessed by spectators at ringside." Gans was awarded the victory and the championship, but the big winner was Tex Rickard. The $72,000 gate was a record, and the fight was the first in a long career of prize-fight promotions that took him from his Northern Saloon at Goldfield to New York City and Madison Square Garden.

So rich was the ore at Goldfield that miners employed hidden overall pockets, hollow pick handles, and false heels on their boots to high-grade the best pieces of it. That practice, combined with growth in influence by the Industrial Workers of the World, prompted the mine operators, under the leadership of George Wingfield, to persuade Governor John Sparks to call for federal troops to maintain order. The move accomplished its intended result, that of crushing the union without open warfare.

By 1910, the Goldfield mines were into decline, but at its peak of prosperity Goldfield was a peculiar combination of wild western mining boomtown and decorous, respectable city. There were miners and prospectors and saloon roughs, plenty of them, but there were also stenographers and telephone operators, bankers and stock exchange brokers. Goldfield was the largest city in Nevada, and the Goldfield Hotel the most opulent stopping place between Kansas City and the Pacific Coast.

George Wingfield was Goldfield's most prominent citizen. In the classic Western tradition, Wingfield had been a buckaroo working at ranches around Burns, Oregon, and Winnemucca, Nevada, in the years before the turn of the century. He rode south when the news of the Tonopah strike got out, stopping in Winnemucca just long enough to borrow $150 from a banker there named George Nixon. Wingfield arrived in Tonopah with most of his stake still intact, but instead of investing it in a prospecting outfit, he put it down on the faro table at the Tonopah Club and ran it up to $2,200; later he acquired a half-interest in the gambling concession at the club and began dabbling in wildcat mining shares.

When the Goldfield bonanza was struck he called for more backing from banker Nixon, and with additional support from eastern capitalists like Bernard Baruch, all but cornered the market in Goldfield mining shares. By the time of the labor troubles with the IWW Wobblies, Wingfield and Nixon were the bonanza kings of Goldfield. When the decline came, Wingfield moved to Reno where he dominated the state's political and economic picture until his banks failed in 1932. His influence on Nevada's development during the first thirty years of this century was incalculable. *Fortune* magazine, in one of its early issues, called him "King George" Wingfield, "Proprietor of Nevada."

After 1918 Goldfield was a stone husk of a city left in the desert to die, and it died badly. In September, 1913, a flash flood wrenched houses from their foundations and laid waste to whole neighborhoods; ten years later a holocaust blazed up to make ashes of fifty-three square blocks. Abandonment and decay have accounted for much of the rest; a small village remains alive at the heart of this once-great city: two or three gas stations, a cafe or two.

But there are landmarks. Principal among them are the mines and dumps at the foot of Columbia Mountain on the north side of town. The Florence Mine is still worked — by a man and his wife. She runs the hoist; he mucks the ore. The Goldfield Hotel still stands at the intersection of Columbia and Crook streets. Built in 1908 at a cost of just under a half-million dollars, the hotel provided accommodation for 150 guests, was appointed with Brussels carpets, mahogany and leather, and ceilings gilded in 22-karat gold. The dining room menu included lobster, squab, and international delicacies. Spared by flood and fire, the hotel survived until 1936, and was reopened during the war to provide housing for Air Force personnel stationed at the base near Tonopah. It has been closed since 1945.

George Wingfield owned the hotel, and it is said that when Goldfield's glory days were over, he had a portfolio of photographs taken to display the building's luxurious appointments to best advantage, took them east, and used them to persuade New York bankers to mortgage the property for $100,000. He then abandoned the place to them, and the hotel passed through several hands, each time at considerable loss. Another story is that in the 1930s the hotel's newest owner, unacquainted with Wingfield's former connection with it, attempted to sell it to him for the bargain price of $50,000. Using a different set of photographs, though. Wingfield refused the bargain.

The brick house with the decorated ridge poles at the corner of Crook and Franklin streets is the Tex Rickard home. It is not open for visitors, however. Neither is the hotel; neither is anything else in Goldfield except the scattering of business houses and the courthouse, a substantial but relatively unremarkable example of post-Victorian public building design.

Some locals say there is damn little reason to stop at

Goldfield except as a lesson in humility; but that is a question of individual taste. This was once the biggest and busiest city in Nevada.

Beatty

117 miles south of Tonopah and 115 miles northwest of Las Vegas via U.S. 95. Four years following the discovery by Jim Butler of silver ore at Tonopah and two years after the fabulous Goldfield strike, prospectors organized the Bullfrog Mining District and established a number of small settlements, Beatty among them. Because of its favored location on the Amargosa River, Beatty survives while the livelier mining towns of Bullfrog and Rhyolite are dead. It is important today principally because it is the first community of any consequence on the highway north out of Las Vegas.

The Amargosa ranks as one of America's driest rivers. Its flow is mostly underground, and its course is usually a long series of puddles and mud streaks. But occasionally the runoff from desert thundershowers transforms the Amargosa into a torrent that washes out roads and causes considerable damage.

The Exchange Club offers a well-stocked bar, an adequate menu, and an excellent source of back-country information about the region. There are a few other cafes, a half-dozen gas stations, but not much of a historic nature within the city limits. Beatty's environs, however, are among the most spectacular in the world: Nevada Route 58 leads to the fascinating ghost city of Rhyolite and over Daylight Pass (or through Titus Canyon when the road is open) into Death Valley.

DEVELOPED CAMPGROUNDS

In the great mountain and valley expanses of central Nevada, developed public outdoor recreation facilities are the exception rather than the rule. This is in itself one of the great attractions of the region, together with the generally permissive attitude toward random camping on the public lands. But as more and more travelers and vacationers avail themselves of the opportunity for wilderness and near-wilderness solitude in the vast emptinesses of Nevada, the opportunities for solitude are dwindling. As trash and rubbish accumulates on the landscape, the attitude toward campers is changing. Eventually, camping in central Nevada will undoubtedly be as institutionalized as it has already become in heavily populated areas. For now at least, it is still possible for a man to step out of time and to absent himself from his kind for a day or a week.

No attempt has been made here to locate undeveloped campsites in Nevada's mining country; there is something more than faintly preposterous about erecting signposts to Shangri-la, and such a list would be virtually endless. To help make finding the developed campgrounds somewhat easier, the sites developed and administered by the Forest Service and the Bureau of Land Management (BLM) are listed indiscriminately together according to the nearest sizable community, rather than segregated by agency. Not included in this list, however, are certain caverns, caves, and archeological sites of such fragile nature as to be jeopardized by casual traffic. The locations of these sites are available on request at the appropriate offices of the BLM, the Humboldt National Forest (HNF), or the Toiyabe National Forest (TNF). State Parks and National Monuments are listed separately. In all cases below, drinking water is available unless its absence is specifically noted.

Walker Lake

The only developed sites along U.S. 95 in Nevada's mining country are on the west shore of Walker Lake about 15 miles north of Hawthorne. Tamarack Point and Sportsmen's Beach are both picnic sites with water, sanitary facilities, and tables, some of them shaded. Tamarack Point also offers a free boat-launching ramp heavily used by water-skiers and fishermen. Fishing is excellent during the fall and winter months. Both areas are open all year. BLM.

Walker Lake, near Hawthorne

Austin Area

Hickison Petroglyph Recreation Site. 20 miles east of Austin via U.S. 50, then north via marked and graded dirt road one-half mile. *No water;* camp sites and picnic units, all shaded, in a thick grove of twenty-foot junipers. Indian rock art is located at several protected places within a few minutes' easy walk from the campground. Open April to November. BLM.

Bob Scott Summit Campground. 6 miles east of Austin via U.S. 50. Family camping units, trailer spaces. Adjacent to, but slightly elevated above, the highway: convenient but hardly secluded. Open May to November. TNF.

Kingston Canyon Campground. 31 miles south of Austin via U.S. 50 (go east for 11 miles) and Nevada Route 8A (for 14 miles), and then west for 6 miles on a marked and graded gravel road. Camp sites in a canyon of remarkable beauty draw heavy use from fishermen who take trout from Kingston Creek and the recently man-made Groves Lake. Open for use from mid-May to mid-October, the Forest Service campground is reached via Kingston Streamsites, a private development which offers bar and restaurant service to the public. This is one of the few places in Nevada where a developed public outdoor recreation site of superior quality exists immediately adjacent to a private development offering the amenities of better-than-average cuisine and a well-stocked bar. See following entry. TNF.

Big Creek Campground. 14 miles south of Austin via U.S. 50 (2 miles), Nevada Route 21 (8 miles), and marked and graded dirt road leading into the west side of the Toiyabes. Family campsites and trailer spaces; open from May to mid-October. The access road to Big Creek Campground continues on to cross the Toiyabes and descends the east side through Kingston Canyon (but is impassible in winter). TNF.

Tonopah Area

Peavine Campground. 48 miles north of Tonopah via U.S. 6 (6 miles) and Nevada Route 8A (34 miles), and then 8 miles west along a marked and graded gravel road. Family campsites open from June to October. Of the nearly two dozen canyons that notch the east face of the Toiyabe range between Austin and Tonopah, only Peavine and Kingston Canyons offer developed facilities. Roads of varying quality give access to the other canyons, and many of them receive relatively heavy use despite the lack of development (or perhaps because of it). Most of these canyons offer fair to good stream fishing, and most support a population of deer, making them at least slightly hazardous during hunting season. TNF.

Pine Creek Campground. About 15 miles north of the ghost town of Belmont (described in detail elsewhere in this section) via unpaved Nevada Route 82. Pine Creek is one of several fair to good fishing streams that course down the east slopes of the Toquima Range into Monitor Valley, and the camping units are satisfyingly remote from the casual traffic of sightseers and highway travelers. TNF.

Cherry Creek Campground. 110 miles east of Tonopah via U.S. 6 (to Warm Springs) and Nevada Route 25 (to the Nyala turnoff), then by dirt and gravel road through Railroad Valley to a point 6 miles beyond Nyala where a marked dirt road climbs into the Quinn Canyon Mountains 15 miles to the campground. Or drive 52 miles southwest from Ely via U.S. 6 to Currant, turn south into Railroad Valley for 33 miles more to the marked road into the Quinn Canyon Mountains. The campsites nestled among the junipers beside Cherry Creek are surely the most remote in Nevada, which is saying a good deal. Fishing is only fair, but deer hunters regard it as a good place to headquarter during hunting season. HNF.

Ely Area

Currant Campground. 42 miles southwest of Ely via U.S. 6. Campsites shaded by cottonwoods growing along the banks of Currant Creek. Adjacency to the highway provides convenience of access but relatively little seclusion. HNF.

White River Campground. 39 miles southwest of Ely via U.S. 6 (for 28 miles) and west along a graded desert road. Campsites under the cottonwoods growing along the White River. The Forest Service has constructed additional "minicamps" along White River and Currant Creek for the use of hunters and fishermen (or anyone else, for that matter). The road to the White River Campground continues northwest for several miles to its intersection with the Currant Creek Road which loops south to the Currant Creek Campground and U.S. 6. Total distance of this loop is 20 miles, all unpaved. It makes an extremely satisfying sidetrip, passing along the base of the sheer rock facade of the Duckwater Range. HNF.

Ward Mountain Campground. 6 miles southwest of Ely via U.S. 6 at Murry Summit. Group picnic areas, playground, barbecue pits, family camping units, and a trailer camping area combine with propinquity to make this a popular outing site for Ely residents as well as for travelers. No firewood available, however; bring your own. HNF.

Schell Creek Area

The following campgrounds are in the Schell Creek Range north and east of Ely, accessible by the scenic Success Summit drive. Take U.S. 6 southeast from Ely 7 miles, and turn east at road marked Success Summit. Continuing along this well-maintained dirt and gravel road will eventually bring you back over the top of the Schell Creek Range to U.S. 93 at a point 5 miles north of McGill. Side roads in the mountains lead to these marvelously situated campgrounds, all maintained by the Humboldt National Forest Service:

Berry Creek. About 23 miles north of the intersection of the Success Summit road with U.S. 6. Campsites and trailer spaces are about 4 miles up the creek.

Timber Creek. About 2 miles north of Berry Creek via Success Summit road. Camping units and trailer spaces are about 3 miles east of the road.

Bird Creek. About 3 miles north of Timber Creek via Success Summit road. Camping units are 2 miles east. Creek water only.

East Creek. About 2 miles north of Bird Creek via Success Summit road. Family camping units and trailer spaces are 3 miles up creek. Creek water only.

Kalamazoo Creek Campground. About 10 miles northeast of East Creek Campground via Success Summit road and graded dirt road leading northeast over the crest of the Schell Creek Range. Campsites are scattered along the length of the creek which trickles down the east side of the range, and development is limited: tables, fireplaces, and pit toilets; creek water only. Because the campsites are dispersed there is little chance of crowding in this relatively isolated campground even during the seasons of peak use.

Cleve Creek Campground. About 42 miles southeast of Ely via U.S. 6/50 (for 28 miles) and north along the Spring Valley road (for 14 miles), which turns off to the north to parallel the Schell Creek Range; or by taking the Success Summit road, turning northeast from it as if to the Kalamazoo Creek

Campground, and continuing down the east side of the Schell Creek Range to join the Spring Valley road at a point about 25 miles north of the Cleve Creek Campground. Camping units in a wide canyon setting attract many repeat visitors. Tables, fireplaces, pit toilets; creek water only.

Wheeler Peak Area

The following campgrounds are located in the Snake Range of mountains south and east of Ely, in the Wheeler Peak Scenic Area of the Humboldt National Forest. The scenic area comprises about 28,000 acres and takes its name from 13,063-foot Wheeler Peak, the second-highest mountain in the state. It is noted for its scenery, its large glacial cirques (one of which still shelters a permanent ice field), lakes and streams, stands of ancient bristlecone pine, and recreational facilities. These include hiking trails and the campgrounds listed below, as well as Lehman Caves National Monument (also detailed below), one of the most beautiful limestone caverns in the world. The campgrounds listed below are accessible from Baker, Nevada, 65 miles southeast of Ely via U.S. 6/50 and Nevada Route 73.

Lehman Trailer Campground. 6 miles west of Baker via Nevada Route 74 and Forest Service Road 446. Units capable of accommodating fairly large trailers and equipped with fireplaces, tables, piped water, and vault toilets. Campsites are shaded and scented by aspens, piñon pine, and wild roses; open for use from mid-May to mid-October.

Wheeler Peak Campground. About 10 miles west of Lehman Creek Campground, at the end of Forest Service Road 446 (Asilo Verde Drive). Family camping units located at ten thousand feet near the headwaters of Lehman Creek in grassy meadows and a fir-spruce forest. Pleasantly cool even on summer afternoons. From the road to the campground the remains of the Osceola Ditch can be seen, a twenty-mile canal built by Chinese hand labor in the middle 1880s to provide water for working the placer mines at Osceola (listed under Ghost Towns in this section). All roads and spurs are paved. Hiking and horseback trails give access to the ancient bristlecone pine forest between the campground and Wheeler Peak, to the icefield beneath the north summit of Wheeler Peak, and to Stella, Teresa, and Brown lakes, a fairly strenuous four-mile round trip. Campground open from late June to November.

Baker Creek Campground. 8 miles southwest of Baker via Nevada Route 74 and Forest Service Road 590. Family camping units located beside Baker Creek among juniper, piñon pine, white fir, and some aspen, and open for use from June to November. From the end of Forest Service Road 590 (about one-quarter mile beyond the campground) a trail leads westward into the mountains about 4 miles to Baker Lake near the crestline of the Snake Range, terminating about 2 miles farther on at Shoshone Campground. Ice Cavern and petroglyph caves are accessible from Forest Service Road 590 between the Lehman Caves Visitor Center and Baker Creek Campground.

Snake Creek Campground. 14 miles southwest of Baker via Nevada Route 73 and Forest Service Road 448. Camping units are scattered along the dirt road paralleling Snake Creek between 6,500 and 8,000 feet in elevation, with fireplaces, tables, and pit toilets; creek water only. Fishing is excellent and seldom crowded. Open for use from June to November.

Shoshone Campground. A western extension of Snake Creek Campground and the point of departure for the trail to Johnson Lake, a highly regarded fishing spot and site of Johnson's Mine and Mill; equipment and materials from the mine are located at several points along the trail to the lake which continues to Baker Creek Campground.

In addition to the trails mentioned above, there are numerous others through the scenic area which offer a dramatic contrast to the desert valleys below, and access to a variety of scenic, historic, and recreation attractions. Detailed, comprehensive information about these trails is available at the Lehman Caves Visitor Center (see following).

OTHER ATTRACTIONS

Lehman Caves National Monument

4 miles west of Baker via Nevada Route 74. A unit of the
National Park Service, Lehman Caves National Monument occupies 640 acres in the piñon-juniper woodlands on the east
flank of the Snake Range. A visitor center, operated jointly by
the Park and Forest Service, contains exhibits relating to the
cavern and to the Wheeler Peak Scenic Area surrounding it.
Picnic facilities are provided but no camping is permitted within
the monument. Evening programs are offered several nights a
week during the summer months and complete information is
readily available. A cafe and souvenir shop operated by con-
cessionaires is open daily from Easter through Veterans Day.
Tours at a modest fee are conducted through the cavern hourly
from 8 A.M. to 5 P.M. from Memorial Day through Labor Day,
and at 9:00, 10:30, 12:30, 2:30 and 4:00 during the remainder of
the year. Because of the monument's relative isolation from
main tourist routes, tour parties are small even during the peak
summer months; in winter you and your party are likely to have
the ranger to yourself. The cave is cool to chilly at any season,
and coats or sweaters should be taken along. Cameras are
permitted, but tripods are not; you'll need flash equipment. The
tour covers about two-thirds of a mile underground, along carefully constructed and maintained pathways, and takes about
forty-five minutes.

The cavern itself (which extends much deeper into the
mountain than tour parties can safely or easily proceed) began
formation tens of thousands of years ago, when the Snake
Range was lower and less rugged, and the climate of the region
much more humid. Carbon-dioxide-charged water, filtering
down through cracks and fissures in the limestone of the mountain, dissolved the stone, widening the cracks. Over a period of
time the more soluble rock was dissolved leaving large vaulted
rooms. Fault and joint planes were widened into connecting
passageways until eventually they formed a labyrinth of cor-

Lehman Caves, near Ely

ridors and smaller winding tunnels connecting larger chambers. As lower channels drained water from the upper levels, the calcium-bearing water gathered as drops or spread out in thin films on the roofs and sides of the caverns, depositing some of the calcium as dripstone. The resulting forms, colors, and textures are at once so spectacular and so exquisitely delicate that a book like this can scarcely do them justice. See them. Entering Lehman Caves is so unexpected an experience after the (inevitably) long, occasionless drive to get there, that it is like meeting a staunch plain ranch wife, and then unaccountably, entering her unconscious, otherwordly, and most wonderfully lovely interior dreams.

Ward Charcoal Ovens State Historical Monument

17 miles southeast of Ely via U.S. 6/93 (for 7 miles) then south on a marked and graded gravel road. Six beehive-shaped charcoal kilns built in 1876 of native rock to provide fuel for the Martin White smelter at Ward (listed separately under Ghost Towns) are the attraction here. About thirty-feet high, each oven enclosed about thirty-five cords of piñon-pine wood, stacked in layers. The wood was kindled and the fire controlled by opening and closing small vents around the base of the ovens.

After the smelter closed in the 1880s, the ovens were used for a variety of purposes: as stables, as campsites for sheep herders and buckaroos, and even, according to the story anyway, as the bridal suite for Addie Hacker and her gambler fiancé, who whitewashed one of the kilns in anticipation of the event. They quarreled, alas, and the marriage did not take place.

Little has been done to "improve" the site for visitors: there is no water; no privies, even. But picnic tables and benches have been placed inside the ovens, providing not only unequalled atmosphere for the afternoon meal, but a welcome cool haven during the summer months. A fence has been erected around the ovens to keep the livestock from interfering with the tourists, but the turnstile remains unlocked. A sidetrip most worthwhile. A Nevada State Park (NSP).

Ward charcoal ovens, near Ely

Ichthyosaur Paleontologic State Monument

63 miles southwest of Austin via U.S. 50 (2 miles), Nevada
Route 2 (8 miles), Nevada Route 21 (50 miles; graded gravel),
then east 3 miles via graded road through the ghost town of
Berlin and into Union Canyon. Or 66 miles northwest of Tonopah via U.S. 6/95 (3 miles), north on Nevada Route 89 (60
miles; graded gravel and dirt), then east 3 miles through Berlin
and into Union Canyon. Or 52 miles northeast of Luning via
Nevada Route 23 (33 miles), Nevada Route 91 (16 miles; graded
dirt), then east 3 miles through Berlin and into Union Canyon.

For a period of approximately 110 million years, beginning about 180 million years ago, when much of Nevada lay beneath the surface of a vast inland sea, sixty-foot-long ichthyosaurs ("fish lizards") were abundant. They were the largest animals of their day (bodies eight feet in diameter, ribs nine feet long), exceeded in size only by some of the dinosaurs of a later period and by some modern whale species. Over the course of time, a number of individual ichthyosaurs became beached along the shoreline of the sea, trapped there to die by the rapidly receding tides. Their bodies, washed parallel with the shoreline by the gentle shoving of the incoming tides, decayed to skeletons which were then buried in the soft alluvial ooze of the shore, eventually being overlaid by as much as three thousand feet of mud and slime that hardened to shale. Ultimately this shale stratum was uplifted and subjected to hundreds of thousands of years of erosion which has exposed the fossil bones again.

Nineteen fossil ichthyosaur skeletons have been excavated in part, and a display quarry containing the remains of six of the huge creatures is maintained as an in-place exhibit for visitors. Tables and charcoal grills are provided for picnicking, water is piped in from springs, and camping is permitted. There are no commercial services available at the monument; the nearest community is the village of Ione, on Nevada Route 21 about 7 miles northwest of the monument. NSP.

GHOST TOWNS

Rhyolite
4 miles west of Beatty via Nevada Route 58 and marked, graded gravel road. Founded in 1905 as the principal townsite in the newly-discovered Bullfrog Mining District, Rhyolite was settled by speculators from Tonopah and Goldfield to the north, and Las Vegas to the south. Many of the district's mines were rich producers, notably the Montgomery-Shoshone, the Original Bullfrog, National Bank, and Tramp, and by 1907 their prosperity had caused Rhyolite to emerge as one of southern

Nevada's principal cities with a population of some six thousand.

Three railroads served Rhyolite, as did four local newspapers, a board of trade, an opera house, four banks, and a telephone exchange. Residential neighborhoods spread out for blocks from the electrically-lighted streets of downtown.

Alas for Rhyolite's fond hopes, the panic of 1907 tipped her mines into bankruptcy, and by 1910 the city had shriveled to barely seven hundred persons. By 1920 it was empty altogether.

Many western towns had homes made of bottles, but the most celebrated is at Rhyolite. Originally constructed during the boom, it was restored during the 1920s by a movie company, and is presently occupied as a residence. So, too, is the ornate Las Vegas & Tonopah Railroad depot at the upper end of town and half a dozen more modest structures still standing intact.

The harsh sun of noontime is unkind to Rhyolite. The old town is better visited by moonlight, or near dusk when the late light of afternoon gilds the desert floor and offers romantic pinks and blues to soften the desolation of old Golden Street. There the Porter Brothers' store stares blankly out at the concrete ruins of the Overbury Block and, farther uphill, the John S. Cook bank building. Few wooden ruins remain; most have gone for firewood and into other buildings elsewhere. Sites of a handful of other ghosts are within a few miles of Rhyolite, though little or nothing remains of them: Bullfrog, Leadfield, and Gold Center are chief among them.

Gold Point

30 miles southwest of Goldfield via U.S. 95 and Nevada Routes 3 and 71. Founded in 1868 as Lime Point, mining proceeded in fits and starts here until after the turn of the century when high-grade silver deposits were found, prompting a rush to the town and a change in its name to Hornsilver. The boom peaked in 1908 when more than two hundred tents and buildings lined the streets of the town; in 1909 lawsuits ended production in many of the most profitable properties and the town entered a

decline. This lasted until 1915 when operations resumed. In 1922 Charles Stoneham of the New York Giants baseball club headed a syndicate which purchased the Great Western mine, and production continued until 1942. The town took its present name in the 1930s. Much of Gold Point remains, perhaps forty buildings or more. And many of the buildings are occupied. Yet the air of abandonment is unmistakable: despite the bright gleam of metal from the newish cars parked behind many of Gold Point's homes, a visitor can hear the lizards scrabbling lightly across the dry sand. No services for the visitor except perhaps a reserved nod of greeting from one of the remaining residents.

Lida

34 miles southwest of Goldfield via U.S. 95 and Nevada Route 3. Founded as Lida Valley in 1872 by miners who thought they were in California. Operations slowed drastically at the end of the decade when the richest of the ore was exhausted, but boomed again in sympathy with the strikes at Goldfield and Tonopah. Production dwindled in 1907, picked up again, fell off, increased — and finally stopped altogether. The town, what is left of it, now serves as the headquarters for Art Linkletter's Nevada ranching operation. Cowpunchers bunk in the old schoolhouse, and horses are corralled in the gaps between buildings on the single street remaining. No services.

Candelaria

22 miles south of Mina via U.S. 95 (for 15 miles) and southwest along a graded dirt road. Founded at the site of a silver strike made by Spanish prospectors in 1863, Candelaria sprang into prominence a decade later when the Northern Belle went into production. In 1876 Candelaria had a two-block business district, but development was limited by the high cost of shipping, materials, and water — drinking water cost four and a half cents a gallon delivered, and a bath was two dollars, retail. Despite its remote and desolate location, the prosperity of the mines

prompted further growth in Candelaria. By 1880 the town had a population of nine hundred, and nearly twice that number three years later.

The arrival of the Carson & Colorado Railroad in 1882 seemed to assure eternal prosperity for Candelaria, which by this time had also developed a municipal water system as well as twenty-seven saloons (and no churches). But fire, mining litigation, and labor disputes combined to end the town's forward motion. By the early 1890s Candelaria had entered a deep and lasting coma, broken only by a few hiccups of activity in the long years since. The cemetery is in relatively good repair, and provides a pleasant hour's browsing for those who take their pleasure this way; of the town itself there are rock ruins and wooden cabins in various stages of decay. Little shade and less water.

Belleville
14 miles southwest of Mina via U.S. 95, Nevada Route 10, and graded dirt road (marked "Marietta"). Located around the mills built in the middle 1870s to serve the mines at Candelaria, Belleville was a wide-open hum-dinger of a town that went on a prolonged binge beginning the day it was founded, and ending when the mills shut down ten years later. Relics here are mostly related to the old mill workings, but a small cemetery remains also.

Marietta
About 9 miles beyond Belleville to the west. Founded in 1877 to serve the borax works at Teel's Marsh to the south and west, Marietta was built largely of adobe and native stone. Even bleaker in its surroundings than Candelaria, Marietta was also visited by gale winds across the dry marsh, carrying suspended within them immense quantities of grit. Adding an extra ingredient of excitement to the life of the community was the fact that the stagecoach from Aurora was robbed thirty times in a single year, and four times in one week.

Abandoned with the richer and more accessible borax discoveries near Death Valley in the 1890s, Marietta's business structures and residences have survived with only marginal success. One of the best-preserved is the store once operated by "Borax" Smith when his borax empire was still young and abuilding. The remnants here are of a little-known town at its best, and they are quite unspectacular. Furthermore they are accessible only by a ten-mile drive across some fairly rough country, and located at the edge of a barren dry lake. There are no distractions once the car's engine is turned off, and the transistor radio, to cushion the impact of the implacable Nevada desert. An hour's meditation at Marietta in mid-day should provide as much understanding about pioneer life in Nevada as a whole library of books on the subject.

Aurora

27 miles southwest of Hawthorne via Nevada Route 31, Lucky Boy Pass road, and marked dirt road. A party of prospectors who had missed their chance at rich ground in Virginia City found exposed quartz ledges bearing heavy deposits of silver and gold while searching for water and game. Their claims attracted many from eastern California as well as more of Virginia City's disappointed, and Aurora began to take shape. Brick from the Pacific Coast was more readily accessible to the town's early entrepreneurs than finished lumber, so Aurora's business district was largely made up of substantial brick buildings.

So rapidly did the town grow that when the California legislature created Mono County in the spring of 1861, Aurora was named its seat. A few months later, the territorial government of Nevada also proclaimed Aurora the seat of Esmeralda County. Thus two county governments, each duly authorized and fully staffed, held sway at opposite ends of town.

In the meantime Aurora continued to grow, and one of the hopefuls who was attracted by the stores of gold and silver was a young Missourian named Sam Clemens. He arrived in the spring of 1862 and worked briefly as a miner, and even more briefly as a mill laborer, before abandoning mining and Aurora altogether for a newspaper job in Virginia City.

All the while, Aurora grew larger and more substantial. By the summer of 1863, its population had soared to nearly ten thousand people and the business district encompassed nearly a dozen square blocks. There were a dozen hotels and as many boarding houses, twenty stores and twenty-one saloons, two newspapers, and a proportionate number of professional offices.

In September of that year county elections were held, and Aurora citizens could vote both for California candidates (at the police station) and for Nevada candidates (at the Armory). Three weeks later the special border survey working south reached the district and drew the state line about four miles west of Aurora. The town was thus firmly within Nevada and the Mono County officials were forced to make the reluctant move west to the small camp of Bodie.

Perhaps because of the sudden reduction in the number of sheriffs from two to one, the rough element in Aurora became increasingly bold and troublesome. Thievery was common, and homicide was ordinary, but when, in Feburary, 1864, a station-keeper named Johnson was shot down in the street, his throat cut, and his clothes set on fire, the townspeople had had enough. After the sheriff arrested three of the murderers and set out in pursuit of the fourth, a special vigilante committee was formed, armed, and deployed through the town. Roughnecks and rowdy characters were escorted to the edge of town or put in jail, and the regular law officers were held in their homes under guard. When the sheriff's posse returned with their quarry, the prisoner was put in jail and the sheriff held in his office.

Governor James Nye, receiving word of the usurpation of government, sent a wire to one of Esmeralda County's commissioners at Aurora urging against violence. He received in reply a telegram reading: "All quiet and orderly. Four men will be hung in half an hour." It was and they were.

But by the end of the year even the most peace-loving citizen might have considered letting the scruffnecks back into Aurora if they would bring prosperity back with them. For Aurora's mines and mills, exuberantly over-promoted, began to fail in the summer of 1864. By the summer of 1865 half the town's population had vanished, and by the end of the decade the richest surface deposits had been worked out (after producing nearly $30 million in bullion). Operations resumed for a few years in the late 1870s, but by the early 1880s the county seat had been lost to Hawthorne, and by the late 1890s the post office was closed.

But Tonopah and Goldfield activity stimulated a renewed optimism in Aurora's mines, and several hundred people reoccupied the old city. The revival held until 1919.

In 1946 Aurora's empty buildings built of brick — much of which had come originally from England as ship's ballast — were demolished by a materials-hungry building contractor and trucked to Southern California where they became part of several large chimneys at Wilmington. Many of the remaining wooden structures have been pulled down by vandals and even cemetery gravestones have been stolen. It is startling (and depressing) to consider how completely the town has been stripped and looted — erased from the landscape as completely as the ores which prompted its building were mined out beneath it.

Rawhide

40 miles northeast of Hawthorne via Nevada Route 31 and marked dirt road; or 57 miles southeast of Fallon via U.S. 50, Nevada Route 31, and marked dirt road. A prospector browsing across the desert near the tent camps of Regent and Reward made the first Rawhide strike on Christmas night, 1906. A few others joned him during the winter, and by August of the following year investors had taken up many of the richest claims in order to bring them into production. In eight months Rawhide had drawn a population of some seven thousand citizens from depression-becalmed Tonopah, Goldfield, and half a hundred

smaller camps, and by the spring of '08 choice downtown lots could not be had for $20,000. Montana mining magnate E. W. King bought into the Rawhide Coalition to the tune of a cool million dollars, Tex Rickard hurried up from Goldfield to open another highly successful Northern Saloon, and Nat Goodwin, a nationally prominent actor and comedian, helped pump up interest in Rawhide mining shares with the notorious promoter George Graham Rice. Rawhide's dizzy pace quickened day by day, principally because of the fact that many of her leading citizens had learned effective promotion techniques at Goldfield, Rhyolite, and Tonopah.

Invited for the sake of publicity by the canny Tex Rickard, Lady Elinor Glyn came jouncing into Rawhide in 1908. The English author was enchanted with Rawhide, a sentiment fervently returned by her hosts, who staged a Wild West shootout over the poker tables at the Northern for her benefit. Lady Glyn learned to roll cigarettes and play roulette. When Governor Denver Dickinson pinned a deputy sheriff's badge to her pal-

Rawhide

pitating breast and authorized her to arrest any man in Nevada, she responded by ecstatically proclaiming Rawhide "a splendid community of real gentlemen."

Most of that splendor went up in smoke on the morning of September 4, 1908, when eight blocks in the business district burned. Business houses were rebuilding even before the embers had completely cooled, but the town's headlong optimism had flickered out with the fire. By 1909 the population had declined to two thousand; by January, 1910 only five hundred remained. Rawhide's last citizen departed in 1966.

Only a few wooden buildings and the stone jail remain intact at Rawhide, but there is still plenty to see, and dedicated ghost-towners can easily spend a day in exploration between Balloon Hill and Stingaree Gulch (Rawhide's quarter-mile-long red light district).

Downeyville
4 miles northeast of Gabbs via Nevada Route 23 and graded dirt road. Site of a silver-lead discovery in the spring of 1877, Downeyville grew slowly, achieving a stagecoach connection with the transcontinental railroad the next year, and a post office the year after that. The town's history was peaceful and unspectacular until it came to an end about 1901, when its few remaining citizens decided they would give Tonopah a try. Recommended principally for its isolation and the relatively large extent of the stone ruins.

Ione
23 miles northeast of Gabbs via Nevada Route 91, or 52 miles southwest of Austin via U.S. 50, and Nevada Routes 2 and 21. Attractively located in a beautiful canyon setting in the autumn of 1863, Ione grew rapidly to a population of about five hundred and was named seat of the newly created Nye County by the territorial legislature. Mining production fell off in 1866 and the county seat was moved to Belmont the year following. Ione's mines never achieved their early promise of richness, but

neither did they altogether give out, and the town has never been completely abandoned. A tiny store, pair of gas pumps, and a bar is Ione's entire business district today, surviving on the occasional trade from visitors to Ichthyosaur State Paleontologic Monument, from its eleven permanent residents, and from the ranchers of the region. The original Nye County courthouse is among the handful of wooden buildings still standing along the ragged street.

Berlin
19 miles east of Gabbs via Nevada Route 91 and graded dirt roads marked Ichthyosaur Paleontologic State Monument. Originally developed in the late 1890s, Berlin's record of production was less than spectacular. The mine and mill attracted a peak population of about 250 people, but by 1909 the operation was closed down. A large mill building, miners' boarding house, assay office, and a handful of cabins are all that remain today. Recently acquired for future development as a state park, Berlin is one of Nevada's ghosts to be spared further wasting. Ichthyosaur Paleontologic State Monument (see listing) is 2 miles east of Berlin through Union Canyon.

Grantsville
21 miles east of Gabbs via Nevada Route 91 and graded dirt road. One of the many camps step-mothered by Austin, Grantsville was established in 1863 but was slow to develop until the late 1870s, when it attracted a population of about eight hundred. Grantsville had nearly twenty stores of various description in its business district as well as a brewery, a bank, a newspaper, a three-times-a-week stage to Austin, and fourteen producing silver mines. The town jail was a tunnel dug in a hillside, and there were forty pupils in the Grantsville school. By 1885 Grantsville's bright prospects had dimmed, and the town slowly slipped into oblivion. Brick, frame, and adobe buildings still stand, and the ruins, including a relatively well-preserved cemetery, are situated in an extremely picturesque canyon.

Manhattan

49 miles north of Tonopah via U.S. 6 and Nevada Routes 8A and 69; 82 miles south of Austin via U.S. 50 and Nevada Routes 8A and 69. Established briefly in 1866 and abandoned three years later, Manhattan burst into life again in 1905 when cattle-chasing buckaroos discovered rich ore. Claims were staked, and by the end of the year several hundred prospectors and miners were in camp. In January, 1906, the camp suddenly boomed. By early spring a business district had taken shape, telephone service and electric lights had been installed, and four thousand people had crowded into Manhattan. Rich discoveries were made in 1906 and 1907, but the San Francisco earthquake of the former year, and the financial panic of the latter, made capital scarce and slowed development. By 1909, however, Manhattan mines were operating at high capacity, producing gold, silver, and copper. Production fell off during the 1920s, but continued through the depression and World War II, and totalled more than $10 million before ceasing altogether in 1947.

Manhattan today is far from a dead town, and there may be some civic upset about being included among the ghost towns of Nevada's mining country. But the fact remains that despite several operating stores, service stations, and saloons, Manhattan's past seems more interesting than her present. In the summertime, Manhattan's long main street is crowded with an armada of travel trailers and campers, neatly parked on campsites of sometimes astonishing complexity in the vacant lots between buildings.

Belmont

14 miles northeast of Manhattan via graded dirt road, or 47 miles northeast of Tonopah via U.S. 6 and Nevada Routes 8A and 82. Another of the many occasions in Nevada history when a mining discovery was made by an Indian for exploitation by white prospectors, this one resulted in the founding of a major Nevada city and, ultimately, its decay into the most interesting of the state's ghost towns. Discovered in 1865 and developed in 1866

Manhattan church

Belmont relic

into the most important community south of Austin, Belmont became the Nye County seat in 1867. In 1868 mining slowed, but it picked up momentum again in the early 1870s, attracting a population of about two thousand until the late 1880s when the mines shut down. In 1905 the county seat was moved to Tonopah. Belmont still has a handful of permanent residents, but recently the only surviving business house, the Desert Bar, still bore a sign reading "Closed for the Winter." The original brick Nye County courthouse still stands, as do many of the buildings along the town's principal business blocks, notably the often-photographed Cosmopolitan Saloon. The cemetery is extensive and still in a relatively undisturbed condition, and the ruins of the large stamp mills are most impressive.

Belmont is scheduled for acquisition by the usually penni-less Nevada State Park System, but until then only the vigilance of its residents has prevented the wholesale looting and vandalism which has resulted in the destruction and disappearance of other Nevada ghosts.

Jefferson

7 miles east of Round Mountain via dirt road. Jefferson was founded in the middle 1860s under the name Green Isle and was thriving by the early 1870s. A Jefferson mine supplied a forty-pound ore sample valued at $400 for the Philadelphia Centennial Exposition in 1876, but by 1878 Jefferson's buildings were shuttered and boarded. Revival attempts, including one in 1917 financed by Charles Stoneham, owner of the New York Giants baseball club, were unprofitable and short-lived. There is an abundance of frame and stone ruins.

Tybo

65 miles northeast of Tonopah via U.S. 6 and a graded dirt road. Tybo grew slowly from the initial discovery of lead and silver in 1870 until 1874, when capital was used in quantity to develop the mines. By 1875 about one thousand residents were supporting an active business district and fighting among themselves along

racial lines — Irishmen against Cornishmen and everyone against the Chinese.

The town withered away after the failure of the Tybo Consolidated and was for all practical purposes dead from 1891 until 1929 when new smelters went into operation and reactivated the mines. Production ceased for the last time in 1937. The brick and frame remnants of the old town date both from its glory days and from later attempts at revival, in addition to the successful one in 1929.

Osceola

39 miles southeast of Ely via U.S. 6/50 and graded dirt road. Organized as a placer mining district in 1872, Osceola staggered along for nearly a decade before canals brought water to the claims in volume enough to permit large-scale operations. In the middle 1880s hydraulic mining started and proved profitable for about fifteen years. In 1886 a $6,000 nugget was washed free from the hillside. After the turn of the century individual placer miners continued active in such numbers that the town survived, but by 1920 the pickings were too slim to support a post office any longer. Still, Osceola never died completely, and a few residents remain today, though the few remaining business buildings are in ruins now.

Cherry Creek

54 miles north of Ely via U.S. 93 and Nevada Route 35. Established at the mouth of Cherry Creek Canyon in the spring of 1873, the town drew a Wells Fargo office, a post office, and about a thousand residents. Two years later a decline in the mines caused a slow dwindling in the town's population until 1880. In that year new ore bodies were located which spurred new excitement, and in 1881 Cherry Creek was revitalized by an upsurge of population to about 1,800 residents. Two years later the mines were again in decline, and the alternation between excitement and decline continued until 1940 when the present period of decline began. Populated now by less than a dozen

residents, Cherry Creek has reached the lowest ebb in its career, but no one is betting that the old camp is through. A number of buildings remain in the decimated business street, including saloons, stores, an assay office, and the town jail. A fire in 1901 accounted for most of the rest.

Hamilton

36 miles west of Ely via U.S. 50 and a graded dirt road; or 45 miles southeast of Eureka via U.S. 50 and a graded dirt road. Founded in 1867 to serve the rich strikes higher up Treasure Hill, Hamilton was first known as Cave City because of the primitive lodgings used by the miners before construction began. The first frame building was a saloon, of course. The rush to Hamilton was violent and quick; six daily stages were not enough to handle the traffic. By the spring of 1868 more than ten thousand miners, prospectors, speculators, and greenhorns were huddled together, most of them in flimsy, makeshift shelters of canvas, twigs, hay, and mud. By the following year a substantial business district had taken shape along Hamilton's main street. Represented there were Wells Fargo & Co., the Bank of California, and dozens of substantial merchants and innkeepers. In that same year Hamilton was selected as the seat of newly-created White Pine County. By the end of the year Hamilton had a new brick courthouse erected at a cost of $55,000 and was the trade and service center for some twenty thousand residents of the White Pine district.

Subsidiary communities sprang up. Near the mines on Treasure Hill, three miles to the south, was Treasure City, a booming town with saloons on one side of its main street, stores and offices on the other. Shermantown was three and a half miles to the southwest of Hamilton, near a cluster of stamp mills that crushed the ore from the Treasure Hill mines. In 1869 Shermantown had about three thousand residents and a business district built largely of quarried sandstone. Eberhardt, five miles to the southeast of Hamilton was another mill town, located three thousand feet below the Eberhardt mine. Connecting the two was the largest cable tramway in the U.S. at the time. Swansea, Picotillo, and Babylon were also centers of population within a few miles of Hamilton, but of even less permanence than the others.

The peak year for all these towns was 1869. Nearly two hundred mining companies were incorporated with a combined list value of more than $70 million. So rich and seemingly inexhaustible were the mines on Treasure Hill that serious consideration was given to the danger of glutting the world money market, and the daily stagecoach connecting with the railroad at Elko carried so much bullion it was held up on an average of twice a week.

By the following year it was apparent that the optimism had been premature. The incredibly rich surface deposits were worked out, and the mines locked in a tangle of litigation. Most of Treasure City's residents had vacated by the end of the year, and Shermantown and Hamilton both declined seriously. In 1873 a near-bankrupt Hamilton businessman set fire to his store, after carefully shutting off the town's water supply. The resulting fire leveled a large portion of the city, and property losses totalled $600,000. Much of Treasure City was burned in 1874. By 1880 all the towns of the district were virtually empty, and by 1885, when another fire swept Hamilton, they were certifiably dead. Attempts at revival, some of them successful, if only briefly and on a small scale, continued until 1925.

Today there are substantial stone ruins in Hamilton, Shermantown, and Treasure City; the principal cemetery of the district is located a mile north of Hamilton. Together, the remnants in the region represent an opportunity for at least a day's browsing. There are no services and no easily accessible water.

Belmont courthourse

NEVADA PROFILE

The state's name is the Spanish word meaning "snow-clad." It appeared on maps as early as the seventeenth century as "Sierra Nevada," the designation for the snow-clad mountains on the eastern horizon of Spanish California. Another early choice, "Washoe," derived from the name of the Indian tribe inhabiting the Tahoe basin, was once the popular name for the mining region of the Comstock Lode.

The Nevada state flower is the sagebrush, and one of the officially approved state nicknames is The Sagebrush State. Others are The Silver State and The Battle Born State. This last is not much used, since the battle referred to is the Civil War, which most Nevadans scrupulously avoided.

The state motto is All For Our Country.

The state tree is the piñon, specifically the single-leaf piñon. This is the sap-drooling, pot-bellied runt that grows, usually in association with the juniper, across the Nevada landscape like tufts in a rumpled bedspread. We think it is beautiful.

The state flag is blue, with a small wreath of sagebrush and a scroll in the upper left corner.

The state bird is not the "desert canary" (the jackass), as it should be, but the mountain bluebird, a blue songbird with a white vest.

The state song is "Home Means Nevada," a syncopated dirge taught to first-graders. You may never be asked to join in singing it, so the words have been omitted from this volume.

Other statistics which may be of interest are as follows:
STATEHOOD: October 31, 1864; thirty-sixth state to join the Union.
AREA: 110,540 square miles; seventh-ranking state.

POPULATION: 488,738; forty-seventh-ranking state (1970 census).

CAPITAL: Carson City.

BOUNDARIES: Idaho and Oregon on the north, Utah and Arizona on the east, California on the south and west.

HIGHEST POINT: 13,145 feet, Boundary Peak.

LOWEST POINT: 470 feet above sea level near the Colorado River in Clark County.

HIGHWAYS: 7,438 miles of paved roads and highways; 9,600 miles of travelable dirt roads (estimates by Highway Department).

CLIMATE: Hot, very dry summers and cold winters with much snow in the Sierra Nevada area; highest recorded temperature, 122° F; lowest recorded temperature, −50° F; average rainfall, 7.4 inches; snowfall from 1 inch in the south to 250 inches in the Sierra Nevada.

PRINCIPAL CITIES (1970 census):

Las Vegas area, including North Las Vegas, 211,347; tourism and resort center, mining, dairy products, beverages, and warehousing.

Reno, 72,863; tourism and resort center, warehousing, lumber products, ranching, and farming.

Sparks, 24,187; tourism and resort center, warehousing, and truck farming.

Henderson, 16,395; manufacturing, chemicals, rocket fuels, research, and engineering.

Carson City, 15,468; government, tourism, ranching, farming, and warehousing.

Elko, 7,621; ranching, farming, tourism, gold and silver mining, and warehousing.

PRINCIPAL LAKES: Mead (man-made), Pyramid, Ruby, Tahoe, and Walker.

PRINCIPAL DAMS AND RESERVOIRS: Hoover Dam, Lahontan Reservoir, Rye Patch Dam, and Wild Horse Dam.

PRINCIPAL MOUNTAIN RANGES: Charleston, Humboldt, Ruby, Schell Creek, Sierra Nevada, and Toiyabe.

PRINCIPAL RIVERS: Carson, Colorado, Humboldt, Moapa, Muddy, Owyhee, Quinn, Truckee, Virgin, and Walker.

MANUFACTURED GOODS: gambling devices, electronic equipment, chemicals, forest products, suntan lotions, stone, glass, and clay products, construction materials, lumber and timber products, and meat products.

AGRICULTURAL PRODUCTS: cattle, sheep and livestock, alfalfa, hay, cotton, dairy products, hogs, and oats.

MINERAL PRODUCTION: copper, gold, mercury, antimony, lithium, barite, clay, fluorspar, salt, silver, sulfur, zinc, and sand.

TOURISM: resort hotels are located in Las Vegas, Reno, Lake Tahoe, and Elko; historic sites include Virginia City, Carson City, Genoa, Tonopah, and Goldfield; there are twenty-three Indian reservations, three national forests, three state forests, and sixteen state parks.

HIGHER EDUCATION:
University of Nevada, Reno.
University of Nevada, Las Vegas.
Northern Nevada Community College, Elko.
Clark County Community College, Las Vegas.
Western Nevada Community College, Carson City and Reno.
Desert Research Institute, Reno, Las Vegas, and Boulder City.

GOVERNMENT: governor, 2 U.S. senators, 1 U.S. congressman, 20 state senators, 40 state assemblymen, 17 counties, 3 electoral votes.

THE CHINESE IN NEVADA

Near the eastern outskirts of Sparks the state of Nevada has erected a concrete plaque honoring the ''heroism and hardihood of the thousands of Chinese who played a major role in the history of Nevada.'' The plaque does not mention the fact that much of the Chinese heroism and hardihood was demonstrated in their resistance to the discrimination, harassment, and violence inflicted upon them both systematically and at random by their white neighbors on the frontier.

The first Chinese in Nevada were about fifty laborers brought to Gold Canyon to dig a ditch from the Carson River through which water could be diverted to the small placer claims along Gold Creek. After the canal had been finished, many of the Chinese camped near McMarlin's trading post on the Carson, picking over the worked-out claims abandoned by the white miners.

With the discovery of the Comstock Lode, the Chinese population in Nevada increased as sharply as did that of every emigrant nationality, but the Chinese were almost wholly confined to the menial pattern already established in California. They worked as wood cutters, peddlers of vegetables grown on tiny plots of hand-irrigated ground, cafe cooks, and laundrymen, and, when possible, as miners. Later, when white men had made fortunes which permitted them to live lavishly, the Chinese were given employment as servants.

In the earliest days of the big grab for the gold ring on the Comstock, the Chinese in Nevada were described in one newspaper editorial as ''frugal, industrious, courteous, patient, willing, cheerful: neither insolent nor quarrelsome.'' Within a decade, however, when the opportunities of the Comstock and of the satellite strikes in the deserts to the south and east had been largely cornered by banking and mining combines, these same qualities were denounced as "slavish virtues," and the Chinese themselves as devious, sly, and serpentine.

The seeds for this shift in attitude toward the Chinese had been early sown. The bylaws of the Gold Hill Mining District, established upon the discovery of the Comstock Lode, forbade Chinese holding claims. Chinese testimony was unacceptable in the courts, a ruling which had the effect of depriving them of legal protection since they could not bring charges or lodge complaints effectively. The 1864 Public School Act prohibited Chinese children from attending the public schools of the state (along with Indians and blacks), and the State Orphanage was closed to them as well.

The rationale for these discriminatory practices and the passionate feelings which inspired them was perhaps best stated by a Nevadan in the late 1870s who observed: "The Chinese drink little and never set 'em up, and in many ways they refuse to yield to the influence of American civilization." Certainly the Chinese clannishness offended the egalitarian spirit of the American frontier; and their outlandish dress and exotic customs only widened the gulf separating them from their European-cultured neighbors.

But it was not their strangeness alone which led to beatings and burnings and shootings. And neither was it that they competed unfairly in the labor market, "stealing" jobs away from honest white workmen, though this claim was leveled against them often. "It is as idle for us to enter into competition with the Chinese in industrial pursuits," harangued a distinguished Nevada politician in search of reelection, "as it would have been for the Kansas farmer a few years ago to compete with the grasshopper in the harvest fields." This theme of unfair competition, working for wages at which a white man would starve — and yet prospering — was heard constantly after the middle 1860s. But that was not the true reason for the hatred.

Convenience was the reason. The Indians were finished

before the Comstock Lode had barely been developed. They were disorganized and demoralized, and no fit object of any but the most casual hatred from any self-respecting white man. The blacks were too scarce to hate with any conviction; a ratio of one in a thousand, or less, is not substantial enough a target for sustained rage. But the Chinese were perfect. Not only did they keep apart from the whites, they had their own quasi-governmental organizations — Tongs — to which they devoted their allegiance. Their language and customs were as foreign as those of the Indians, their skins as noticeably pigmented as those of the blacks. Thus they were the perfect scapegoats.

By 1870, the Chinese accounted for nearly 7.5 percent of the Nevada population, and far outnumbered any other single nationality represented in the state. By 1870 also, organized anti-Chinese sentiment had begun to express itself openly. Anti-Chinese associations were formed in Carson City, Eureka, Tuscarora, Dayton, and other Nevada communities. At Empire, on the Carson River, a group of vigilantes burned the local Chinatown to the ground and chased its residents away. The Colombo Restaurant in Virginia City advertised virtuously that "No Chinamen" were employed on the premises, and the 1871 legislature passed an act prohibiting the employment of Chinese on state property. In 1879 the law was tightened even further: no state contracts were permitted to firms employing Chinese labor, and no Chinese could be employed in or about state public works projects, directly or indirectly.

By 1879 both major parties in the state had adopted a strong anti-Chinese plank in their platforms, and the question of Chinese immigration had become one of national importance, resulting in the passage of the Chinese Exclusion Act of 1882.

Nevadans were already practicing some informal exclusion of their own, principally along the line established at Empire. In the summer of 1876, when a construction train carrying a Chinese work gang approached the tunnel at the Storey County line, it was stopped by an armed mob of whites and ordered back to Carson City. The whites claimed that they should have preference for the laboring jobs done by the Chinese, and refused to allow them into Storey County. On the following day about 150 armed white men descended on a wood camp operated by H. M. Yerington and drove eighty Chinese woodcutters into the desert. They also made a blanket demand that any firm using Chinese labor replace them with white workers within forty-eight hours. The ultimatum was ignored, but tension remained high.

The press at first deplored the raids on the Chinese, but by the middle seventies, when the Workingmen's party issued an ultimatum to Reno's Chinese residents to leave or be driven out, the press had generally assumed a vigorous anti-Chinese attitude. The *Gold Hill News* informed its readership in 1877 that the Chinese steal by instinct; theft was as natural to them as eating.

The Chinese met the continuing campaign of violence and vituperation with determination. Not only did they refuse to panic, they did what they could to resist. When Carson City elected a solid slate of anti-Chinese candidates to the Board of Trustees unopposed, the local Chinese merchants lodged a claim for $50,000 in damages resulting from the raids of white hooligans. The claim was rejected without consideration. When a boycott was launched against the Chinese in Carson, the Chinese responded with a boycott of their own against any merchant participating in the anti-Chinese agitation.

Not surprisingly, the anti-Chinese campaign faltered with the first signs that the Comstock mines were petering out. Suddenly workingmen and merchants alike had some serious problems to deal with, problems that no number of house burnings or beatings could pretend to solve: the ore was giving out, and nobody could make a convincing case against the Chinese for that unhappy fact. By the end of the 1880s, anti-Chinese associations, raids, and harassments were forgotten as the whites scrambled to save themselves from economic collapse.

By the turn of the century, when the Chinese amounted to scarcely more than 3 percent of the state population, harassment had virtually ended, though social constraints were still strong, as a Carson City newspaper headline demonstrated in 1903. A story noting the marriage of a white woman and a Chinese man was headed, "Marries a Chink." Roughnecks raided Chinatown in Tonopah during the same year, but it was the last of such antics, and Chinese thereafter were allowed to exist more or less without unwelcome attention.

Unlike California, though, where the Chinese had experienced much the same kind of vicious treatment, Nevada does not now have a large Chinese population. Presently, less than two-tenths of a percent of the state population — about a thousand individuals — are of Chinese ancestry.

Despite their small numbers, today's Chinese Nevadans occupy positions of influence and prestige in the financial, political and professional hierarchies of the state.

BIG BONANZA COUNTRY

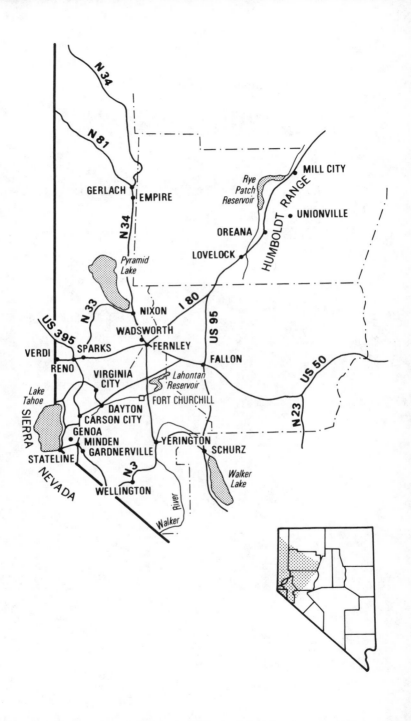

In its western slopes the Sierra Nevada range rises gently upward in a rumpled succession of foothills from California's great central valley to peaks more than two miles above the level of the sea. In the east the mountains drop sharply away from the summits in a sheer, slightly scalloped, granite scarp into the high desert valleys of Nevada. The majestic presence of the Sierra at Nevada's western boundary is responsible for much of the character of this portion of the state.

Warm moist air traveling inland from the sea is nudged upward above the inclined foothills as it travels eastward. As it rises the air cools and its moisture condenses, falling as rain at first, and then as snow. As the chilled sea air scrubs across the summits in winter, its moisture is plundered by the high forest lands. Beyond the crests, where the air swoops down again into the high-floored Nevada valleys, it is relatively dry. As a consequence, the characteristic vegetation of the region east of the Sierra Nevada is low-growing scrub brush, shading upward to piñon-juniper woodlands on the slopes of the low ranges enclosing the valleys. The broad expanses of gray brush are broken here and there by grassy meadows and alkaline playas, and striped occasionally by meandering lines of cottonwoods and willows that mark the courses of rivulets and shallow streams. Only three rivers plunge down the steep stone face of the Sierra to flow east into Nevada. The Walker and the Truckee curl between the humped and bulged desert mountains before damming up in Walker and Pyramid lakes. The Carson, until the construction of Lahontan Dam in 1915, simply spread out across a broad reedy marsh and vanished into the grey desert sand.

Jedediah Smith passed through this country, and so did a few other wide-ranging trapping parties. But the first Americans to enter it in numbers were the California-bound wagon trains pioneering the Humboldt Trail west from Salt Lake City. After the first of these had come and gone, Frémont came to name and map the rivers, the valleys, the mountains, and the passes. On his heels came the gold rushers. Few of them found the area (still part of Utah Territory then) of any interest except at its far western edge where forage for starved and exhausted animals was relatively abundant.

Recognizing an opportunity, in 1851 a party of Mormons established a tiny trading post and corral where a small trickle splashed down out of the heights to soak a natural meadow at the foot of the mountains. Here they provisioned the westward-bound wagon trains with staples hauled the long, dusty way from Salt Lake City, and with wild hay for the animals. These first merchants prospered, and in the spring of the following year a half-dozen more enterprising men established themselves along the route of the wagon trains where there was reliable water and good grass. The original trading post at Mormon Station became the center of population and activity between Placerville and Salt Lake City as farmers came out from Salt Lake City to occupy the fertile ground at the base of the mountains. At the same time a few Gentiles began prospecting the runty hills to the northeast. By 1853, despite the laborious passage of tens of thousands of gold rushers through northwestern Nevada, the non-Indian population of the region — the only permanently settled region within the present boundaries of the state — was fewer than three hundred.

In the following year Mormon Station became the seat of Carson County, Utah Territory, and its name was changed to Genoa. With characteristic energy in the face of incredible isolation and privation, the predominantly Mormon farming population had created a narrow green strip of attractive and productive croplands between the looming mass of the Sierra and the vast desert distances to the east.

At the same time the small number of prospectors working placer claims on Gold Creek, a tributary stream of the Carson, was slowly increasing as unsuccessful miners from the California gold fields began drifting back across the spine of the Sierra Nevada. Few of them braved the bleak winters, choosing to return to California until spring.

But by 1857 the population of Johntown, scarcely more than a tent camp, numbered in the hundreds durings the season of good weather. In that year the steadily disintegrating relations between Brigham Young's Utah theocracy and the federal government in Washington threatened to result in violence. Troops were marched toward Salt Lake City to impose the federal will, and to strengthen his hand in the impending confrontation, Young recalled many of the farflung Mormon colonists home to Zion. Among them were the farmers at the foot of the Sierra. All but one family abandoned what they had built and trailed out into the desert for home.

Thus the society of far western Utah Territory was largely secularized when, in January, 1859, rich gold placers were discovered near the headsprings of the willowed stream meandering past Johntown. Within a few weeks most of the settlement's population decamped for the new diggings on the flank of Sun Mountain, but several months of furious development passed before the miners realized that the gold-rich rock into which they were digging was the source of the free gold they had been panning for years downcanyon.

And it was several months more before it became clear that the heavy "blue mud," which fouled their gear and frustrated their efforts to get at the gold, was silver. Both of these discoveries had been made by the summer of 1859, and the ripple of glad news which arrived in California produced a shudder of excitement which sent thousands in a frenzied rush across the Sierra to Washoe. The Johnson Cutoff Trail became the most heavily traveled highway in the West.

As ecstatic an effect as the gold discovery had upon the white population, its effect upon the Indians was catastrophic. The white intrusion in such numbers was disrupting and destroying the delicate desert ecological patterns upon which the Indian survival techniques were based. The white man's livestock devoured the desert forage plants far faster and more completely than the Indians could themselves; the white man's rifles decimated the available game and drove away what wasn't shot; the white man's axes felled whole forests to provide timbers for the mines and lumber for the settlements. As white preemption of the Indians' survival resources accelerated, the Paiute population grew simultaneously more resentful toward the intruders and more dependent upon them.

In May of 1860 the thickening stream of traffic over the Sierra brought even more of the gold-hungry from California. As a number of the leading men among the Paiutes were meeting at Pyramid Lake to discuss their plight, nine young braves raided Williams' Station on the Carson River, burned down the buildings and corrals, and killed four whites. On the following day, word of the attack (but not of the abduction and repeated rape of two young Indian girls which inspired it) reached the settlements on the Comstock Lode. A panicky defiance suffused the populace. Men mustered themselves awkwardly into companies and set out toward Pyramid Lake to have "an Indian for breakfast and a pony to ride."

At the ensuing battle, however, the Paiutes breakfasted on the punitive expedition, annihilating about half of them in a day-long battle and sending the survivors limping back toward home. In June a more businesslike force composed of regular soldiers as well as volunteers drove the Paiutes into the mountains rimming Pyramid Lake and exhibited such military might that the Paiutes never again challenged the settlers in force. Nevada's brief "Indian War" was over.

The era of exploitation which had inspired the war was just beginning. For more than twenty years the immense wealth of the Comstock Lode drew settlers into the state. Many of them were miners and mill workers, but there were loggers and sawyers to supply the mines with timber, railroaders to freight in supplies, farmers and ranchers to provide food. New communities were founded and prospered: Carson City, first as a freight and staging center for the mines and then as capital of the Nevada Territory and of the state, Reno as the transcontinental railhead for the mines. Other small towns huddled along the railroad line to the east like beads on a string, and other mining strikes were made in the mountains of northwestern Nevada. For the forty years beginning with its discovery, however, the Comstock Lode dominated the affairs of the state.

By the turn of the century the Comstock mines had been 20 years in irreversible decline. Between 1880 and 1890 the state's population had dwindled 25 percent and by 10 percent more from 1890 to 1900. It was then that the great gold and silver strikes were made at Tonopah and Goldfield, fanning the mining excitements as hot as ever and inflaming the national imagination the way the Comstock had done just four decades earlier. The principal benefits of the new strikes, though, were largely confined to the southern section of the state. Northwestern Nevada continued in depression, and Reno replaced Virginia City as the principal community and focal point for the variety of efforts made to revive the region's economy.

Reno in 1900 was a dusty little roughneck town dominated by the railroad and thriving on its traffic. After barely two years of existence, Reno by 1871 had snatched the county seat away from the elder Washoe City. Reno suffered disastrous fires in 1873 and 1879, and in 1874 was the scene of a concerted vigilante movement to rid itself of hoodlums and scavengers.

The presence of the University of Nevada prompted residents of other communities to call Reno, snickeringly, the "Athens of Nevada." Despite the university and an increasing "polite" population, the life force of the town remained centered on the railroad, and its heartbeat was most evident in the mud-or-dust streets near the depot. This was where saloons, hurdy-gurdy houses, gambling halls, and hotels of varying degrees of elegance were concentrated. There too were the offices of the State Board of Trade, an organization devoted to promoting the exploitation of the one great untapped resource which the region possessed in abundance: empty land.

Founded in 1889 by Francis G. Newlands to encourage rural settlement, the Board of Trade had the active cooperation of U.S. Senators Jones and Stewart, both of them leading figures in Nevada politics since the hey-day of the Comstock. Jones and Stewart proposed a variety of measures in Congress to bolster the state's agricultural economy. Despite their efforts, and despite the interest shown by cooperatives and farm colonists ranging from the Hebrew Agricultural Society to the Dunkards, agricultural development was slow and failure-prone. There was simply too little irrigation water. When Newlands won election to the House of Representatives, it was largely on the basis of his proposal to get federal sponsorship for local irrigation programs.

This proposal was strongly supported by the congressional delegations of other arid western states, but just as firmly opposed by President McKinley. With the succession of Theodore Roosevelt, however, the agricultural problems of the western states found a sympathetic ear and the Newlands Reclamation Act was passed by Congress and signed into law.

In the autumn of 1903 the first federal reclamation project undertaken in the U.S. was begun about a dozen miles east of Reno. There a diversion dam was built to shunt Truckee River water into a thirty-three-mile-long canal which carried it to the Carson River. Feeder canals were constructed to bring more than twenty thousand acres of desert soil under irrigation. About 90 percent of the new arable land lay within Churchill County, and the population there rose from 831 in 1900 to nearly 3,000 in 1910.

The canal construction project, occurring simultaneously with the Southern Pacific's program to double the track over the Sierra, helped make Reno more raffish a town than ever as scores of footloose men roamed from saloon to bawdy house to gambling hall. Such a Sodom of gambling, liquor, and prostitution had it become, in fact, that in 1904 the president of the university restricted his students to the campus to protect their virtue.

Four years later the Reno mayor was still making vague promises to improve the situation, but another man was already embarked on a program which would revolutionize the town. W. H. Schnitzer was a lawyer with more genius than clients, and he hit upon the brilliant notion of advertising his services as a divorce lawyer in New York newspapers, periodicals, and theater programs. It was Schnitzer who publicized the advantages to a Nevada divorce: a relatively brief six-month residence requirement and an abundance of grounds versus the sole New York ground of adultery. Just how many thoughtful New Yorkers availed themselves of Schnitzer's services is not known; probably not many, as his name is not prominent in the annals of the divorce bonanza which followed.

The lode was not struck until 1906. By then Schnitzer may already have packed his shingle and left, for the divorcees who brought Reno into pay-dirt and prominence were not New Yorkers at all. Laura Corey had been a New Yorker once, when she was still a showgirl, but her most recent address was Pittsburgh, Pennsylvania, where she was wife of the president of U.S. Steel. Her arrival, her establishment of residence, and her eventual divorce were big news back East and provided precisely the right mixture of elegant naughtiness to elevate Reno into the prominence that the Comstock Lode and the Tonopah-Goldfield boom had inspired in the national consciousness. While the Nevada Commercial League was exalting the city's prosperous future as "encircled by live mining camps . . . camps that will make of Reno another Denver," the real source of prosperity began to appear at the railroad station, beminked, bejewelled, and bewildered at the rough little city peopled by cowboys, Indians, sheepherders, canal diggers, tracklayers, hay buckers, and silver miners, shy desert creatures who gazed timidly and appreciatively out at them from the barrel houses along Commercial Row.

Silent screen star Mary Pickford moved to Nevada in 1920 to wait out the six-month residency required by Nevada law for her divorce from actor Owen Moore. Much of the publicity surrounding the event emanated from Reno, which by then had become the most interesting city between Chicago and San Francisco. Goldfield and Tonopah were waning, and their leading citizens had moved north to continue their management of the state's political and economic life from Reno.

The giant among them was George Wingfield, the Oregon buckaroo-turned-gambler-turned-mining-share-speculator who had virtually cornered the market in Goldfield mining stocks and come away with a staggering fortune. With him came a half-dozen others of large fortune or influence: Tasker Oddie, who had seen to the original Tonopah assays for Jim Butler and who was later elected governor; Key Pittman, an Alaskan mining lawyer who had championed the small operations in Nome (and inspired the Rex Beach novel, *The Spoilers*) before moving to Tonopah and getting elected to the U.S. Senate; George Bartlett, another lawyer who served a term in the House of Representatives before moving to Reno to become the most prominent figure in divorce law as both attorney and judge; and Patrick McCarran, yet another Tonopah lawyer who had been Nye County district attorney and a member of the Nevada Supreme Court before moving to Reno and serving twenty years in the U.S. Senate. From Tonopah and Goldfield, too, came squadrons of businessmen and entrepreneurs eager to stay at the center of the action; hotelkeeper Frank Golden was probably the best-known among them, but there were dozens.

Reno had already become a pint-sized little city by the time the Tonopah bunch settled in. Downtown was a little sprucer than it had been in the earliest years, but about as coarse and rowdy as ever after dark. Polite society kept itself carefully aloof from the carryings-on, settling principally in the southwest beyond the river, or in the vicinity of the university: businessmen, bankers, doctors, lawyers, railroad officials. A few of them, especially those associated in one way or another with George Wingfield, were prominent beyond the borders of the state. Only Wingfield himself, however, could match the prominence of a pair of boyos from downtown: Big Bill Graham and Jimmy the Cinch McKay.

Damon Runyon would have felt right at home with Graham and McKay. Indeed, they had many friends in common. When Jack Dempsey got a Nevada divorce in 1931, it was McKay who testified to his bona fides as a Nevada resident. Graham was a big breezy man who liked to hold court at the Grand Cafe bar; McKay was smaller, brainier, and more aloof. Together they almost ran Reno.

The 1909 Nevada legislature had outlawed gambling, but Graham and McKay made up only one partnership among many that operated gambling parlors in Reno. They ran the Bank Club, which (with the Palace and the Waldorf) was one of the town's leading gambling houses. When Prohibition became the law of the land in 1919, the two men immediately became leading bootleggers, serving not only Reno and Lake Tahoe (where they ran the Cal Neva Lodge), but other communities in northwestern Nevada as well. They also dominated prostitution in Reno as proprietors of the Stockade, a fenced warren of tiny brick cribs on the eastern outskirts of town — each containing a bed, a wood-stove, and a whore. They also owned The Willows, a clubby bar, restaurant, and gambling parlor.

In New York they might have remained virtually anonymous; in Reno they were — well, not leading citizens exactly, but prominent men who commanded respect. When McKay shot Blackie McCracken to death in Douglas Alley that respect was so commanding that a coroner's jury ruled self-defense as a matter of course.

A couple of blocks from the Bank Club was the building in which George Wingfield kept the offices from which he ran Nevada. His old partner, George Nixon, had died in 1912, leaving behind him a chain of banks and a seat in the U.S. Senate in addition to a number of other profitable enterprises. Most of them became Wingfield's, though he spurned the Senate seat when it was offered to him by the governor. Instead, he served as the state's Republican National Committeeman. One of his lawyers, whose offices were a few doors down the hall, was the Democratic National Committeeman. Thus Wingfield was in a position to dominate both political parties in Nevada without the inconvenience of running for election or traveling to Washington.

So pervasive was Wingfield's power in Nevada during the quarter-century beginning about 1906, when he managed to consolidate ownership of every productive mine in Goldfield but one, that even though his empire crumbled almost forty years ago, and he has been dead for twenty years, the mention of his name still raises the neck hair of old-time Nevadans. He is still passionately hated and extravagantly admired today. He took long chances his whole life through, and he kept a poker face throughout.

With Wingfield running Nevada and Graham and McKay running Reno, the 1920s were golden years. The city was not only the center of political and financial power in Nevada, and as wide-open as any frontier town had ever been, it was also graced by the presence of the *haut monde* of the eastern seaboard and the gaudiest of Hollywood's celebrities. The daughter of Reno's mayor married Walter Johnson, the "Big Train" of the Washington Senators, who thereafter made annual visits to Reno and hummed the high fast one past ecstatic Reno youngsters before going on to spring training. There was so much going on in Reno, in fact, on every level of activity, that the brag coined for the Transcontinental Highway Exposition of 1927 (when U.S. 40 was paved through town) was more than justified: "Biggest Little City in the World."

But in the thirties things began to go haywire for the men who had done so much to create Reno's character. A decline in livestock prices had begun in the 1920s and continued without letup. 1929 was a drought year, and the state's cattle and sheep men were in serious trouble by then. The stock market crash increased the calamity, and Wingfield, a major lender, was forced to decide between foreclosing the bankrupt ranches or advancing more funds to tide the helpless ranchers over until prices improved. Unwilling to see a leading industry crippled, Wingfield granted more loans. But his own finances had reached a critical position by this time. His investments in every aspect of the Nevada economy were formidable, and as a consequence so was his power and influence. But a serious setback in any part of his empire could topple the entire interlocking structure.

1930 was another year of drought. And 1931. By now the state's stockmen were in desperate trouble, and Wingfield with them. With his characteristic daring, he provided the cash necessary to ship Nevada's herds east to out-of-state grazing lands. Wingfield had called the bet and played his hole card. But to do it he had to siphon funds from his savings banks through his commercial banks. Under the banking laws of the time this was an illegal transaction, and when it came to light the next year, the governor (ironically, a sheriff who had ridden into office on Wingfield's coattails) was forced to declare a twelve-day bank holiday. Wingfield's banks never reopened. Of the $4 million he had advanced to the state's stockmen by 1932, the bank's receivers recovered only $200,000. An avalanche of ranching bankruptcies followed, and Nevada was once again deep in depression.

Graham and McKay also overreached themselves. By the late 1920s their reputation had filtered east, and gangsters from New York, Chicago, and elsewhere began to visit Reno when the heat was on at home. The Graham and McKay fix was so good in Reno that as long as, say, Baby Face Nelson kept his nose clean while he was in town, he was safe from annoyance by the police. This kind of activity led to closer association with the out-of-town underworld, and soon the two — by this time in partnership with Scarface Sullivan, proprietor of the Palace Club — entered into the money-laundering business. By presenting the proper introductions a man with hot money could bring it to Reno, stand by as Graham and McKay doled it out to winning customers at their gambling tables, and take new currency home again — less, of course, a modest commission for the service. Alvin Karpis brought the $100,000 Hamm kidnaping ransom to Reno and hid out in a cabin on Walker Lake provided by Graham and McKay while the money was being disbursed to the innocents.

Then, according to a Reno newspaperman of the times, egotism led them astray: "hot shot eastern gangsters came in here and blew smoke at them, made them think they controlled the state." They began to function as switch men in confidence games. As early as 1929 the two were acting as bankers for con artists working the "wrong horse" or "wrong stock" switcheroo. Federal investigators ultimately pinned more than forty transactions of this kind to their door, with a take totalling more than a million dollars.

The Wingfield empire and the Graham and McKay satrapy fell apart almost simultaneously. By 1933 Wingfield stated phlegmatically that he was reduced to only a Packard automobile and membership in a duck hunting club. He was forced to go to Graham and McKay to borrow a couple of thousand dollars for walking around money.

In January of the next year federal agents grabbed Graham and McKay for mail fraud. A subpoena was issued for Roy Frisch, the Reno banker who had witnessed them receiving $117,000 from one of their suckers. Frisch's testimony would have locked up the case against the two so tight that even their high-powered lawyers couldn't squeeze them out.

A few nights later, before the subpoena had been served, Frisch left his home to walk the few blocks downtown to see a picture show. He never arrived at the movies and he never returned home. His disappearance, though, is not an utter mystery. It is known that Baby Face Nelson was in Reno the night Frisch vanished, and that he was an old friend of Graham and McKay. He also owed them a favor.

No one was ever charged with Frisch's murder (Nelson was shot to death by FBI agents in Illinois a few weeks later), and his absence did not ultimately affect the outcome of the government case. Graham and McKay were tried three times, twice getting hung juries and the third time drawing a conviction. Each of them was sentenced to nine years in federal prison and fined $11,000. They were pardoned, old men, by President Truman upon petition by Senator McCarran, and lived quietly in Reno until they died.

The Reno to which they returned was an utterly different city from that they had left. They had seen the legalization of gambling and the six-week divorce law, but they had been sequestered in stony lonesome when the effects of these revolutionary changes began to impinge themselves on their old wide-open town.

The immediate effect of the legalization of gambling was to remove the fix. It became obsolete. And just as repeal had legitimized formerly underworld occupations — bootleggers became distributors and saloonkeepers again — gamblers at once joined other businessmen in respectability. Even more important, legalization took gambling and drinking out of the vest pockets of a few men with connections and made them generally accessible occupations. Anyone could get into the business. To the rest of the nation, ready and eager to be scandalized, it seemed that Reno had suddenly become the most interesting vacation stop-over since Sodom, but in fact legalization toned Reno down considerably. Instead of Graham, McKay, and Baby Face Nelson, Reno now had prime movers like Raymond Smith, who put his carny-based knack for show business to work at creating games like Mouse Roulette, in which players bet on the number or color on which a live mouse would stop its scampering. Reno gambling was on its way to becoming a volume business.

Other changes were in the wind. In 1927 an ex-cab driver, ex-skating instructor, ex-engine room wiper named Norman Biltz had come to northwestern Nevada to head the 105-man sales force of a Lake Tahoe subdivider. He sold thousands of Tahoe lots at $500 each. With the Depression, however, the market for Tahoe property dwindled to nearly nothing, and Biltz thereupon concocted a plan which not only revitalized his own flagging career but also pumped new capital into Nevada's moribund economy.

Biltz compiled a list of the two hundred people in the U.S. who had personal fortunes of $10 million or more and set about selling them Nevada domiciles with high-priced real estate thrown in. His sales pitch was based on the fact that many states, floundering to maintain services which Nevada had never provided at all, were tinkering with their tax structures in ways that pinched the wealthy. Nevada did not. To a man or woman with $10 million, Biltz reasoned, the difference should be appealing. It was. By combining an encyclopedic understanding of tax laws, exhaustive research into the personal foibles of his millionaire prospects, and an endless willingness to take pains on their behalf, Biltz enticed an estimated fifty to sixty multimillionaires to Nevada. He settled them at Lake Tahoe, in exclusive Reno neighborhoods (Doris Duke, Jello heir O. F. Woodward, A. K. Bourne of the Singer sewing machine family, auto and aircraft magnate E. L. Cord, the Salt Lake City *Tribune's* Kearns family, and the steamship-owning Dants, all Biltz clients, maintained homes within sight of one another), and on the great ranches in Nevada's interior.

With the notable exception of Max Fleischmann (Fleischmann's Yeast), however, few of these immigrant millionaires put their money where their mailbox was. Most of them were content to remain as Nevada's star boarders, free to come and go as they pleased, but without kitchen privileges in state politics.

Upon the collapse of the Wingfield empire, Biltz himself came into considerable influence, but he was overshadowed by one of Wingfield's old Tonopah neighbors and bitterest enemies: Pat McCarran. McCarran leapt into the political vacuum created by Wingfield's disaster to win a U.S. Senate seat in 1932, and from that moment became the leading political force in the state and an increasingly influential figure in Washington. By the end of World War II northwestern Nevada had been returned to prosperity by the accumulated efforts of McCarran, the enterprising 1931 legislature, steady agriculture development, a resurgent livestock industry, and the celebrated reputation for frolicsome naughtiness that the Smith family and their colleagues had provided to Reno.

But the war's end accelerated the changes taking place in Reno. The city was no longer isolated. An increasingly affluent and mobile California population discovered that the long drive up over the looping Sierra highways was a small price to pay for a weekend of more or less innocent hilarity in the busy little casinos on Virginia Street. Ironically, this surge of prosperity presented the new generation of Reno gamblers with a new problem. Reno's conservative element had been content to look the other way when gambling had been largely confined to the rowdy element. But as gambling joined divorce as big business in the city, genteel society began to harrumph. The gamblers, not yet big enough to be influential, heard the rumblings of discontent and heeded them. They became more concerned with appearances than the people they were at pains to appease. They policed their operations carefully, not merely to prevent cheating, but to eliminate any hint of the unsavory. Prostitutes were made unwelcome and loud drunks were quieted quickly or hustled out the back door. Sizeable contributions were made to good causes (the recruiting fund of the University of Nevada football team and student scholarships are two examples), and in every way possible the gamblers behaved as the model citizens they were striving to become.

Their efforts have paid off. If none of them were ever admitted into the inner circle of old-line Reno society, neither were they badgered as they might have been. They have kept their place with restraint — two or three bright, brash blocks of Virginia Street — and left the bulk of the city alone. Bill Harrah, who scandalized his colleagues by employing efficiency experts to study his gambling operations as if it were a factory, and who was one of the first to refer to his business by the blander name of "gaming," became the biggest gambler in the world until

Howard Hughes went on his Las Vegas buying spree. The Smith family's Harolds Club was the only northern Nevada casino to attract Hughes' acquisitive eye.

CITIES AND TOWNS

Reno

Today Reno's setting, despite its occasional pall of smog, is one of the most magnificent of any American city, and weekending Californians no longer worry (if they ever did) that a part of a kidnapping ransom will turn up in the winnings they take home with them. It has been years since anyone was shot to death by a gambling man in Douglas Alley. Nevertheless, in making Reno safe and respectable — a job the polite element in Reno society could never have accomplished — the gamblers have ended forever a unique and fascinating chapter in the history of the West.

Virginia Street. Reno is more like a great big Elko than a small Las Vegas. It began as a railroad town, between the tracks and the Truckee River. A bridge across the Truckee carried traffic to and from the Comstock mines, and the road across it was named for its principal destination, Virginia City.

Virginia is still the principal north-south arterial street in Reno, and the old downtown between the river and the railroad is where most of Reno's action is still going strong. Besides the gaudy accumulation of gambling casinos, this is the locale of most of the city's banks, a handful of movie theaters, and shops and stores ranging from an elegant furrier to J. C. Penney.

Harrah's is a dominating presence in downtown Reno: a twenty-four-story, 325-room hotel that sticks up out of the city like a tusk. Old time Nevadans like to say that Californians got all the millions from the Comstock, but that they've been paying it back a quarter at a time since gambling was legalized. By 1965, Bill Harrah had accumulated enough of those quarters to be acknowledged the biggest gambler in the world. Howard Hughes has since purchased that title, but Harrah hasn't gotten any smaller.

Reno

Harolds Club, a few steps north from Harrah's, is still the friendly, folksy-western place that the publicity-wise Smith family created and operated until its sale to Howard Hughes (his last casino purchase, and the only one outside of Las Vegas). There is a magnificent gun collection exhibited on the second floor, with W. S. Hart's Peacemaker and a revolver of Wild Bill Hickock's among the thousands of weapons on display.

The Mapes was the first of Reno's post-war gambling palaces and still occupies a commanding place on the downtown skyline. The Holiday, a block to the east, was built to be Reno's non-gambling hotel, for maiden aunts to stay in. It turned out that maiden aunts like to be where the action is, and the Holiday nearly went broke. As a former owner put it, "You could fire a cannon through the main floor and never hurt a soul." When a small casino was installed six months after opening, the hotel perked up considerably.

The Riverside, across the Truckee, was Reno's premiere hotel through the twenties and thirties. By the 1950s the Riverside had lost some of its glamorous reputation, and by the late 1960s it had been cast into limbo by a succession of underfinanced or unlucky owners. A new owner and extensive remodeling have revived the Riverside in good style.

There are other good hotels, downtown and elsewhere. Eating places are plentiful and varied; a surprisingly cosmopolitan selection in this provincial city. Go exploring. Good streets to try: Virginia Street south of 4th; 4th, east and west of Virginia; Wells Avenue from 4th to South Virginia. There are eating places in the downtown casinos ranging from mediocre to superb.

Other Sights. There are a couple of outstanding attractions in Reno beyond eating, drinking, sleeping, and gambling. One is the Atmospherium-Planetarium on North Virginia, an easily recognizable building that looks like a warped frisbee. The building contains a domed theater in which a unique cinematic process provides visitors with the "experience" of space flight, an eagle's eye view of the formation of a fierce thunderstorm as it grows from a small pufferbelly cloud, the cosmic process of the birth and death of a star, and other marvels and wonders.

Across the way from the Atmospherium-Planetarium is the State Historical Society Museum. It is open without charge weekdays from 8 A.M. to 5 P.M. and weekends from 9 A.M. to 5 P.M. An excellent collection interestingly displayed.

The main part of the University of Nevada, Reno, campus lies back toward town. Its art galleries, theatrical productions, and sporting events are open to visitors. The Mineralogy Museum of the Mackay School of Mines is open to the public without charge 8-12 A.M. and 1-5 P.M. on weekdays.

Reno fields a California League baseball team, the Silver Sox. There are the usual bowling alleys, golf courses, pool halls, swimming pools, and similar recreational areas. Live it up.

The Chamber of Commerce has designated a meandering, forty-eight-mile round trip drive through the city as a "Scenic Drive." It takes about two and one half hours to negotiate, and as a spokesman puts it, "On your Reno Scenic Drive you'll see facets of the city that no cursory visit can provide." That's the truth.

Sparks

Adjacent to Reno on the east. Sparks was an afterthought of the railroad's, created in 1904 to replace Wadsworth as the big switching yard, repair facility, and crew change station on this section of the Southern Pacific line. Never prepossessing, Sparks is a quiet, largely residential community. It is nevertheless graced by the presence of The Nugget, one of northern Nevada's largest casinos which boasts a great variety of specialty restaurants under its enormous roof.

The second of Sparks's two principal visitor attractions is Harrah's Auto Collection on Glendale Road (take 2nd Street east from Reno; it becomes Glendale Road as it crosses Kietzke Lane: then watch for the signs. For the Nugget, take 4th Street east from Reno. It will bend and jog as it transforms itself into B Street, Sparks, but it will lead you past the big front doors that never close.

Harrah's Automobile Collection is Nevada's Grand Canyon: it presents a view of such shimmering diversity that the eye cannot take it in, and the mind is numbed. It is described as the most complete chronicle and collection of any object in history, and if that is an overstatement, it can't miss by much. The collection comprises about fourteen hundred automobiles, more than a thousand of which are on display at any given time. Each car is utterly authentic, from the precise shade and brilliance of the paint, to the stuffing in the upholstery: the showroom is a symphony in blacks and reds and ivories, tans and greys, brass and nickel and chrome.

There is the 1907 Thomas Flyer which won the 1908 New York to Paris race and still bears the scars of that momentous journey. There are two of the only seven Type 41 Bugatti Royales ever built. On hand is the last known Atlas passenger car in existence. There's Al Jolson's custom Cadillac, and Lana Turner's 1941 dual-cowl phaeton Chrysler Newport, one of five built. A 1913 Coey Flyer touring car is the oldest one still in existence, and the 1906 Compound is the last one in the world. The 1936 supercharged Cord limousine was the property of Mr. Cord himself, and Mr. Doble's 1925 Doble steam coupe is prominently displayed. The '57 Jaguar XK "SS" was Steve McQueen's. The 1911 Maxwell is what started the whole thing, the first antique Bill Harrah acquired, back in 1948. The 1933 Stutz was owned by Death Valley Scotty, and the Tucker was number thirty-two out of about fifty. Remember the 1966 Studebaker Wagonaire with the sliding roof panel? This particular one was the next to last to come off the assembly line.

That's fifteen cars already; only 985 or so to go, and each of them (except the Thomas Flyer) exactly like new. In addition to the cars, visitors may inspect the restoration facilities where, after painstaking research in the vast library archives maintained by the collection, parts are fabricated and finished to duplicate irreplaceable original equipment. Craftsmen make radiators, hub caps, radiator ornaments, any part that can no longer be dredged up from the back lots of old wrecking yards,

*Winning car in the New York
to Paris race of 1908; part of the massive
Harrah's Automobile Collection, Reno*

and they make them to the precise specifications of the original equipment. Restoration proceeds at the rate of about twenty to twenty-five cars a year; about 150 men and women are employed at the collection in various capacities.

Admission to the collection is nominal, with youngsters under six admitted free and family and group rates available. You may drive yourself and park free, or you may take free transportation from Harrah's Club downtown, riding in a motorized 1906 San Francisco cable car (California Street line) or one of the various antique buses the collection keeps in service, depending on the weather.

Harrah is convinced that the collection says more about craftsmanship, culture, and the industrial revolution than any other kind of museum which attempts to record the progress of man. A writer for *Autoweek* described it as the only non-neon monument the gaming industry has ever erected to itself. I say that if it is true that America has been conducting a love affair with the automobile since those first tinkerers began producing them, then this is where the love letters are stored.

Carson City

30 miles south of Reno, 38 miles north of the California state line via U.S. 395; 26 miles northeast of Stateline, Lake Tahoe. Located in the Eagle Valley, which had been settled by ranchers in the autumn of 1851, Carson City was established by Abe Curry, who paid $500 in gold coin and a remuda of horses for the richest part of the valley in the middle '50s. Curry's townsite was platted in 1858, several miles to the west of "Dutch Nick" Ambrosia's trading post on the Carson River. With the discovery of the Comstock Lode a few months later, Carson City began to outstrip Genoa as the freighting and transportation center of the new district. In 1861 the Territorial legislature created Ormsby County with Carson City as its seat. The following year Curry's Warm Springs Hotel, where the first Territorial legislature had met, was leased to serve as the Territorial Prison, with Curry its warden. The property was later pur-

chased by the state, and still serves as the site of the maximum-security penitentiary. Prison labor later supplied the quarried and faced sandstones used to construct many of the city's government buildings, notably the Capitol Building and the U.S. Mint (now the Nevada State Museum).

Carson City was established as Nevada's capital in 1864, and its growth afterward was no longer wholly dependent upon the health of the Comstock mines. The mines, nevertheless, provided Carson with most of its economic importance during the early years when, in addition to freight and staging lines, the city served as a marshalling point for the prodigious timber cut in the Sierra Nevada. Long flumes capable of carrying great pine logs were constructed from the lumber camps near the Sierra summits to swoop down the steep eastern slopes, ending north of Carson City where saw mills were erected. The logs, swept along on a rushing stream of water in the flume during their swift flight down the mountainside, were fed into the sawmills to make timbers for the ever deepening Comstock mines, and then loaded onto flatcars of the Virginia & Truckee Railroad for the trip to Virginia City and Gold Hill.

In November, 1869, the V&T was completed between Virginia City and Carson City, with the company's shops and main offices located in Carson. When the V&T pushed its line north to Reno in 1872, Carson City was linked by rail with the rest of the nation by the connection at Reno with the Central Pacific. By 1874, thirty-six trains a day were passing through Carson City, which was by then a town of considerable vigor.

Like many other Nevada towns in their youth, Carson was made lively, and occasionally dangerous, by the presence of hundreds of rootless, restless men. Shootings, stabbings, and street brawls were commonplace. But Carson was unique in contending with outbreaks from the state prison, several of which provided the young city with memorable moments. In the spring of 1873, for example, when new Warden P. C. Hyman presented himself at the prison, he was refused admittance by the man he was to replace. When the governor, the attorney general, and the secretary of state drove out to straighten things out, they too were turned away. Not until a force of sixty riflemen and a cannon had been drawn up before the prison gate did the retiring warden surrender and permit himself to be relieved of his office.

But by and large the roughhouse was confined to clearly demarcated sections of the town, and the city's character and appearance was largely the consequence of its large government and mercantile population which lived circumspectly.

Carson's fortunes were affected by the decline of the Comstock, but the steady business of government prevented catastrophe as trade and traffic fell off. Carson participated vicariously in the Tonopah and Goldfield booms far to the south after the turn of the century by virtue of the fact that much of the traffic for those cities was routed to Reno, then through Carson via the V&T to the Carson & Colorado RR connection at Mound House a few miles east. This traffic ended suddenly when the Southern Pacific (successor to the Central Pacific) built a line connecting with the C&C from the east, thus bypassing the V&T altogether. Carson then resumed the quiet style of life that had evolved since the decline of the Comstock, only recently progressing to a brisk period of growth and development which has increased its population to more than 27,000.

Carson no longer innocently advertises itself as the nation's smallest state capital, but much of its appeal is the product of the long, lazy years when it did. The long-established Nugget on the city's main street has been joined by a new hostelry with an old name, the Ormsby House, to provide big casino action. Carson City is essentially a quiet and orderly settlement, with file clerks and bureaucrats far outnumbering the night-life crowd. And it is probably the most tourable town of its size in seven states.

Walking Tour. It is Carson's good fortune to have had no other significant industry than government since the Bonanza years of the Comstock, for the combination of gradual growth and the relatively conservative nature of the citizenry has contributed to the preservation and prettification of dozens of homes and other buildings dating from the nineteenth century. *Sunset Magazine* has devoted pages to Carson's attractive architecture, and as a consequence an hour's strolling tour along some of the older streets has become a pleasing experience for many visitors.

Here is one brief walking tour covering a dozen short blocks, about a half an hour's worth if taken at a slow dawdle (remember, though, all but a few of these "exhibits" are private homes; the residents don't relish strangers trampling their flowers or peering in their windows any more than you would: be discreet).

Park your car behind the supreme court building (across from the capitol building) and begin by walking east from the corner of Curry and Spear streets. The tan brick building at the southeast corner of that intersection was Wells Fargo & Co.'s Carson City office, and its Mother Lode architecture is considered a relative rarity in Nevada. Across the street is the Rinckel Mansion, built in 1874 by a local butcher. It is open for tours; times and seasons announced on the sign at the edge of the property.

At the eastern end of the block, at 214 King, is a pleasingly rococo home built by the Alcovitch brothers in 1880. Very nice millwork.

Continue east along King Street crossing Nevada and Division streets to the former Nevada *Appeal* building. In palmier days, this structure housed the Tahoe Brewery which, despite its name, used water from King's Creek for its beer. The slogan "Famous as the Lake" can still be seen painted on a few old buildings in the region, and a six-pack recently discovered in the basement of a Virginia City saloon went for $15, but Tahoe beer is no more, alas. Turn north at the next corner.

At King and Minnesota streets the present Catholic rectory was the residence of James Nye, the territorial governor appointed by Lincoln and later one of the state's first U.S. senators. "The Grey Eagle," as he was called, later lost a bid for reelection to the Senate, and upon his return to the family home in Virginia lost his reason and died insane.

At the next corner, 204 N. Minnesota was built by an early-day district judge using native sandstone quarried at the state prison and was erected with prison labor. This last caused a sprightly scandal over the private use of public energy.

Beyond Proctor Street stand 302 and 340 N. Minnesota. The former is distinguished by its "widow's walk" and round, conical-roofed porch. The octagonal structure out back with the stovepipe stack is a smokehouse built when a man could shoot game as he pleased, but could not refrigerate it even if he were a millionaire. The latter structure stands on the site of Carson's first school house, and is built of materials salvaged when the school building was torn down. It housed Dr. Simeon Lem Lee and his family. Dr. Lee was a Union war hero from Illinois who came to Nevada in the 1870s, settling permanently in Carson in 1879 after an extended residence in Pioche. He is remembered as a fiery, crochety fellow, but a good surgeon. The house was built in 1898 and has solid mahogany paneling in the dining room. Double back and walk east on Proctor Street.

On the next corner, Proctor and Division, are another pair of interesting homes. 212 N. Division is a six-room home built in 1874 and distinguished by the bay window on the front wall and the bird bath in the yard. Across Proctor Street, the Episcopal Rectory dates from 1868 and is one of the oldest residences in the city still standing on its original location. Turn north on Division, crossing Telegraph and Spear streets.

The stucco covering the two-story house on the northeast corner of Division and Spear streets is an anachronism, added years after it had been vacated by Orion Clemens, the territorial secretary of Nevada, whose younger brother became known as Mark Twain. The local people refer fondly to the place as the Mark Twain house because young Clemens was his brother's house guest on occasion.

Next door to the north is the marvelously decorative home built for H. M. Yerington, the superintendent of the Virginia &

Truckee Railroad. Fireplaces in this twelve-room structure are of marble, and its elegance is unmistakable inside or out. Double back to Spear Street and walk a block east to Nevada.

412 N. Nevada was built in 1870; its architecture is both intriguing and appealing.

406 N. Nevada, next door, to the south, was the home of Abe Curry, the founding genius of Carson City, and is built of sandstone quarried at the prison. The original front porch and a skylighted cupola have been removed. Continue south on Nevada Street.

308 N. Nevada is cottage-sized Victorian, small but flawless in its evocation of a vanished era in both design and workmanship. A feast for the eyes. You are now standing three short blocks from the point at which you began. Walk one block east and two blocks south to return to the beginning. This stroll covers only about half of Carson's homes considered in one way or another significant. To assist you in seeing them all, the Chamber of Commerce makes a detailed map available for the asking (at their office in the shopping center at the south end of Carson Street, or, during the peak tourist season, at the yellow caboose parked on the lawn at Spear and Carson streets in the center of town).

If many of Carson's older residential neighborhoods seem to comprise an outdoor museum, there are some extraordinary indoor ones too.

The Nevada State Museum. On N. Carson Street, between Robinson and Caroline, this handsome stone structure was built of prison-quarried sandstone in 1866 as a branch of the U.S. Mint, coining nearly $50 million in gold and silver before operation was discontinued. The building served as a federal assay office until 1933, then stood vacant until a local circuit judge, Clark Guild, persuaded the legislature to purchase it for use as a museum. Several new additions have been made to the old building, substantially enlarging it without sacrificing the solemn character of the original building unduly. It is open to visitors seven days a week from 9 A.M. to 5 P.M. As you might

State Museum, Carson City

expect, the mineral exhibits are among the finest of the museum's displays, and the unique "mine" in the basement is worth a visit even if museums are not your favorite pastime. Also recommended: the startling life-size diorama of a Paiute camp and the Dat-So-La-Lee woven baskets (many appraised at more than $10,000) in the Indian Hall.

The State Capitol Building. On Carson Street. Completed in 1870, and with a decorative iron fence contracted and installed by a female contractor — virtually unheard of at the time — the building is still used by leading state officers including the governor. Tours are provided in the summer months, but visitors are invited to prowl through the building by day in any season.

The Governor's Mansion. From Carson Street take Robinson Street west to Mountain. Nevada's governors have resided here since 1908, but the building was remodeled and refurnished during the incumbency of Paul Laxalt with $250,000, much of

Capitol, Carson City

Governor's Mansion, Carson City

which was raised by public subscription. The building is open for tours one day each week; arrangements and reservations must be made through the governor's office at the Capitol. It is a strikingly attractive example of formal Georgian design.

The Warren Engine Company Museum. Upstairs above the fire station at Curry and Musser streets. Open daily from 1 P.M. to 4 P.M., admission free. Except when a fire has everyone occupied, you'll get a guided tour of this small but intriguing museum by one of the twenty paid firemen who staff the Warren Engine Co. along with an approximately equal number of volunteers. The Warrens are the oldest established volunteer fire brigade in the U.S. (established 1863) and understandably proud of the fact. The materials they have assembled for display range from a meticulously restored 1912 chain-driven Seagraves fire truck to smaller, but equally colorful, memorabilia such as antique uniforms, lithographs, alarm systems, and the like. A delightful twenty minutes.

The V&T Repair Shops. On Stewart Street south of its intersection with U.S. 50. Not a museum, but structures impossible to pass without a close look, these immense buildings once housed the considerable shops of the Virginia & Truckee Railroad. Now occupied by a commercial firm, entrance is restricted. V&T machinists in these shops constructed and repaired much of the machinery used in the Mint, as well as maintaining the railroad's locomotives and rolling stock.

Carson offers a full range of automotive, medical, and professional services. In addition to the major new Ormsby House, there are more than a dozen good motels, most of them on Carson Street. The city also offers a surprisingly wide selection of good dining places.

Prison Store. Carson has the number and kinds of stores you would expect in a city of its size, but it also has one which is out of the orindary: the Inmate Store just outside the gate at the penitentiary. Drive east on Fifth Street and turn off into the prison parking lot. You'll see the small store building just to the left of the prison gate. Hours are from 8 A.M. to 7:45 P.M., seven days a week.

The store sells inmate-made handicrafts, art work, clothing, jewelry, and the like, and you can buy from the large selection on hand or have what you want made to order. Convicts can — and do — repair saddles, make personalized belts and purses, address invitations in excellent calligraphy, and knit caps and socks. The workmanship ranges from adequate to exquisite, and the inmate clerk (#10674: manslaughter) assured me when I last visited the store that, "I've been in other penitentiaries, but I've never seen such nice work as this in any of them."

Minden/Gardnerville

15 miles south of Carson City, 23 miles north of the California state line via U.S. 395; 12 miles north of the California state line via Nevada Route 88. Gardnerville is the elder of these two sibling towns, founded to serve the agricultural population of

the Carson Valley in a more conveniently central location than the long-established Genoa at the valley's western edge. The Carson Valley is one of the earliest-settled, richest, and most productive of the state's agricultural regions. The sharp-eyed travelers who notice the small signs alongside U.S. 395 at each end of the valley, welcoming travelers to Nevada's Garden Spot, may be tempted to take it lightly, particularly if they are passing through in winter; the signs, after all, poke up from a tangle of gnarled sagebrush. But in spring, summer, and autumn, when the valley is bursting with life, the vast irrigated tracts are a green velvet patchwork quilt upon which the stacks of baled hay stand like giant cheeses, and cottonwoods and poplars rise up like flashing green flames. The meadows are sopped with water from the Sierra, and fat and languid cattle browse placidly everywhere.

Gardnerville had its share of rough characters in its youth, but the farmfolk, often German or Danish in origin, were generally less frivolous and more peaceful than their mining town counterparts. So genteel were the residents of Sheridan, a nearby hamlet, in the years around the turn of the century, that when a U.S. senator came to campaign for reelection, the townspeople nailed the town drunk inside a piano crate. The old farm town of the nineteenth century has been elongated by the presence of U.S. 395, and most of the business enterprises face the highway.

Most services are available in Gardnerville, including a small shopping center, antique shops, and the inevitable neon-walled casino. Of special interest, however, are the Basque restaurants which cluster near the south end of town and which have provided Gardnerville with such fame as it enjoys beyond the confines of the valley. These Basque places were originally established to serve the large population of sheepherders from the Pyrenees who husbanded the bands of sheep, taking them high into the mountains in summer, and far down into the empty eastern valleys in winter. In Gardnerville, as in many of northern Nevada's smaller towns, Basques established hotels where the sheepherders could stay when they were laying over between jobs or taking a two-weeks' vacation. For the non-English-speaking sheepherders the hotels were a special convenience, as well as being inexpensive and hearty feeders. In time, other townsfolk came to appreciate the modestly priced suppers served at these workingmen's hotels, and today dining out at one of them is considered a substantial treat. Most of them are still small family operations, with mom and dad supervising a work force of sons, daughters, aunts, and nephews. Most places still reserve the first serving to the Basque boarders with rooms upstairs. All of them have bars, and except in the peak summer months, the clientele is largely local. They have deserved reputations for excellence. And as long as you are there, skip martinis for the evening and order a Picon Punch. It's a traditional Basque cocktail that doesn't affect your head as much as it does your knees.

Washoe Valley ranch scene

Minden adjoins Gardnerville to the north. These once-separate communities have fused together the way Reno and Sparks have done, and to visitors the demarcation line is of little importance. Nevertheless, Minden is worth a look on its own merit, for unlike the rather more haphazard quality that Gardnerville projects, Minden is as neat and quiet as a turn-of-the-century picture postcard town.

It was established in 1905 when the V&T, its profitable Tonopah–Goldfield traffic snatched away by the new SP spur through Hazen, decided to extend a line southward from Carson City to harvest the Carson Valley trade. By 1904, however, the only feasible right-of-way had long been in the possession of the Dangberg family. The Dangbergs were agreeable to the railroad's laying track across their ground — but only if certain conditions were met. The principal one was that the railroad must build its terminal, too, on Dangberg land, adjoining Gardnerville on the north. The railroad was agreeable, and when its small brick depot was constructed, a townsite had been platted around it and christened Minden. A two-block business district arose along Esmeralda Street, with a large grassy park separating it from the neat grid of residential neighborhoods. This tiny enclave still retains much of its quiet charm; the telephone company workers who eat their lunches in the park on warm spring and summer days often get up scratch softball games during the noon hour, and tourists who use the picnic tables there are often invited to join in. Except for this mild excitement, the town is magnificently quiet. You can hear the bees buzzing in the gardens and the children playing in the schoolyard.

Minden's old main street, angling away from the highway as it does, is quiet too. The sensation of traveling back to the turn of the century is the product not only of the architecture, which is superbly evocative, but also of numerous less intrusive facts about Minden: there are no parking meters on the business street, for example.

Minden has been the Douglas County seat since Genoa

gave up the stature it had once held as Utah Territory's principal settlement west of Salt Lake City, but its virtues do not much lend themselves to the tourist trade. Even the old Minden Inn, once a favored retreat for honeymooning movie stars, is less a resort than a curiosity these days. Built as a solidly unpretentious commercial hotel comfortably close to the railroad depot, the plain old structure has been remodeled so that it resembles a grandmother in hotpants.

Lacking any specific tourist attractions aside from its tidy air of the departed "good old days," Minden is still a point of more than casual interest to travelers, since three of the most scenic highways in the world intersect there, and it is the nearest Nevada settlement to a fourth.

Nevada Route 88, leading south from Minden and U.S. 395 at the north end of town, proceeds to the California state line, and there becomes California Route 88 through Woodford's and over Carson Pass in the high summits of the Sierra Nevada to California's Mother Lode and great central valley. This road, and California Route 4, which originates at Woodford's and jogs south to Markleeville before curling up over the mountains at Ebbett's Pass, are incredibly beautiful. California Route 89, which doubles with Route 4 between Woodford's and Markleeville, terminating at Topaz Lake in the south and circling the west shore of Tahoe in the north before continuing on through Truckee, Quincy, and a score of tiny mountain villages, is scarcely less magnificent. Nevada Route 19, climbing the sheer eastern face of the Sierra to drop directly into the Tahoe basin, provides motorists not merely an airliner's view of the Carson Valley as it soars upward, but a close experience of the mountain wall, thrilling and beautiful at once.

Genoa

(pronounced Juh-NO-uh). 7 miles northwest of Minden, 12 miles southwest of Carson City via U.S. 395 and any of several signed, paved roads leading west to the foot of the Sierra. Genoa is the oldest permanent settlement within the borders of

Nevada, and one of the most attractive villages anywhere in the American West. Established as a trading post in 1851 to serve the wagon trains as a resting and reprovisioning place between the deserts of the Great Basin and the granite barricade of the Sierra, Mormon Station, as the original settlement was named, became the nucleus of a small farming population. The town that grew up around the old Mormon stockade was named the seat of Carson County, Utah Territory, in 1854, and of Douglas County, Nevada Territory, in 1861.

With the discovery of the Comstock Lode, Genoa's importance was reduced. Carson City was closer to the mines, as convenient to California, and more energetically promoted. Genoa's importance had become largely local by the time statehood was granted in 1864, and even that local importance had been superseded to a great extent by Minden and Gardnerville in 1910, when a resident of the county poor house, tormented by bedbugs, attempted to fumigate his mattress by lighting a pan of sulfur beneath it and succeeded in burning half the business district, the county court house, and the original Mormon fort. The fort had never managed to acquire a patina of historical reverence; by the time it burned it had been used as a cafe, a chicken coop, and a pig barn. The present structure is a replica.

In 1916 Genoa had lost the county seat to the up-and-coming burg of Minden, and the town dwindled further in size and importance. There are only about fifty dwellings in the place now, and perhaps a half-dozen business establishments, but each of them is attractive, and taken all together they comprise a village of extraordinary charm. Of special interest to visitors are:

Mormon Station. The replica of the original Reese store and stockade (which burned in 1910) are now operated as a museum; open daily from 9 A.M. to 5 P.M. except during the peak summer months, when it stays open until 7 P.M. The museum is devoted to the memorabilia of Carson Valley history, both the spectacular aspects, such as the Pony Express (Genoa served as a way station), Indian relics and firearms, and the homelier side as well: farmhouse furniture, tools, and other domestic articles. It is a small museum, but it hints at the quality of life in the region it represents better than many larger museums do elsewhere. There is a grassy picnic area alongside the old stockade with drinking water and a few tree-shaded picnic tables.

Across the street from the fort are the remnants of Genoa's business district, the principal features of which are the old brick building which served in turn as court house and school until 1956, and the oldest saloon in the state. A frog-jumping contest is held in the place every summer, but visitors in the off-season are also invited to bring their frogs in if they wish.

The pink house across the way was built as the home of John Reese, a Mormon entrepreneur who developed Mormon Station in 1851; in it the early settlers of the valley wrote a petition to the state of California asking for annexation. When the petition went unanswered, they organized a ''squatter's government'' of their own, mainly to protect their title to the land they had put under cultivation. Today the pink house is a

Mormon Station, Genoa

dining room, and cocktails are served on the back lawn on warm summer evenings.

The road south along the base of the Sierra passes Walley's Hot Spring, a resort of some fame in years past, with pools, a hotel, ballroom, and gardens. A fire destroyed most of the elegance in 1935, and the pools are now devoted to hydroponic farming. The nearest natural hot-water pools open to the public are at Grover's Hot Spring State Park across the California state line, about four miles west of Markleeville. A short distance south beyond Walley's Hot Spring is the foot of Nevada Route 19, the Kingsbury Grade, which scales the Sierra to Lake Tahoe.

Verdi

(pronounced VUR-dye). 10 miles west of Reno, 2 miles east of the California state line via Interstate 80 and marked access road. In 1864 a California lumber company established a logging and sawmill town at Crystal Peak on the eastern flank of the Sierra Nevada a short distance north of O'Neil's Crossing on the Truckee River. By 1868 the town had grown to fifteen hundred people, most of them engaged in cutting and sawing the timbers required by the eastward-snaking Central Pacific Railroad, and in working small gold and silver deposits. The CPRR tracks bypassed the town, however, and by 1869 most of Crystal Peak's vitality had been transplanted to the new railroad townsite at the old crossing on the Truckee half a mile to the southeast. Saw, lath, and shingle mills buzzed incessantly to serve the California market, and by the 1880s Verdi had become one of the main collection and storage points for winter ice which found ready markets in California's valley and coastal towns during the summer.

Verdi was never a metropolis, but its place in history is secure as the site of the first train robbery in the West. Shortly after midnight on the morning of November 5, 1870, five men boarded the east-bound train at Verdi. When the locomotive left the station, the passenger cars had been uncoupled and left standing on the track. The locomotive, pulling only the mail car and express car, chuffed eastward to a stone culvert, where the engineer was ordered to stop. A sixth man lunged up the bank carrying an armload of guns and tools, and the robbers opened both cars, putting the train crew in the mail car under guard while they struggled to open the Wells Fargo & Co. treasure boxes which another member of the gang had telegraphed from San Francisco would be especially rich. The robbers found $41,600 in the shipment, hurriedly divided it at the edge of the roadbed, and scattered into the night after barricading the track to prevent immediate pursuit.

Within a week every member of the gang had been captured and $39,500 of the stolen money recovered. Two of the men turned state's evidence against the rest during their trial at Washoe City and were released; the others drew sentences of from five to twenty-three and a half years in the state penitentiary.

The train robbery was only a single exciting moment in an otherwise uneventful history, however. Verdi could boast of a short-line logging railroad of its own before the twentieth century was very old, but by the 1930s logging had virtually ceased and Verdi was subsisting on the railroad and highway traffic. U.S. 40 uncoiled itself after its sinuous passage over Donner Summit to pass through the town, and by the late 1940s and early 1950s the town was best known for the large truck stop there; at any given moment there were likely to be more diesel tractor-trailer rigs parked in Verdi than private passenger cars.

More recently a metal company has built a small plant near the Truckee. The Donner Trails Guest Ranch, one of the few remaining dude ranches in the state, stands in a meadow on the outskirts of Verdi, and the Verdi Inn, a remnant of the earlier prosperity which accompanied the railroad, is a noted dinner house of old and exceptional charm. The town shows evidence of its ups and downs, but the setting alone is worth the short detour from the freeway. A dirt road leads into the Sierra by way of Dog Valley, and at several scenic points along its length the

Forest Service has developed campgrounds. The Washoe County Park Department maintains the beautiful Crystal Peak Park at the river's edge just south of town as a picnic area and fishing spot.

Wadsworth

34 miles east of Reno, 63 miles southwest of Lovelock via Interstate 80 and paved, marked access road. Established at the Big Bend of the Truckee River as a principal construction camp for the CPRR, the Wadsworth townsite was platted on the location of Lower Crossing, a place of recuperation for wagon trains cutting westward from the Humboldt Sink in the 1850s and '60s. As the last source of wood and reliable water before the hundred miles of desert separating Wadsworth and Humboldt (northeast of Lovelock), the town was an important base camp during construction of the railroad.

It retained its importance after construction had been completed, for the repair shops of the railroad's Truckee division were located there in 1868. A roundhouse containing twenty stalls was built at Wadsworth, as well as numerous other railroad buildings. The railroad payroll attracted a fair business community, and by the 1880s, when the town was serving as railhead for numerous settlements far to the south, the population had reached about five hundred. It never grew much larger, and in 1904, when the railroad relocated its Truckee division shops in Sparks, it grew decidedly smaller. Whole buildings and entire neighborhoods were dismantled and loaded onto flatcars; even shade trees were uprooted and shipped westward to the new town. Wadsworth was relieved of all the burdens of importance by the change, but the remnants of the old town linger on the attractive riverside setting. The relocation of the highway has deprived the town of the bulk of the traffic it served when U.S. 40 passed through the main street, and things are pleasantly quiet in Wadsworth these days.

Nixon

16 miles north of Wadsworth via Nevada Route 34; or 48 miles northeast of Reno via Nevada Routes 33 and 34. Nixon (named for a former Nevada senator) is the headquarters town of the Pyramid Lake Paiute Indian Reservation, and is situated on the Truckee River at a point about two miles from the river's outlet into the lake. It is a small town, but made interesting recently by the construction of a Tribal Crafts Store to complement the small general store and gas pump across the road which had been the town's only enterprise for many years. Available at the store is a good assortment of Indian-made goods, principally beadwork and leather. There isn't as much there as you'd like to select from, but the store carries one of the most embracing stocks of Indian-made goods that you are likely to find in Nevada.

Gerlach

59 miles north of Nixon via Nevada Route 34. Gerlach is a village with a small store, cafe, and gasoline pump which derives its meager living from the gypsum mine at Empire (a few miles down the road toward Nixon), from the Western Pacific Railroad, which maintains a small switching yard and crew-change facility there, and from the few hardy off-the-beaten-path visitors who pass through the town bound for the Smoke Creek and Black Rock deserts or for the nearer Fly Geyser. It is of little interest to the casual visitor except that Fly Geyser — a prominent landmark discovered by Frémont during his 1843–44 expedition which also took him to Pyramid Lake — is one of the best natural hot springs in the state for bathing.

Numerous pools, each of them fed by hot-water springs, are scattered over a wide area. Most of them are *very* hot, but some can be found which are only comfortably warm, and others in which currents circulate randomly and in discernible patterns. There are hundreds of natural hot springs in Nevada, but Fly Geyser is among the very finest. Some sheds have been thrown together, and there is no admission charge. The experience of bathing here will leave the visitor with a new respect for the Indian way of life, and perhaps even a sharper awareness of the Indian's difficulty in making peace with the white man's style of living. Which, with all its plumbing fixtures, is as far from providing a bath like this one as earth is from heaven.

Fallon

61 miles northeast of Carson City, 110 miles west of Austin via U.S. 50; 62 miles east of Reno via Interstate 80 and U.S. 95 Alternate; 56 miles south of Lovelock via Interstate 80 and U.S. 95; 72 miles north of Hawthorne via U.S. 95.

When Mike Fallon built a crossroads store on his ranch property in 1896, the sparsely settled region of the Carson Sink had a nucleus for the first time since Kenyon's trading post at Ragtown, to the west, served the wagon trains. In the same year the county renovated the old Virginia City-to-Fairview telegraph line (for which it had paid $975 in 1889) to serve as a single-line telephone system linking the farms and ranches in the area.

Creation of the Truckee-Carson irrigation project by the U.S. Reclamation Service shortly after the turn of the century prompted a tremendous spurt of settlement in the region to be provided with irrigation water, and the tiny settlement at Fallon became the seat of suddenly vigorous Churchill County. By 1902 a post office had been opened there and a switchboard installed on the telephone system. The courthouse was completed the following year, and a newspaper established. By 1904 there were more than a dozen businesses in the settlement, including a hotel, and a volunteer fire department had been organized. A bank was established in 1908, and Fallon was incorporated. By this time the intensive agricultural development held promise of satisfying dividends. Fallon's Hearts O' Gold cantaloupes graced the menus of fine hotels and restaurants in the biggest cities of the nation, and Fallon turkeys brought premium prices.

For the Fourth of July celebration in 1911 the town fathers

imported a wrestler who challenged all comers after lying down in the dirt and gravel of Maine Street and permitting his trainer to drive an automobile over his rigid body. In 1915 the Nevada State Fair was held in Fallon, and townspeople built an enormous "palace" of hay bales at the intersection of Maine and Center. The structure measured sixty-by-sixty feet and its walls rose eighteen feet high. At night dances were held within it while the king and queen of the fair presided on thrones of Fallon hay.

Prices turned down after World War I, and Fallon fell into dull times. Even the small mining excitements in the nearby hills did not entirely lift the depression. In June of '42, however, the Navy began construction of a small air station southeast of town, and Fallon's economy jumped up again. The station was closed in 1946, but reopened during the Korean War. In 1960 it was dedicated to Lt. Cdr. Bruce Van Voorhis, a Navy Medal of Honor winner from Fallon. The fourteen-thousand-foot runway is the Navy's longest.

Fallon today wears a look of quiet satisfaction; a quiet tree-shaded town as easy and amiable as a well-to-do farmer's wife who still wears her old gingham apron but has an all-electric kitchen to take the backache out of the chores. The telephone system is still owned and operated by the county, the only one in the nation run as a public utility. At the city park on summer afternoons visitors can take the kids swimming at the pool or watch Little League games, with fielders wearing mitts they could use equally well as chest protectors. In a game I watched one day the centerfielder was so short that when he threw up his glove to catch a fly ball he looked like a microwave relay station. The tail end of the number 7 on his back was tucked halfway down into his pants. On warm July nights, when a brief thundershower has wetted down the fresh-cut hay and alfalfa in the fields and the frogs and crickets serenade, Fallon is at its drowsy, comfortable best.

There are a small handful of gambling parlors on Maine Street, but most of Fallon's attractions are related in one way or another to agriculture. In August, after the middle of the month, fresh picked cantaloupes are sold at the Workman Ranch on Soda Lake Road. Dairy tours can be arranged on short notice at the Chamber of Commerce office. And most interesting of all, perhaps, are the weekly livestock auctions held on Allen Road beginning at 11:00 A.M. every Wesnesday. Livestock buyers from all over the country attend, and in busy seasons the sale continues late into the night. Cattle are the principal attraction, but sheep, hogs, and horses are auctioned as well, and occasionally more exotic creatures like a goat or burro. It is a fascinating experience.

Fallon's motels are good and accommodations are plentiful except on rodeo weekends, of which there are many in Fallon.

The Churchill County Museum, quartered in a former grocery store on south Maine Street, is open from 9 A.M. to 5 P.M. weekdays, 10 A.M. to 5 P.M. Saturdays and Sundays. Admission is free, and exhibits include such oddities as leather post cards and a hand-operated vacuum cleaner as well as the more usual collections of frontier Americana. It is an excellent museum.

Lovelock

92 miles northeast of Reno, 72 miles southwest of Winnemucca via Interstate 80. Named for an early homesteader in the valley through which the Central Pacific Railroad drove its tracks in 1868, Lovelock became a way station of some significance during the early years of the twentieth century when it served as railhead for a handful of small mining settlements in the hills. Most of the mining production ended by the early 1920s and Lovelock's economy became largely agricultural again. Some forty thousand acres are under cultivation in the Lovelock Valley, most of it devoted to hay and grain.

In recent years experimentation with alfalfa has begun to pay off, as the 18 percent protein content of the Lovelock alfalfa is richer than most of the Western crop. Alfalfa and seed have been exported in quantity to California for several years, and twenty-five pounds of seed were recently furnished to experimental farms in mainland China where agronomists are making test plantings at Peking, Chengchow, and elsewhere while considering the purchase of about nine million pounds more.

Lovelock alfalfa growers also raise leaf-cutter bees, which trip the blossoms of the plant during pollination, and it is a peculiar characteristic of these creatures that they plug holes. Soda straws left unattended, for example, may be clogged with bee eggs and other junk (no honey, alas), and one local man had to give up on the gas burner for his outdoor barbecue when the leaf-cutters persisted in stuffing the jets with gunk.

The town of Lovelock can boast a pair of architectural treasures at opposite ends of Main Street (which crosses the highway at the flasher-light). To the north is the Pershing County courthouse, erected when Lovelock was named seat of the newly-created county in 1919. It is round. There is another round courthouse somewhere in the U.S., the local people think, but no one can recall where. The other gem is the Southern Pacific Railroad station. Its glory is that it is like small-town turn-of-the-century railroad stations everywhere in the West, but is painted mint green and pistachio rather than the usual ochre yellow, providing a pleasantly imaginative appearance setting off the Gothic simplicity of the design.

Lovelock provides all services to travelers, up to and including a small casino. There were two, but the Pershing Hotel burned a few years ago and has not been rebuilt. Night life, consequently, is not Lovelock's strong point. In fact, Lovelock may be the plainest town in Nevada, its heteroclite courthouse and Erewhonian railroad station notwithstanding.

Wellington

26 miles southwest of Yerington via Nevada Route 3; 14 miles northeast of the California line, 30 miles southeast of Gardnerville via U.S. 395 and Nevada Route 3. Established in the early 1860s as a station on the Carson City–Aurora stage line, Wellington is situated on the West Walker River at the head of Smith Valley. With the dwindling of Aurora's prosperity in the early

1870s, Wellington became altogether a farm settlement with a post office, gas station, general store, and cafe. It remains today much as it has been for years, and the general store, with wash boards, horse tack, and galvanized tubs suspended from the rafters, is one of the few authentic cow-country general stores still operating in the state. The proprietor is friendly to strangers unless they show an inclination to settle nearby or to encourage tourists to flock there; he is a refugee from city life and in no hurry to experience the rush and bustle again. If he seems glum, it may be because of the new subdivision being scratched into the hillside just out of sight to the west. The Wellington Cafe is famous in the region for its hearty meals, and the reputation is deserved.

Yerington

67 miles southeast of Carson City via U.S. 50 and U.S. 95 Alternate (or 73 miles via U.S. 395 and Nevada Route 3); 57 miles northwest of Hawthorne via U.S. 95 and U.S. 95 Alternate. Situated on the East Walker River in Mason Valley, Yerington began as a small store and trading post called Pizen Switch. When the settlement had grown to hamlet size, municipal pride demanded a more genteel handle for the little burg, and the citizens agreed on Greenfield. But a little later on, the citizens gambled their gentility for a chance at profit by renaming the town Yerington, after the superintendent of the Virginia & Truckee Railroad. It was hoped that by this gesture of amiability, and certain other inducements, the road might extend a line into Mason Valley. It didn't work.

Yerington did get a railroad, but not until early in the second decade of the twentieth century when the copper deposits worked briefly and unprofitably in the 1860s were subjected to wholesale exploitation. Smelters were built and the Nevada Copper Belt RR completed from Wabuska, where it connected with the SP, through Yerington and around the base of the Singatse Range where a number of mines were being worked. For the remainder of the decade the district produced copper valued at several millions, but production dwindled with the twenties. With the outbreak of World War II, the Anaconda Copper Mining Company bought control of the principal copper properties, but decided against bringing them into production because of the large lag-time involved. When the Korean War broke out in 1950, however, Anaconda resumed large-scale production under contract with the government. An open pit was dug into the side of the mountains west of Yerington in 1952, and ore production began two years later.

The development of the lode came too late to save the NCBRR, which tore up its tracks in 1947 and died, but it did foster the establishment of Weed Heights, a pleasantly planned, rather prim company town just west of Yerington. Precipitated copper and concentrates are trucked from Weed Heights to Wabuska, where they are trans-shipped by rail to the Anaconda smelter in Montana.

Despite the establishment of the company town, Yerington has benefited from Anaconda's presence. Local boosters refer to the region as the ''Cattle Kingdom in the Copper Hills.'' Rich farms extend southward through Mason and Smith valleys to within sight of the Sierra Nevada. Nevertheless, Yerington is the only Nevada community of any size which does not lie on one of the main tourist thoroughfares. There is no place in town which can properly be called a casino, and a large, clean, and well-appointed motel room could be had for less than $10 when I last visited town.

The country club is open to the public, and is where Yerington folk take out-of-town visitors to supper. There are perhaps a dozen more restaurants in town, most of them adequate. Yerington offers all services, but only a single tourist attraction: the daily guided tour of the Anaconda mining operation at Weed Heights. Unless you are willing to consider as an attraction the friendly, slow-paced, small-town quality of life there. Spend fifteen minutes on the main street about five o'clock in the afternoon and count the number of people who stop and chat with one another as they pursue their errands. I watched one man spend ten minutes traversing a single block, amiably passing the time of day with four different neighbors. It should be a sight for sore eyes for anyone with the urban whips-and-jingles.

LAKE TAHOE

Some 35 miles southwest of Reno via U.S. 395 and Nevada Route 27 (to Incline); 16 miles west of Carson City via U.S. 50 (to Glenbrook); 14 miles west of Minden via Nevada Route 19 (to Stateline); and accessible from Interstate 80 via California Routes 89 (14 miles to Tahoe City, California) or 267 (13 miles to King's Beach, California).

Tahoe lies at the back of California's neck just where Nevada's elbow juts into it, a bright blue eye staring upward from its granite socket like an outsized parody on Picasso. At an elevation of 6,229 feet it is an alpine sea ranking with the most spectacular mountain lakes in the world and spreading across nearly two hundred square miles of mountain grandeur well over a mile above the level of the ocean. To the west of Tahoe the peaks of the Sierra Nevada rise up to four thousand feet above the lake, and to the east the craggy summits of the Carson Range soar even higher. Tahoe is cupped between them, nearly forty cubic miles of water, in a pine-blanketed setting of such compelling majesty that within twenty years of its discovery in the virgin, virtually inaccessible wilderness, by John C. Frémont in 1844, the lake had become one of the West's leading vacation spots. Today, after more than a century of development, Tahoe and its basin rank as one of the finest all-season recreation areas in the world, but the matchless scenic beauty of the region is being exploited at such a pace that the sight of the lake through the pines is as likely to inspire depression as exhilaration.

Lake Tahoe's modern history began in 1844 when Frémont spied it from a pinnacle in the Carson Range to the east. It accelerated four years later when John Calhoun "Cock-Eye"

Johnson connected Placerville, California, with the Carson Valley by a looping trail across the portion of the Sierra that skirted Tahoe's south shore. Mart Smith arrived to open a small trading post at the present site of Meyers, California, in 1851 and became Tahoe's first permanent settler — excluding the peaceful Washoe Indians whose claim to the region was considered no better than that of the other forms of wildlife which inhabited it.

When the first trans-Sierra stagecoach run was made in 1857 it followed the Johnson Cutoff Trail with a stop at Smith's Station. Two years later, when the discovery of the Comstock Lode drastically swelled traffic over the road, two competing stagecoach lines maintained regular schedules with Tahoe stops, and when the Pony Express was inaugurated in 1860, the route followed the old Johnson Cutoff as well.

By 1861 the Comstock's voracious need of timbers and fuel had prompted the beginning of a logging industry in the Tahoe Basin. One of the early prospectors for productive timberland at Tahoe was young Sam Clemens who hiked up to the east shore of the lake from Carson City in 1861. After finding what seemed to be a goodly stand of trees, Clemens and his companions spent several memorable days vacationing. "So singularly clear was the water," he wrote years later in *Roughing It*, "that where it was only twenty or thirty feet deep the bottom was so perfectly distinct that the boat seemed floating in the air! Yes, where it was even *eighty* feet deep. Every little pebble was distinct, every speckled trout, every hand's-breadth of sand. Often, as we lay on our faces, a granite boulder, as large as a village church, would start out of the bottom apparently, and seem climbing up rapidly to the surface, till presently it threatened to touch our faces, and we could not resist the impulse to seize an oar and avert the danger. But the boat would float on, and the boulder descend again, and then we could see that when we had been exactly above it, it must still have been twenty or thirty feet below the surface. Down through the transparency of these great depths, the water was not *merely* transparent, but dazzlingly, brilliantly so. All objects seen through it had a bright,

Lake Tahoe

strong vividness, not only of outline, but of every minute detail, which they would not have had when seen simply through the same depth of atmosphere. So empty and airy did all spaces seem below us, and so strong was the sense of floating high aloft in mid-nothingness that we called these boat-excursions 'balloon-voyages.' " Clemens left Tahoe to more business-like developers after inadvertently starting a small forest fire in his camp.

By the middle 1860s, few Tahoe visitors took much time to admire the scenery. Comstock-bound traffic past the lake had become incessant, and a string of hotels, corrals, stores, and businesses had been established along the lake's south shore to cater to the travelers. In a single three-month period in 1864, 6,667 men afoot, 883 more on horseback, and another 3,164 in stagecoaches paraded past the lakeshore. Plodding along with them were five thousand pack animals and nearly that many cattle. A daily average of 320 tons of freight was drayed past by 2,564 teams. One entrepreneur even drove a flock of turkeys from California to Virginia City by way of Lake Tahoe. Hay to feed this endless stream of beasts was grown, harvested, and hand-baled at the west shore of the lake for delivery by two-masted schooner to the docks on the south shore where it sold for as much as $250 a ton.

Tahoe's first resort had been built in 1863, at Glenbrook, to provide the leisured aristocracy of the booming Comstock with a vacation spot conveniently located at the head of the new turnpike to Carson City. It was a spa which could compare with the celebrated Saratoga in New York for elegance, gaiety, and the beauty of its surroundings. The first privately owned vacation "cottage" was built at the lake that same year at Emerald Bay, for stagecoach magnate Ben Holladay.

The phenomenal lakeshore traffic slowed to a trickle with the completion of the transcontinental railroad in 1869, and the lake settled down to a dreamy existence of summer frolics and winter hibernation. Only the prodigious logging industry, centered at Glenbrook, but with crews working everywhere in the basin, and the commercial fishermen who shipped trout by rail from Truckee to the coast and to the Comstock (at fifteen cents a pound) broke the idyllic calm. These activities went largely unreported in San Francisco and Sacramento, and as far as the outside world was concerned, Tahoe was for play. The elegant new Grand Central Hotel, erected at Tahoe City in 1871, with walnut furniture, Brussels carpets, and an ornate cast iron kitchen range that cost $800, eclipsed Glenbrook House as Tahoe's toniest resort the day it opened. The Grand Central was superseded in its turn by Elias J. "Lucky" Baldwin's Tallac House farther down the beach.

As early as 1879, when Baldwin purchased "Yank" Clement's hotel, the property was one of the few which had not been logged by timber cruisers, and by the early 1880s, Tahoe folk were remarking on the obvious decline in numbers of the native trout. They were affected both by the efficiency of the market fishermen (commercial fishing was not outlawed until 1917) and by the effect of the logging and sawmill operations on the spawning creeks, which became choked with sawdust, slash, and other debris.

The first tangible demonstration of what the future held in store for Tahoe did not arrive until 1900, but when it came it was right on schedule, shrieking and clicking and belching smoke: a narrow-gauge railroad that connected Tahoe City with the Southern Pacific's main line at Truckee. The arrival of the railroad prompted construction of the marvelously gabled four-story Tahoe Tavern a little south of town to set the new standard of elegance at the lake, and increasingly more people enjoyed Tahoe excursions and vacations. The lake steamers glided across the smooth summer surface of the lake as before, trailing languid plumes of black smoke. Logging at the east shore had largely ended with the decline of the Comstock and conversion of the railroads to coal.

Just then, enterprising eyes began to squint at Tahoe's water. In 1900 A.W. Von Schmidt, president of the Lake Tahoe and San Francisco Water Works, proposed to furnish the city of

San Francisco with a water system capable of delivering thirty million gallons of Lake Tahoe water a day in return for $17,690,000. He was agreeable to building a system which could deliver up to a hundred million gallons a day, for that matter, at a proportional increase in price. The San Francisco County Board of Supervisors went so far as to visit the proposed site of his diversion dam on the Truckee before allowing the idea to lapse. Three years later a San Francisco attorney named Waymire proposed a tunnel through the side of the Tahoe basin to drain the lake into the Rubicon branch of the American River and thus supply limitless power and water to San Francisco. The Waymire project made even less headway than Von Schmidt's.

The third attempt to drain Tahoe was backed by the Department of the Interior, and it nearly succeeded. The U.S. Reclamation Service, discovering it had made massive miscalculations in estimating the amount of water required to make the Truckee-Carson Irrigation District in Nevada a success, moved to acquire the outlet dam and control gates in 1903. With control of the outlet, Reclamation Service engineers could release whatever amounts of water were needed downriver, and thereby wash the egg from their chins.

The Truckee Electric Company refused $40,000 for the property on which the dam was located but made a counter-proposal. The company would present the Reclamation Service with the dam and gates gratis in return for rights to a guaranteed flow of four hundred cubic feet of Tahoe water a second. The anxious Reclamation Service engineers agreed at once.

Negotiations dragged, however, and it was not until after Taft's election to the presidency in 1908 that an amended contract was agreed upon. In it, further concessions were granted to the utility company. The company could locate pipes and reservoirs anywhere it might choose on public land. Most important, it was granted the right to locate another outlet diversion at any depth below the lake's surface. This concession amounted to blanket permission from the federal government to drain Lake

Tahoe into the Nevada desert for the purpose of generating electricity for sale.

The chief forester for the Department of Agriculture got wind of the contract before it could be signed, and waged a vigorous delaying battle against it. In 1912, property owners at the lake succeeded in getting an injunction against the power company preventing it from cutting into the rim of the lake.

One side-effect of the affair was to raise again the question of ownership of Tahoe's water. Not until 1935 was agreement finally reached. It provided that the level of the lake was to be maintained at a minimum elevation of 6,223 feet above sea level and allowed to fluctuate upward to as high as 6,229.1 feet. Thus the top six feet of Tahoe are in essence reserved for the down-river farmers in Nevada — less the million and a half tons a day that are lost to evaporation.

An even more portentous herald of the future arrived at Tallac House in 1905 in the person of Mrs. Joseph Chanslor, a merry woman of almost oppressive determination who had clattered and churned up over the summits from Sacramento, all alone, in her chain-driven Simplex. She made the trip in the remarkably fast time of eight hours. The automobile had come to Lake Tahoe. When Mrs. Chanslor sputtered off toward Sacramento again, no one realized the significance of her visit.

Still another hint of the future was dropped in 1911 when lots were subdivided at Tahoe Vista on California's north shore. But to the horror of the proprietors, the first purchaser turned out to be a notorious Sacramento madam named Cherry de St. Maurice. A pall fell over further sales in the "exclusive" sub-division.

Nevertheless, in 1927 Tahoe land was being subdivided in earnest. Forty thousand lots were carved out of Robert Sherman's holdings at King's Beach, Tahoe Visita, and Brockway, not for the Crockers, Yeringtons, and Birdsalls who had purchased spacious lots at Idlewild in the 1880s, but for citizens of more modest means who could afford $500 for a smaller slice of paradise. A hundred and five salesmen were selling those lots, many of them never laying eyes on the property itself but selling from maps set up in San Francisco hotel suites. By the time the stock market fell to pieces in 1929, seventeen thousand lots had been sold. Most of them reverted to the subdividers when the new owners could not meet their small payments during the Depression. In an awkward, painful way, the Depression had saved the lake from wholesale exploitation, at least temporarily.

As early as 1900, bills had been introduced in Congress to create a national park at the lake in order to preserve it forever, but not until the middle 1930s did the proposal reach even the investigative stage. In 1935 an inspector for the national park system reported his conclusions in Washington: ". . . in its pristine state, the proposed Lake Tahoe National Park area was worthy of recognition as a national park; however, under the present conditions, I do not feel justified in recommending this area for future consideration as a national park." The inspector cited as reasons the facts that (1) more than 90 percent of the proposed park area, slightly less than two hundred square miles along the lakeshore, was already in the private hands of about two thousand invididual owners; (2) the speculative prices on lake frontage made acquisition costs prohibitive; (3) "ruthless commercial enterprises . . . have destroyed to a great extent the natural character and charm of the most valuable portion of the proposed national park site — the land immediately adjacent to the lake." Despite the urgings of other park service personnel, notably wildlife technician Robert T. Orr, who saw in the Tahoe basin a unique and relatively pristine alpine habitat "which might well be considered as of National Park merit," the recommendations of the inspector were accepted and the proposal for a Lake Tahoe National Park was shelved for good.

Nevertheless, by the end of World War II Tahoe still had only about a thousand permanent residents in the villages and hamlets rimming the lake. But in 1945 the twentieth century began to arrive at Tahoe with such rapidity and with such impact that conditions at the lake went rapidly out of control.

By the late 1940s Tahoe vacation resorts were turning away

customers, and new ones were being built to accommodate the overflow. Skiing, never popular on the West Coast except as a "hillbilly" pastime in isolated mountain communities, became the fashionable wintertime equivalent of tennis. By the early 1950s Tahoe's recreation potential had caught the attention of everyone on the coast — including that of the Nevada gamblers. In 1954 Harvey Gross tore down the little cafe-cum-slot machines he had been operating at the state line on the South Shore and erected an eight-floor gambling hall and hotel. The next year, Bill Harrah built a sprawling casino across the street, its gambling rooms in Nevada and its parking lot in California. At once the character of the adjoining California shore began to change. With millions of new weekend visitors driving to the lake from California's coastal and valley towns to gamble, hundreds of Tahoe property owners began a scramble to provide them with the other services they required for a comfortable visit: motels, stores, restaurants, auto garages.

Logged-over land at Bijou, on California's south shore, had sold for less than two dollars an acre in the late nineteenth century. By the end of WW II it brought as much as $150 per front foot, and by the early and middle 1950s had leapt in value to $500 per front foot. A vacant lot which sold for $3,800 in 1954 increased in value to $18,000 by 1957, inspiring a San Francisco newsman to write, "If you have some money in the bank, run — don't walk — to the south end of Lake Tahoe. Millions have already been made. More is waiting if you know what you are doing."

At about the same time, ski developments began to multiply, gradually transforming Tahoe's "season" from a busy four-month summer to a brawling year-round affair. When the 1960 Winter Olympics were held in Squaw Valley, winter recreation in the Tahoe basin and its adjacent slopes became big business, and Tahoe's exploitation accelerated in quantum jumps.

New subdivisions were carved out of the forests, whole new communities were established. Glaring neon signs were stuck onto raw concrete cubes looming up out of the pines like anti-parks. Roads were cut, hills were leveled, trees were felled. Slash and debris found its way into the lake. And in 1967 Dr. Charles Goldman, professor of zoology and director of the Institute of Ecology at the University of California, Davis, wrote a magazine article about his studies at Tahoe. "Nine years ago," he wrote, "when I first started studying Lake Tahoe, the rocks along the shore showed only a slight growth of attached algae. Last spring, one could collect handsful almost anywhere in the shallows, and waves piled up mats of the detached material along the shore." If permitted to continue unchecked, Goldman warned, the buildup of algae would eventually change the lake waters from clear blue to turbid green. "Tahoe is being polluted," he insisted. "To deny this fact is comparable to saying that a man receiving a daily dose of arsenic in his breakfast coffee is not being slowly poisoned. If the poisoning continues, the steady accumulation in the man's system will eventually kill him. . . . Those who claim Tahoe is not being polluted are applying the irrelevant standards commonly applied to water used for domestic purposes."

Goldman's warning did not go unheard, but response to it varied from the concern of conservationists to the indignation of the developers. In the summer of 1969, a California Water Quality Control engineer issued a report refuting Goldman's findings: "We define for our use at Lake Tahoe any measureable, visibly or otherwise, change in the lake's water quality. Using this definition one must conclude after reviewing all available data that Tahoe is not polluted, and furthermore is not measurably different in quality than when first discovered by John C. Frémont on February 14, 1844." Less than a year and a half later, however, the same engineer reversed himself utterly in a new memorandum.

"Water quality degradation caused by erosion in the Tahoe Basin is much broader than the nutrient contribution alone. Turbid or muddy waters now enter the lake through many of the streams where development is proceeding in the watershed.

This turbid water resulted in a large mat of algae floating to the shore at King's Beach during the summer of 1967. The algae mat was not supported by a controllable nutrient inflow but rather was killed by a turbid water inflow from a stream which reduced the clarity of the water and thereby did not permit the penetration of light necessary for plant life.

"The first recorded algae bloom in Lake Tahoe occurred during the summer of 1969 along the south shore. It is my opinion that such blooms will occur annually and will become more extensive in area and in algae density. . . . This problem can be corrected only through complete control of all man-caused erosion in the watershed."

In December, 1969, President Nixon signed a Congressional Act establishing the bi-state Tahoe Regional Planning Agency, a board composed of members from California and Nevada who would oversee development at the lake as a whole, thus superseding the more than seventy federal, state, county, and local agencies which had exercised separate control in the past. The agency has not yet established itself as a forceful voice for conservation.

Because Nevada's Lake Tahoe shoreline is reasonably compact, its communities, recreation facilities, and other attractions are here grouped together rather than listed separately:

Stateline

26 miles southwest of Carson City via U.S. 50, at the California state line on Tahoe's south shore. The present community of Stateline sprawls across the area occupied in Tahoe's quiet past by a pair of settlements called Lakeside and Edgewood. Lakeside was centered upon Carney's (formerly Lapham's) Stateline House, an inn built in the early 1860s to serve the flood of Comstock traffic and bisected by the California–Nevada boundary survey of 1873. The inn burned in 1876 and was not rebuilt until 1892, by which time a small settlement had grown up on the site. By 1901 Lakeside had flourished to the extent of

having a post office and a boat landing with regular steamer service. A new survey in 1899 placed the heart of the community a half mile deeper into California, and as the years passed in tranquility, Lakeside became an attractive little enclave of summer cottages. With the scrambling dash toward exploitation which began in the early 1950s, Lakeside property values soared enormously because of the proximity to the Nevada casino developments. It is now a clutter of motels, gift stores, cafes, and other enterprises auxiliary to the gambling trade next door in Nevada.

Edgewood originated in yet another of the strategically located stations on the Johnson Pass Road, the renowned Friday's Station, established by "Friday" Burke and "Big Jim" Small in 1860. As soon as a log barn and a shed could be thrown together to accommodate, respectively, horses and men, Friday's served as Nevada's westernmost relay station for the Pony Express. Friday's was home station for Pony Bob Haslam, the messenger whose famous ride — 380 miles on horseback through hostile Indian territory — ranks as the outstanding feat of that spectacular organization. Burke and Small also controlled the toll road franchise past their expanded station, and collected as much as $1,500 a day in the peak months of the Comstock traffic before the railroad. The Pioneer Stage Line used the station as a horse change and dinner station as well.

When the railroad destroyed the lake's roadside prosperity, the partners split their holdings, Small keeping the old station and Burke the lakefront land farther to the east as far as Round Hill. By the 1880s Small was publicizing his "Buttermilk Bonanza Ranch" by reporting tongue-in-cheek sightings of a mermaid "with a fine chest development, beautiful white mustache one and one-half inches long, and of a most amenable nature" frolicking just offshore. Remarkably enough, considering the rush to "improve" the area by creating neon-coated cubes of concrete everywhere along the lakefront, the old Friday's Station still stands. Its original hand-hewn interior walls and floors are intact. It goes virtually unnoticed by the iron tide of traffic that floods past it each day, bound for the hard glare of lights just down the road.

Stateline today is connected politically with Nevada, but economically with California. Most of the millions who visit the large casinos at the south shore have driven up from northern and central California communities, and most of the employees who deal them cards, serve them drinks, and carry their luggage live across the line in California.

There are several gargantuan casinos at Stateline and a handful of smaller clubs, all of them on U.S. 50 in the half mile east of the Nevada state line.

These casinos, and Tahoe's legendary beauty, draw as many as fifty thousand visitors a day into the Tahoe basin, where about six thousand hotel rooms are available to accommodate them. The public campgrounds around the lake turn visitors away at the rate of thousands a day during the warm-weather months. Many people who head for Tahoe without lodging reservations find themselves staying in Gardnerville, Carson City, or Truckee. Perfectly nice places, but not Tahoe.

At Timber Cove Marina, just west of Stateline in California, the stern-wheeler M. S. Dixie leaves three times daily for three-hour lake cruises (June 1 through Labor Day). The itinerary varies according to the weather, but Emerald Bay is usually included, and the scenic north and west shores. The experience is delightful and as close as possible to a glimpse of Tahoe's appearance before the exploitation of the last two or three decades.

The East Shore

U.S. 50 proceeds around the eastern lake shore from Stateline. A mile or two along the road is Round Hill Village, a shopping center of uniquely charming design, managing at once to appear both modern and comfortable. The enclosed mall houses a variety of shops, cafes, and restaurants.

A paved road to the lakeshore provides access to Nevada Beach for swimming, boating, and picnicking. The network of roads serving the residential area above the shopping center provides any number of magnificent views of the lake.

Commercial development of the Nevada shore is relatively sparse except at the California state line north and south, but there are a number of excellent dining places.

Glenbrook, once Tahoe's most renowned resort, and later the scene of intensive logging and sawmill operations, is quiet now. Bliss Country Club, an excellent nine-hole golf course is the settlement's only attraction to visitors these days.

Beyond Glenbrook, U.S. 50 climbs to Spooner's Summit, where a small settlement had grown up in the 1860s around the saw mill operated by Michel Spooner, a French-Canadian. The Pioneer Stage Line kept horses and feed here, serving its route to Carson City. Just below the summit to the west, Tahoe traffic takes a left turn and continues north on Highway 28.

The North Shore

Highway 28 is a two-lane road which meanders along the lake's eastern shore, much of it altogether undeveloped and part of it included within the Nevada State Park system. Sand Harbor State Park has been created as a swimming beach and boat launching facility at one of the loveliest sites on the lake. Design and construction of the facilities has been carried out with an obvious concern for the integrity of the region. A nominal per-car fee is charged at the entrance gate for day use of the park, and another for use of the boat launch ramp. No camping is permitted in the park in any season; the park is open the year around.

A short distance north of Lake Tahoe State Park, at the outskirts of Incline Village, stands the Ponderosa Ranch, an amusement park which derives its "authenticity" from its fidelity to the sets of a television program.

The community of Incline Village itself spreads north and east away from the Ponderosa Ranch, along the Tahoe shore and into the pine-forested slopes above it. It is a far more pleasant settlement than the LA-in-the-Pines on the south shore. No traffic jams here, no parking messes, no slurban sprawl.

Crystal Bay begins where Incline Village leaves off, and the center of this small community is located at the California state line where a concentration of gambling houses has been doing a seasonal business since before WW II. Here the famous Cal-Neva Lodge no longer suggests much of its raffish past. During Prohibition the bar at the Cal-Neva was an uproarious rendez-vous, one of the most stylish speakeasies in the American West. More recently it was partly-owned, briefly, by Frank Sinatra before the State Gaming Commission yanked his gambling license for having unsuitable playmates. Presently the Cal-Neva is as respectable a gambling hall as exists in the state. It is also the newest hotel at Crystal Bay, with two hundred rooms built in 1969 in a ten-story addition overlooking the lake.

Several of the smaller north-shore clubs still shut down for the winter, but there is a growing optimism here that "the season" will soon become a twelve-month affair. Most of that hopefulness stems from the perpetual development of new ski areas in the vicinity and the opening of a new paved highway which put Interstate 80 only 12 miles away.

California begins at the west end of Crystal Bay.

THE COMSTOCK

Peter O'Riley and Patrick McLaughlin were a pair of prospec-tors whose luck had thinned out in California. Like a few dozen others, they had abandoned the increasingly company-dominated Mother Lode to prospect across the Sierra Nevada where a man alone or in a small partnership could still count on washing good wages out of a streambed. They had worked their way up near the head of Six-Mile Canyon by early 1859, and were excavating a small reservoir to store water for their placer-ing when they discovered gold-rich gravel that rivaled the dis-coveries a month or so earlier at the head of Gold Creek. Henry Comstock, one of the original locators at Gold Hill, cut himself in on their claim by insisting the men were digging on his "ranch," and a settlement began taking form at once.

James Fenimore, a bibulous Virginian, was making his way to his brush-roofed dugout one evening, staggering drunkenly over the rough ground, when he stumbled and fell, breaking the bottle of whisky in his coat pocket. Staring ruefully down at the whisky soaking into the yellow dirt he made the best of a bad situation by "christening" the new camp "Virginny," after his home state.

And thus was founded the west's most extravagantly rich mining camp, Virginia City. As the wealth and the extent of the lode (to which Comstock's name early became attached) was recognized, Virginia became less a camp and more a city by leaps and bounds. By 1862, as the helter-skelter of discovery began to give way to the more formal rhythm of steady production, many of the mines tangled together in litigation and starved for the ready cash required to sink shafts, extend tunnels, and ship ore to the mills.

By bringing order to the chaos, William Sharon and the Bank of California came into control of many of the lode's leading properties. As in California a decade earlier, the Comstock had passed from the era of the individual prospector into the era of large corporations and syndicates. The economic cycles smoothed after an extended period of readjustment, and in 1871 an enormous body of high-grade ore discovered at the nine hundred-foot level of the Crown Point brought that mine's stock up from a low of $2 a share to more than $1,800 a share. Other stocks rose in sympathy, and almost at once other new discoveries were made.

The $35 million extracted from the Crown Point was matched by the Belcher, and in 1873 the "Big Bonanza" was struck deep in the Consolidated Virginia, a concentration of ore that yielded $105 million in gold and silver. By the middle 1870s there were twenty-five thousand permanent residents in Virginia City, another nine or ten thousand in Gold Canyon, and thousands more in smaller communities in Six-Mile, Seven-

Mile, Flowery, and other nearby canyons. In Virginia City alone there were over a hundred saloons, six churches, four banks, and a railroad with as many as fifty trains a day during the busy peaks. When a great fire destroyed three-quarters of the city in 1875, rebuilding began immediately.

But the "new" Virginia City never matched the old. Mining continued unabated, but the ore was thinner in its values and no vast new discoveries were made. In 1878, after nineteen years of production in which nearly $300 million dollars in gold and silver had been bucketed up from the shafts, the lode entered decline.

The Sutro Tunnel was completed the following year, too late to have an appreciable effect on the fortunes of the lode. Pumping the water from the mines was made easier, but without the high-grade ore to send to the mills, production continued to lag. By the 1890s the Comstock mines were largely moribund, though more than $400,000 was extracted in 1899 and production continued more or less sporadically until 1942. In its later phases the Comstock was a travesty of its youthful self.

Mining after the turn of the century was largely low-grade, but with realistic values to the ore, so that for many years after it had ceased to be the wonder-of-the-world, the Comstock was still producing at a rate of better than a million dollars a year. Only small and short-lived attempts have been made at revival since World War II, though exploration advances and recedes like the tide at fluctuations in the price of silver.

Virginia City

24 miles southeast of Reno via U.S. 395 and Nevada Route 17; 16 miles northeast of Carson City via U.S. 50 and Nevada Route 17. For twenty-five glorious years the leading city in the state and the most important community between Denver and San Francisco, Virginia City began to falter in the middle 1880s, slipped deep into decline ten years later, but did not ever altogether die, even when mining was curtailed by government fiat in 1942. Mining never resumed except in small and sporadic operations, and by 1950 Virginia City was fairly well on its way

to being a ghost. But in 1952 Lucius Beebe, former New York City society columnist and authoritative railroad buff and author, rediscovered it, restored a ramshackle mansion in the upper reaches of the town, and reactivated the *Territorial Enterprise* in the tradition of Dan De Quille and Mark Twain. Beebe's presence, and the interest he aroused in the frowsy old mining town, prompted the beginnings of a tourist boom which accelerated beyond all anticipation with the debut and continuing popularity of *Bonanza* on television.

It is fashionable these days to lift a genteel lip at Virginia City, to dismiss it as honky-tonk and cheapjack, to deplore the use of so many of its impressive old buildings for the sale of carnival slum souvenirs to weary and travel-stunned tourists, and to wrinkle a concerned forehead over the debauch of a rich historical property.

Nuts to that.

Virginia City is still extraordinary. It is its own true descendant; a feeble and degenerate descendant, perhaps, but still firmly and organically connected to its own nineteenth-century beginnings.

It is true enough that Virginia City is no longer the brutal amalgam of a San Francisco and a Gary, Indiana, that it was in its heyday. Its industries are dead and its elegance is faded. But that is to be expected: the Comstock area has been reduced to less than a fiftieth of its peak population during the years of the Big Bonanza. What makes Virginia City remarkable today is the fidelity with which it represents its own robust youth. And it is interesting that much of the criticism leveled at the community is based precisely on this fidelity to the past.

The principal denouncement of Virginia City concerns its commercialism, as if the mining men who built the city were propelled by the tenderest and most sublime of motives. Visitors offended by the eager greed of contemporary Virginia City would faint dead away at the sight of the original. In a magazine article recently, the author announced a wistful concern over the choice Virginia City had to make between being ''honest''

Virginia City

and "hokum." That is as nonsensical as asking an orange to choose between being round and being orange. In its glory Virginia City was one of the great hokum capitals of the world, as crude and as brash a city as ever rooted itself to a western mountainside. So thick was the hokum there that many a good man — and his money — was mired down in it forever. Most of it took the form of worthless or fraudulent mining stocks, but it embraced the whole spectrum of get-rich-quick or get-something-for-nearly-nothing schemes that quick and devious minds could invent. Lacking a general interest in mining shares these days, local entrepreneurs have simply taken to retailing hokum across the counter. That hokum is quite properly "honest" and appropriate to Virginia City.

The signs which bristle above the board sidewalks and line the roads into town constitute another common objection to Virginia City. They are considered garish and given large responsibility for creating a "Coney Island" atmosphere. Quite so. Here is what a visiting journalist wrote about Virginia City in 1863: "One of the most characteristic features of Virginia City is the inordinate passion of the inhabitants for advertising. Not only are the columns of the newspapers filled with every species of advertisement, but the streets and hillsides are pasted all over with flaming bills." So for authenticity's sake there should probably be more signs, certainly not fewer, and more telephone and electric lines strung from poles along the streets. Any post-fire (1876) photograph shows them clearly, festooning every intersection like clumsy midair cat's cradles.

Some of Virginia City's signs are neon now, and that is clearly an anachronism, as are the automobiles creeping through town at a snail's pace, their drivers in search of a place to park. But neon instead of paint and board, and automobiles instead of wagons and buggies (traffic was worse when fifteen thousand people lived in the city, and parking utterly impossible) — these are consequences of Virginia City's survival as a living community, a place where old traditions remain intact, not through the efforts of historical boards or restoration specialists or educators, but in the very fabric of the lives of its citizens.

In the recent magazine article referred to, the author suggested that Virginia City "in the offseason feels more like it must have been. . . . In most saloons along the board sidewalks two or three natives huddle around a lone bartender and a heater." That's wrong too. From the day of its founding Virginia City was an enormous carnival of frenetic activity. To quote the journalist of 1863: "Entering the main street the saloons along the board sidewalks are glittering with their gaudy bars and fancy glasses, and many-colored liquors, and thirsty men are swilling the burning poison; organ grinders are grinding their organs and torturing their consumptive monkeys; hurdy-gurdy girls are singing bacchanalian songs in bacchanalian dens. All is life, excitement, avarice, lust, deviltry, and enterprise." Or in other words, allowing for contraction, just like a peak tourist-season Sunday today.

There is another point which needs to be stressed in Virginia City's favor. The town can still boast a broad and distinguished variety of eating and drinking establishments, perhaps even a better ration than in the boom days.

Virginia City's museums have a distinctive appeal. "Most of them break every rule that has been devised for good museum operation," a lifelong professional in the field told me, "but people love them: they can touch things, turn cranks, flip switches, just fiddle." There are half a dozen such museums, including the life-sized "dioramas" of mining life offered in several of the ancient buildings on C Street. If there seem to be an imposing number of desks that used to belong to Mark Twain, well . . . he was a prolific writer after all — and hokum is a natural part of Virginia City's heritage.

Most of Virginia City's business houses are stretched along the length of C Street, and the steepness of the cross streets discourages many visitors from exploring further. That is regrettable, since much of Virginia City's charm and character does not emerge from a single view. A half hour spent touring

the rest of the town by car or on foot is well worth the investment; many of the Victorian homes on the hill above town, most
of them dating from the 1870s and '80s, have recently been
restored and stand in rather splendid fashion once again.

B Street, the next above C, is well worth a stroll. The Court
House is a distinguished example of western Victorian public-
building architecture, and visitors are encouraged to view the
building which still houses the machinery of county government. The building, like most of those now standing in Virginia
City, was constructed after the great fire of 1875. It is distinguished not only by its impressive dimensions and spacious
elegance, but by the statue of justice above the main entrance: it
wears no blindfold.

Chief among the attractions along this promenade is Piper's
Opera House, once the leading theatre on the lode. The opulent
International Hotel stood across the street from it (until it
burned in 1914), making B and Union streets the toniest corner
on the Comstock during the glory years. Internationally famous
actors, singers, musicians, and troupes played Piper's, and one
of its impresarios was the young David Belasco. Next to Piper's
stands a row of often-photographed buildings, including the
Knights of Pythias Hall (still used by an active aerie of Eagles)
and the Miner's Union Hall (occasionally serving as a theatre
for melodrama or as a dance hall).

Below C Street the attractions are as compelling. St.
Mary's In The Mountains on E Street, and St. Paul's Episcopal
Church on F are both open to worshippers and casual visitors
alike during seasons of good weather, and services are still
conducted on Sundays, as they are in the old Presbyterian
Church on south C Street. St. Mary's In The Mountains, rebuilt
by Father (later Bishop) Patrick Manogue after the great fire of
1875, was recently remodeled by Father Paul Meinecke. It is a
structure of grace and eloquence, and has long been considered
one of the finest remaining examples of western Victorian
church architecture.

The large, rather forbidding brick building visible below the

Virginia City graveyard

town is the former St. Mary's Hospital. Operated by an order of nuns until shortly before the turn of the century, it became the Storey County Hospital until it finally closed in the middle 1930s. It now houses a year-round caretaker and an active summer arts program.

A number of mines are open to visitors (signs are everywhere) as are the homes of a number of its leading citizens from the bonanza years. The restored and refurbished Savage, Mackay, and Chollar "mansions" — they actually combined the functions of residences and mining offices — are spotted along D Street south of the brick school buildings.

Below town to the north are a number of Virginia City's cemeteries. The Jewish cemetery is located below the highway north of town and is difficult of access: ask directions if it interests you. The burying grounds visible from the north end of town (please don't call them Boot Hill; Boot Hill is in Tombstone, Arizona, a bumptious little town that never aspired to anything like Virginia City's refinement) number among their population Catholics, Masons, members of the Miner's Union, and other fraternal organizations and have been rescued from abandonment in recent years by a team of convicts from the State Prison working under the direction of the pastor at St. Mary's.

Virginia City is still protected by a volunteer fire department in which membership is a matter of significant local prestige. The nearest emergency medical help is in Carson City, but an ambulance is on call at the fire house on C Street and manned full-time. There are service stations, at opposite ends of C Street, open seven days a week.

The Divide
At the south end of Virginia City. Everything south of the intersection of Nevada Routes 17 and 80 was once a separate satellite community with its own small business section. It was here that Mark Twain was "held up" by old cronies when he returned to the Comstock as a lecturer after becoming a nationally popular writer. He was not amused. Here too was kept the equipment to ease laden wagons down the steep grade toward Carson. The great frame structure off to the east was an ice house. The Divide's hundreds of houses are nearly gone now; its separate identity faded into that of Virginia City long ago.

Gold Hill
2 miles south of Virginia City via Nevada Route 80. *This road not recommended for trailers or other vehicles with a tendency to fading brakes, overheating, or vapor lock.* It is *very* steep.

Gold Hill was the site of the original discovery of the Comstock Lode, at a point on the hill behind the small pink and yellow houses at the lower leg of the S turn below the Divide. A former Gold Hill resident invested great research and no small amount of money to place the signs identifying historic sites. Though nine thousand people once lived in Gold Canyon, only about thirty remain today, and Gold Hill's business directory has dwindled in proportion. The California Bank building, now a gallery for contemporary western artists, is open daily during seasons of good weather, weekends at other times. A hundred yards farther down the canyon, the Gold Hill Hotel is the state's oldest. Built of brick and stone in 1859, it has been renovated without the sacrifice of its pioneer character. A small stone bar adjoins. Open daily during the season of demand, weekends at other times.

Behind the hotel, and continuing down the west wall of Gold Canyon, are a number of the great mines of the Comstock: the Yellow Jacket, the Crown Point, the Kentuck, Belcher, and Overman. Most of these mines were in production as recently as 1942, and none is abandoned. Mining will amost certainly resume again just as soon as the price of silver rises to the point to make it profitable once more. Geologists are continually sampling and drilling; that day may not be far away.

American Flat
4 miles south of Virginia City via an unmarked dirt road leaving Nevada Route 80 to the west (second road west below the rock shop). Located in a basin out of sight of Gold Canyon, American City was built around the great cyanide mill still standing in impressive ruin. It is a favorite location for photographers, for neckers (does anybody still call them that?), and for the Storey County Jeep Posse which holds its annual barbecue and dance in the old mill. Small children should be closely attended, since they can step through a hole in the floor and simply vanish.

Silver City

6 miles south of Virginia City via Nevada Routes 80 or 17; 17 is the easy road: buses, trailers, laden trucks, and untrustworthy automobiles should use it in either direction. Silver City is the third of the three principal communities on the Comstock Lode, but it was never any great shakes and it has been reduced to a single business house today. Nevertheless, the proprietor of the Golden Gate Bar exhibits one of the finest collections of baby rattlers to be seen anywhere in the West. Inquire locally about details of the unusual Silver City Garden Tour.

A toll gate once stood at the head of town, in the rock formation called Devil's Gate, and extra teams were stabled here to help drag the heavy freight wagons up the long, steep grade to Virginia City. No mining is being done now, though the original silver strike of the Grosch brothers was made within sight of the town. Hosea Grosch was laid to rest in the Silver City cemetery (to the east of town, reached by an unmarked dirt road leading north from Nevada Route 17), and his grave marked with an impressive monument placed in 1865 by a member of Abraham Lincoln's cabinet.

Johntown

2 miles south of Silver City via marked dirt road. The Y intersection of Nevada Routes 17 and 80 at the lower end of Silver City is actually an X; the fourth leg, though, is a dirt road which continues south down Gold Canyon after the paved highway abandons it. It departs at the small plaque-bearing monument and meanders down the stream through extremely pleasant scenery. Just beyond a small (and getting smaller every year) earth-and-timber bridge, Johntown is off to the west: a heap of stones at the edge of the willow-shaded stream. It is still possible to see the remnants of wall poking up out of the rubble, but Johntown was built with rock and mud and has not weathered well. This was Nevada's first mining town; it enjoyed a certain feeble revival in the 1930s when gold dredging operations were

being carried on downstream, but nothing of this more recent activity is evident except to sharp and persistent searching. The Johntown road continues south to Dayton or to U.S. 50, depending on which turns you take; none of them are marked. If you can get as far as Johntown in the vehicle you are driving, you can make it the rest of the way, but you may decide it isn't worth it. This was once a major thoroughfare.

Dayton
12 miles east of Carson City via U.S. 50. Originally a trading post at the junction of Gold Creek with the Carson River, Dayton had a Pony Express station at the edge of town and flourished as a mill town during the early years of Comstock development. It was the first seat of Lyon County.

Dayton's place in Nevada history is secure as the site of the first marriage, first divorce, and first public entertainment, all of them occurring in 1853. The wedding occurred when a prospector injudiciously left his fourteen-year-old daughter with friends while he searched for placer claims. When he returned to town he found his daughter had been married to another prospector. He at once took her off to California, pursued by the bridegroom and by a party of townspeople whose motive was to prevent bloodshed. All the travelers met on the trail and after a heated discussion it was agreed that the girl be given her choice of continuing on with her father or returning with her new husband. She elected to go on, thus becoming Nevada's first bride and first divorcee within the space of a few days. Later in the year a New Year's Eve party was held at which some 150 prospectors swapped lies about their claims, news from the states, and danced with the females (four women and five little girls) present. After so dramatic a beginning it has been mostly downhill for Dayton. The town achieved its present configuration by the middle 1860s, after which Comstock milling was done at more convenient places.

The most vivid municipal event since the mills closed occurred in 1960 when John Huston, Clark Gable, Marilyn Monroe, Arthur Miller, Montgomery Clift, Eli Wallach, and Thelma Ritter came to town to film the rodeo scenes for *The Misfits*. Marilyn Monroe's paddle-ball performance at the Odeon Saloon marks the high point of the twentieth century in Dayton so far.

A service station, two small grocery stores, a garage (ask for Wheels), and a number of saloons comprise Dayton's business district. No listing can communicate the drowsy charm of the place, however, or its attractive setting. The old cemetery above the town provides not only a pleasant diversion for those who enjoy wandering in pioneer burying grounds, but a beautiful overview of Dayton and the rich river-bottom country in which it is situated. A most satisfying panorama.

STATE PARKS AND RECREATION AREAS

Pyramid Lake

33 miles northeast of Reno via Nevada Route 33; 16 miles north of Wadsworth via Nevada Route 34.

The drive to Pyramid Lake from Reno carries the motorist through a succession of shallow depressions between low, brush-stubbled hills. It is a pleasant drive, but long enough to create an awareness of the desert's monotony. To those whose tolerance of the desert is low, the half-hour drive may be enough to permit that monotony to become oppressive. But when the last rise is topped, the eye-searing expanse of Pyramid Lake stretching out before you is a stunning, staggering sight: a sheet of electric blue cupped between pastel mountains of chalky pinks and greys.

John C. Frémont was the first non-Indian to gaze down at Pyramid Lake, and his journal entry of 10 January 1844 records his impressions of the lake: ". . . we continued our way up the hollow, intending to see what lay beyond the mountain. The hollow was several miles long, forming a good pass; the snow deepening to about a foot as we neared the summit. Beyond, a defile between the mountains descended rapidly about two thousand feet; and, filling up all the lower space, was a sheet of green water, some twenty miles broad. It broke upon our eyes like the ocean. The neighboring peaks rose high above us, and we ascended one of them to obtain a better view. The waves were curling in the breeze, and their dark-green color showed it to be a body of deep water. For a long time we sat enjoying the view, for we had become fatigued with mountains, and the free expanse of moving waves was very grateful. It was set like a gem in the mountains, which, from our position, seemed to enclose it almost entirely. . . . On our road down, the next day, we saw herds of mountain sheep. . . ."

The sheep are gone now, and the descendants of the Indians, with whom Frémont feasted on trout (measuring as long as four feet!) a few days later, are now fighting to preserve the lake against further shrinkage caused by the diversion of water out of the Truckee River. Despite the enormous changes which have overtaken the world since Frémont's visit in 1844, Pyramid Lake (which he named for a tufa rock formation on the eastern shore) remains as strikingly beautiful and as uniquely enchanting as it was when he first saw it.

Pyramid Lake is unlike Tahoe. It is shallower, warmer, and substantially more alkaline than Tahoe, lower in elevation, and not so easily accessible. But these differences are not the decisive ones. Tahoe is charmingly beautiful. Pyramid is a shock; in addition to its primitive, challenging beauty, it projects a profound sense of antiquity. Gazing out across its surface is an experience almost three-dimensional.

There is more to Pyramid than meets the eye. From long before Frémont's visit, fishing has always been one of the lake's most highly-regarded characteristics. The cui-ui and the Pyramid cutthroat (called hoopigaih by the Paiute Indians) had long supported a relatively large and concentrated native population comprising several overlapping cultures. The arrival of white settlers began the exploitation of the fishery in earnest. Commercial fishermen harvested one hundred tons of trout between Winter 1888 and Spring 1889, for shipment all over the

Pelicans on their Anahoe Island retreat at Pyramid Lake, north of Reno

U.S. By 1912 a local entrepreneur was hiring as many as fifty Paiute fishermen to catch and ship from ten to fifteen tons of trout a week for sale in the southern Nevada mining camps. But already other of the white man's activities were affecting the fishery. The dam at Derby, so great a boon to the farmlands of Churchill County, was completed in 1905 and thereafter diverted not only Truckee River water, but thousands of trout returning toward Pyramid from upriver spawning beds. Even worse, the drop in the lake's level resulting from the diversion of water left sandbars exposed at the Truckee's mouth. They, and the diminished water below Derby Dam, frustrated the cutthroat spawning. The native cutthroat population began to dwindle. Nevertheless, in 1925 a Paiute named Johnny Skimmerhorn caught the world's record cutthroat there; a forty-one-pounder. Photographs taken in the twenties and thirties show celebrities like Clark Gable struggling manfully to show off a pair of enormous cutthroat, or a group of Nevadans peeking out from behind a curtain of silvery fish that stretches eight feet long: a day's catch. But by the 1940s the cutthroats were gone.

Restocking began in the early 1950s, and today five to ten pounders are not uncommon at Pyramid. Crosby's resort, at Sutcliffe on the west shore, is a source not only of fishing information, but of both the Nevada fishing license and the special Indian reservation permit required to fish at Pyramid. Crosby's and the trading post at Nixon are the only sources of food, drink, and gasoline closer than Interstate 80.

Three cautions regarding Pyramid Lake. It is 300 feet deep, and despite the protective mountains it can be extremely dangerous when the wind is up. Scarcely a season passes without at least one boat foundering in the chop of a sudden storm. *Heed all weather warnings instantly.* They are not provided capriciously. Next, regard all surfaces off well-traveled roads with extreme suspicion. There is a great deal of loose shifting sand, often just at the edge of the road. If you bog down in it you are in for less fishing and more digging. And third, give Anaho Island a wide berth. It is the site of the largest white pelican nesting colony in North America and has been a National Wildlife Refuge since 1913. Visitors are not permitted without special federal permit, and even "buzzing" the shoreline can cause a destructive panic among the birds.

Warrior Point Park. 9 miles north of Sutcliffe on Pyramid Lake road. Open all year; drinking water, hot showers, and sewage dump. Family picnicking and camping units available Boating, swimming, fishing. Administered by the Washoe County Parks and Recreation Department (WCPR).

Lahontan State Recreation Area

3 miles southeast of Silver Springs, 28 miles north of Yerington, via U.S. 95 Alternate and marked, paved access road. 17 miles west of Fallon, 38 miles east of Carson City, via U.S. 50, U.S. 95 Alternate and recreation area access road. Administered by the Nevada State Park System (NSP).

Before the construction of Lahontan Dam in 1915 to contain the waters of the Carson River, they ponded out in the desert northwest of Fallon in the Carson Sink. With the completion of the dam, a ten thousand surface acre reservoir was created with nearly seventy miles of excellent sandy shoreline. Like Rye Patch far to the north, this reservoir has only recently come under state care, and development is limited. There are no formal campsites in the recreation area, but camping is permitted almost anywhere visitors may care to set up. Boat camping is especially popular because of the many secluded coves and islands inaccessible by car. A great many picnic tables are provided, and a boat launch ramp is located near the entrance where the resident supervisor and rangers are headquartered. Fishing is excellent at Lahontan, with both warm and cold water species in residence. Trout fishing is especially good at the upper end of the reservoir and below the dam, but there are bass, crappie, carp, and catfish too.

Fees are charged at Lahontan, but the schedule is a little complicated, and an annual permit allowing unlimited use of the recreation area is available.

Lahontan Reservoir State Park

Rye Patch State Recreation Area

22 miles northeast of Lovelock and 47 miles southwest of Winnemucca, via Interstate 80.

Rye Patch Dam was constructed to store the waters of the Humboldt River, which formerly spread out in a broad, reeded sink south of Lovelock. The resulting reservoir, when full, comprises some eleven thousand surface acres. All developed recreation facilities at the present time are located near the dam at the south end of the reservoir where a resident ranger is on hand to collect entrance fees (an annual permit for unlimited use is available) and to assist visitors. There are primitive overnight campsites with tables, pit toilets, and fireplaces and a large picnic ground, also near the dam. Rye Patch offers excellent fishing (trout and wall-eye pike are planted) as well as all water sports.

Pitt-Taylor Cove, near the upper end of the reservoir, is a favorite fishing spot, though without developed facilities. Majuba Bay, at the extreme northwestern end of the reservoir, provides the best sandy beach around the shore line. Access to Majuba Bay, however, is presently limited to four-wheel drive vehicles: twelve miles of bad road, no developed facilities, just the experience of swimming at the shore of a desert island. Visitors are not permitted to gather rocks within the recreation area boundaries, but the ranger will provide information about nearby rockhounding opportunities. The recreation area is open the year around. (NSP).

Sand Mountain

Some 25 miles southeast of Fallon, off U.S. Highway 50. Sand Mountain lies in a valley between the southern edge of the Stillwater Mountains and Four Mile Flats. About two miles long and almost a mile wide, it rises hundreds of feet out of the valley floor. This Sahara-like sand dune was formed by wind-carried sand particles which accumulated over a vast number of years.

The unique appearance of the mountain allowed early-day emigrants on the Overland Trail to use it as a landmark on their westward trek. About one mile southwest of the mountain is the site of the Sand Springs Pony Express station. The Four Mile Flats produced thousands of tons of salt used to extract gold and silver from the ores of the Comstock Lode.

Facilities are scarce in this area, and those planning to visit should bring their own drinking water, firewood, and other needs for day or overnight use. In the area you can picnic, hike, go rockhounding, or simply camp. One of the favorite pastimes which the area facilitates is off-road vehicle operation. Administered by the Bureau of Land Management (BLM).

DEVELOPED CAMPGROUNDS

Desert Creek Campground. 10 miles south of Wellington via Nevada Route 22 (for 4 miles) and marked, unpaved road leading south. Campsites situated on an excellent fishing stream. Open from mid-April through October. Administered by the Toiyabe National Forest (TNF).

Davis Creek Campground. 12 miles north of Carson City, 18 miles south of Reno via U.S. 395 and Bowers Mansion access road. Campsites, including designated trailer spaces; picnic areas, sewage dump, hot showers. Fair to good fishing in Davis Creek, and Bowers Mansion is only a pleasant stroll away. WCPR.

Tahoe Area

Nevada Beach. On Tahoe's east shore, directly below the Round Hill Village Shopping Center on U.S. 50. The pine forested site, sloping sandy beach, and closure of the adjacent waters to power and sail boats make this campground one of the most popular in Nevada, particularly during the summer. Campsites, picnic areas, and a picnic pavilion available for large-group reservation. No boat launch facilities, and a seven-day limit on camping is imposed to make the units accessible to as many people as possible. TNF.

Spooner Summit Rest Area. Adjacent to U.S. 50 at Spooner Summit between Carson City and Lake Tahoe. Picnic tables, water, and modern restrooms. Not a campground as such, but a convenient haven that may come in handy. No one will object if you stay the night here. Pleasantly situated in a grove of aspens on the site of a historic inn and sawmill.

Clear Creek Campground. 10 miles west of Carson City, 2 miles east of Spooner Summit via U.S. 50. Campsites of rustic appearance in dense stands of pine and aspen. *No trailers* permitted: they jack-knife on the narrow, winding access roads. Open June through September.

Mount Rose Campground. 20 miles southwest of Reno, or 6

miles northeast of Incline Village via Nevada Route 27. Campsites at the head of a natural meadow surrounded by granite peaks dappled with sub-alpine forest groves. A number of small streams provide good fishing. Open from mid-June to early Setpember.

GHOST TOWNS

Fort Churchill

8½ miles south of Silver Springs, about 24 miles north of Yerington via U.S. 95 Alternate, or, better, 34 miles northeast of Carson City via U.S. 50 and Nevada Route 2B (graded but unpaved, passing along the course of the Carson River for most of its length).

Established in the aftermath of the short-lived Paiute War of 1860, Fort Churchill garrisoned about six hundred officers and troops by the end of 1861. As the Civil War demanded increasing numbers of seasoned troops in the eastern battlefields, elements of the California Volunteers replaced the regulars at garrison duty. When the federal government refused the offer of a group of Nevada patriots to arm and equip a unit for service against the rebels, most Nevadans serving the Union during the war enlisted in companies at Fort Churchill. Co. F of the 2nd Calif. Vol. Infantry, in fact, was an all-Nevada company. By 1863 Nevada volunteers, most of whom had enlisted at Fort Churchill, comprised two companies of infantry and two of cavalry. Nevada troopers received their first brass-hat inspection in September of that year, during the course of which an aide-de-camp with the rank of major staggered through a second story doorway at a Carson City inn, apparently under the impression that there was a balcony outside. There wasn't.

Most of the military activity at Fort Churchill consisted of patrolling the Overland Stage route, the only transcontinental stagecoach route since the closing of the more southerly Butterfield route by the war, and in chasing after small bands of Indians who made occasional forays against isolated settlers. It

Fort Churchill, near Yerington

was inglorious, unglamorous, boring, and largely unproductive duty, and of the twelve hundred Nevadans in federal service during the Civil War, nearly a third deserted. One of them was apprehended as he was negotiating the sale of his troop's horses to the stage line. Nine Nevadans were killed or died in service, and virtually all of the survivors had been mustered out of service by Christmas of 1865.

By 1867 the adobe buildings of the fort housed only a single company and in 1869, when the railroad superseded the stage line, the fort was abandoned. It was ultimately purchased for $750 by the proprietor of Buckland's Station, a half mile to the south. Acquired in the recent past as a state park, the fort was declared a national historic landmark in 1964.

Despite the fact that the roofs and many of the timbers were removed after its abandonment, thus leaving the thick adobe walls unprotected and exposed to the elements, enough of the old fort remains in gaunt and melted ruin to be impressive. The park rangers have identified the remaining structures and the sites of those buildings which have not survived, and a model in the visitor's center reconstructs the old outpost in small scale to aid visitors in their explorations.

The cottonwood-shaded camp sites near the river are provided with piped drinking water, as are the group and individual picnic areas.

Fort Churchill was the first military post in the state, and Nevada never had a larger or more important one; today it is one of the state's most interesting state parks, open the year around.

Buckland's Station

Now called Weeks, about ½ mile south of Fort Churchill via U.S. 95 Alternate. Established on the Carson River as a trading post in 1859, Buckland's had grown by the following year to include a tavern and a hotel as well as the proprietor's ranching headquarters. By the time a blacksmith shop and wagon repair facilities were added, Buckland's had been selected as the seat of Churchill County. This exalted status lapsed when a change in county boundaries put Buckland's in Lyon County. The station continued to prosper, largely because of the nearby presence of the Fort Churchill garrison.

In 1870 the two-story frame building which dominates the tiny settlement was erected as a hotel serving stagecoach travelers with its bar and dining room, and the local ranching population with the large dance hall. With a decline in stagecoach traffic, Buckland's faded, losing its status as a community and surviving as a ranching headquarters. Buildings are occupied, and tourists are not invited to prowl through the grounds. Nevertheless, because the old place sits just at the side of the highway, a few minutes parked at the edge of the road will provide a glimpse into the way things looked at an isolated nineteenth-century stage station. Several more recent buildings interfere somewhat with the reverie.

Como

About 10 miles southeast of Dayton via unmarked dirt road. Ask for detailed directions in Dayton. Located high in the Pine Nut Range, south of the Carson River, Como for a time shared in the early excitement of the Comstock's rich strikes. Discovered by prospectors in 1860, the Palmyra Mining District attracted hundreds to the village of Palmyra and the town of Como which eventually outstripped it.

Noted in its day for the luxury of its principal hotel (which had carpets in the bedrooms) and for the secessionist sympathies of many of its citizens, Como hit its peak in 1864, when it could boast of having a newspaper. By 1865 Como was dead, and despite efforts to reopen the mines in 1879 and in the early years of this century, Como is even deader today. There is little of the old town left standing after more than a century of weather and looters, but the drive up the mountain (remember to check about road conditions in Dayton) and the view from the townsite ruins are exceptional.

Ragtown

8 miles west of Fallon, 18 miles east of Silver Springs via U.S. 50, then a few hundred yards south to the bank of the Carson River. Ragtown was the first place where water and forage were available to the wagon train pioneers after the exhausting crossing of the Forty Mile Desert between the Humboldt and the Carson Rivers. The settlement took its name from the fact that the women, after washing their ragged clothes in the river, spread them to dry across the humpy bushes growing abundantly in the sandy soil. More than two hundred emigrants were buried in Ragtown, though until the middle 1860s there was only a single permanent building there. By the end of that decade, Ragtown had lost most of its early transient character, and by the turn of the century, when the hamlet of Leeteville existed on the former watering place, it had become indistinguishable from any other farming locale in the region. Today nothing remains to mark the site except a state historical marker and the descen-

dants of the bushes across which the pioneer women draped their tattered laundry.

Franktown

18 miles south of Reno, 12 miles north of Carson City, via U.S. 395 and paved, marked access road leading toward the base of the Sierra. Like Mormon Station, Franktown achieved the status of settlement when Mormon pioneers cleared farms in the stream-watered valley near the foot of the mountains. The community was Nevada's second largest within a year of its establishment in 1852, and three years later the townsite had been surveyed and platted. With the return of the Mormons to Zion in 1857, most of the properties in Franktown passed into Gentile hands, and by 1860, when the mines on the Comstock were beginning to produce the first of their seemingly inexhaustible shipments of bonanza ore, much of it was freighted over the Virginia Range and across Washoe Valley to Franktown for milling in the sixty-stamp mill built there. The wagons returned to Virginia City and Gold Hill loaded with lumber cut at Franktown sawmills, and the settlement, though still small, was quite prosperous.

By the middle of the decade, though, Comstock mining bosses had shifted their milling business to the more convenient Dayton mills, and Franktown began a slow decline. By 1880 the small business district had become vestigial despite the Virginia & Truckee RR spur built for the shipment of fruits and vegetables for which the community was well-known.

Franktown today no longer exists as a community, though the old V&T water tank marks the townsite location. Several ranching operations are headquartered there, and on the grounds of one of them, a short distance to the south of the old townsite proper, is the log cabin in which Will James wrote *Smoky* and several other of the stories which launched his career as a western writer and artist.

Bowers Mansion

20 miles south of Reno, 10 miles north of Carson City via U.S. 395 and marked, paved access road. Though not a "ghost town," Bowers Mansion is nevertheless a fascinating remnant of the early days of the Comstock boom. Built in the middle 1860s by Sandy and Eilley Bowers, the structure represented an attempt by the illiterate Scots prospector and his boardinghouse-keeper bride to live as grandly as their new-found Comstock wealth allowed. Furniture and appointments were shipped around Cape Horn from Europe as the couple embarked on a Continental shopping spree after Sandy had sold his Gold Hill claim for enough money, as he said "to throw at the birds." Throw it they did, much of it coming to rest in their two-story stone mansion.

Sandy died within a few years of striking it rich, but Eilley lived on long after the wealth had all been spent. She closed off

Bowers Mansion, Washoe Valley

progressively more and more of the immense stone house, but ultimately could not afford to exist there on even the meagerest scale. She sold the monument to grandeur and moved back to Virginia City where she lived out her years telling fortunes. "The Washoe Seeress," as she was known as an old woman, eked out a slender living by whispering of fortune coming to her gullible clientele. She died broke in a furnished room.

The mansion passed through a number of hands before being acquired by Washoe County; for a time during Prohibition it was operated as a road house and earned a faintly notorious reputation. The county has restored the old home to a condition approximating its grandeur, and tours are conducted.

There are picnic areas, for groups and for families, a swimming pool, and a snack bar is open during seasons of good weather. Campsites are available at nearby Davis Creek Campground.

Washoe City

15 miles south of Reno, 15 miles north of Carson City via U.S. 395. Established on the north shore of shallow Washoe Lake as an ore-milling and sawmill center to serve the Comstock, Washoe City dates from 1861. By the end of that year it had been selected as the seat of Washoe County government and had attracted a sizeable professional community to augment its busy mercantile and industrial life. By 1863 or so, Washoe City's population hovered at about six thousand, but by 1869, its mills idle, Washoe City was on the skids. When the county seat was moved to Reno in 1871, the town was clearly doomed, and by 1880 the population had dipped to barely two hundred. Finally, in 1894, even the post office was declared a dead letter and Washoe City was finished.

Traffic between Reno and Carson City has prompted some building in the area in recent years, but the stone building standing at the east of the highway is all that remains of the original city. Even that will not last much longer, as plans have been submitted for a trailer park on the property. The swaybacked log cabin across the road is not original, but a structure built for a movie in relatively recent years.

Glendale

Take Boynton Lane about a mile southeast from Sparks. Originally Stone & Gates' Station on the Truckee, an emigrant trading post established in 1857, the place became a favored river crossing, and by 1860 a bridge had been built to replace the primitive ferry. By the middle 1860s Glendale was the leading settlement in the Truckee Meadows, with a hotel, several stores, a post office and blacksmith shop, even a school. With the founding of Reno by the Central Pacific RR a few miles to the east in 1868, Glendale reverted to being a crossroads hamlet, but the schoolhouse there (recently moved to a site near the Centennial Coliseum convention center on south Virginia Street in Reno) continued in use until the late 1960s and was the oldest school in continuous operation in the state, one of the last one-room school houses in service in Nevada.

Unionville

39 miles northeast of Lovelock, via Interstate 80 and Nevada Route 50 (turn east at Oreana); 48 miles south of Winnemucca via Interstate 80 and Nevada Route 50 at the Mill City offramp. Nevada Route 50 is paved to within 3 miles of Unionville from the north (Mill City) end, unpaved from the south (Oreana-Rochester) end.

Established in May, 1861, by a party of prospectors whose interest had been stimulated by the arrival of a small band of Paiutes in Silver City carrying rich ore samples, the Buena Vista Mining District had, by early July, spawned the small community of Unionville in Buena Vista Canyon, beyond the Humboldt Mountains from the Humboldt River. In the autumn of 1861, Unionville consisted of "eleven cabins and a liberty pole" but was selected over the smaller Star City to serve as the first Humboldt County seat.

By early 1863 Unionville was a substantial town of some

two hundred residences, a horse-drawn omnibus line, a municipal government, a newspaper, nearly fifty business houses of
every description, and a new schoolhouse already in need of
repair. A slapdash quality of construction was characteristic of
most early mining camps, but Unionville seems to have been a
champion in this regard. A visitor to the county offices during a
summer rainshower found the county clerk huddled with his
records in the one corner of the room "where the rain didn't
come any thicker than it did outside." Construction difficulties
largely stemmed from the scarcity of local lumber and the poor
quality of materials shipped in. The subject excited the editorial
interest of the *Register,* which noted in 1863 that about half the
lumber shipped to Unionville was "just what it was cracked up
to be" and the other half was "knot." The paper also com-
mented ruefully that it was often difficult to distinguish between
loads of firewood and hay, since some of the trees were so
slender and some of the hay so coarse.

Despite the town's rapid growth, and the rich assay reports, development of the mines at Unionville proceeded
slowly, the owners being more concerned with promoting stock
than in excavating ore. When Sam Clemens made a prospecting
trip to the town in the winter of 1861–62, he took claims, but
then succumbed to the stock fever and abandoned the shaft at a
depth of twelve feet in order to trade in shares of the district. He
and his partners bought into the Columbiana, the Branch Mint,
the Universe, the Grand Mogul, the Great Republic, the Root
Hog Or Die, and more than a score of mines before departing
after a stay of a few weeks.

Nevertheless, by 1864 a number of Unionville's mines had
begun to produce substantial quantities of rich ore, and in 1868
the Arizona began to show signs of the ore which would ultimately bring nearly $6 million dollars up in the skips. The
Arizona, the National, the Manitowoc, and the Gem of the
Sierra were all producing well in the late 1860s. But when a
slowdown in mining coincided with a disastrous Unionville fire
and an upswing in vigor at Winnemucca, a brawling way station

on the CPRR at the big bend of the Humboldt, the county seat was lost. With it went much of the town's prosperity, in spite of continuing good production from many of its mines through the 1870s. By 1881 Unionville was down to about two hundred residents, most of whom were engaged in small-scale mining operations. By 1939 the tailing piles of the Arizona mine alone had been reworked fourteen times, each time at a profit.

Unionville today is largely in ruins, a slender chain of jutting walls and foundation holes extending almost three miles up the length of the narrow Buena Vista Canyon. Cattle browse among the remains of the old city, and poplars have grown tall where wagons once clattered down toward the mills at the canyon mouth. About a dozen residences remain tenanted in Unionville, and the fruit from the trees in the canyon is considered superior. A small but interesting museum is housed in the old schoolhouse, and a small fee is charged for admission. There is no other business remaining in Unionville, and no source of food or drink. If you come prepared, however, the friendly folks at the museum will offer detailed directions to the mines and other points of interest around Unionville, including several lovely picnic spots along Buena Vista Creek. After the dusty desert drive, Unionville is a refreshing oasis of green. Remember, though, that the residents are not in the business of catering to tourists (the museum excepted), and mind your manners.

Pine Grove

25 miles south of Yerington via Nevada Route 3, Pine Flat Road, and marked dirt road. Founded in 1866 by a prospector led to the spot by an Indian, Pine Grove had grown to about two hundred population by the end of the decade. The lively little camp swelled to about six hundred early in the following decade when, in addition to mining, it served as supply and service center for the ranchers and farmers in the surrounding valleys. The town reached its peak during the seventies but decline was slow and work continued in the mines and mills until they were

closed by the demonetization of silver in 1893. Intermittent small-scale operations continued afterward, including one just a few years ago, but the town itself never recovered. Today there is little evidence of the bustling camp that extended almost a mile along the narrow canyon, but enough to provide an eventful afternoon of browsing.

SKI AREAS

The largest and most sophisticated complex of ski facilities in the world is located within a ninety-minute drive of Reno and Carson City.

Sierra Nevada skiing began in 1854 when a Norwegian-born goldrusher-turned-farmer applied for the contract to carry mail from Placerville, California, to Genoa, Utah Territory (now Nevada). He arrived with a pair of twenty-five-pound oak skis, ten feet long and an inch and a half thick under the toe strap, and a new name: John A. Thompson. He had been worried that his actual name, Jon Torsteinson Rui, would prove unpronounceable to an Anglo-Saxon postmaster. He needn't have worried; he was the only applicant for the mail contract and the postmaster hired him on the spot.

He departed Placerville on his first trip over the mountains on January 3, 1856 and reappeared two weeks later, having completed the return leg of the journey in the incredible time of three and a half days. Thompson became an immediate hero in the mining camps on both sides of the Sierra. He not only provided a tenuous link of communication with the outside world, he demonstrated that the killing mid-winter snows could be conquered.

His pack, often loaded to a hundred pounds, contained a great deal besides mail. He carried assay reports, ore samples, medicines, even — in installments — machinery and the type for the *Territorial Enterprise*, Nevada's first newspaper. His visits were eagerly awaited events in the isolated mountain households. One Cisco Grove resident, recalling the 1860s, wrote:

"Snowshoe Thompson passed us daily carrying the mail between Meadow Lake Valley and Cisco. After each storm he
would carefully make his track in the soft snow. Starting at the
top of Red Mountain he would glide along the mountainside at a
consistent grade. A frosty night would freeze the track, which
would thereupon guide him as the steel rails do the locomotive.
We would watch him sail down the four mile grade at great
speed, cross the ice-frozen river, throw our mail toward the
house and glide over a hill by the momentum gathered in the
descent."

After two years on the Placerville-Genoa route, Thompson
transferred to increasingly more remote runs, carrying mail and
supplies into the highlands for twenty winters. Everywhere he
went he took the time to teach the eager settlers the use of his
famous "Norwegian snowshoes." There were several characteristics in common among these otherwise highly individualistic little towns served by Thompson: small size, crude construction, and a dread of winter which brought with it crushingly deep
snows, imprisonment, possible hunger, and interminable bore-
dom. Thompson's Norwegian snowshoes helped combat each
of the defects of the season.

A newspaper of the time once described the residents of
Jamison City, a Plumas County, California, mining settlement,
as rough folk who "are not of a quarrelsome disposition . . . but
on Sunday they meet at the saloon, drink 'tanglefoot,' black
each other's eyes, bite off ears, etc., merely for amusement."
After the introduction of Thompson's long oak snowshoes the
paper lifted its editorial eyebrows in pleased surprise: "Jamison
City had an excitement, and singularly enough for the place, it
was unattended with the annual spring fighting, though whiskey
flowed in profusion, and almost every person felt its enlivening
influence. The event was a snowshoe race."

These ski races took place at dozens of mountain villages
besides Jamison City. They originated simply as friendly out-
ings. Later, as skiers in Gibsonville, Sawpit, Port Wine,
Johnsville, Table Flat, and Onion Valley acquired polish,

inter-village meets were arranged. In 1863 the St. Louis men lost a best-four-of-seven downhill race to the men from Pine Grove and provided a champagne supper as their forfeit. By 1867 (some authorities say it was as early as 1853) the Alturas Snow-shoe Club had been formally organized as the first ski club in the U.S. and the third in all the world. The Alturas men organized ski meetings, the first club-sponsored skiing events anywhere. And because contestants traveled hundreds of miles, there is a case for considering the inns and boarding houses in these tiny Sierra Nevada hamlets as the world's first ski lodges. The little town of Johnsville has even launched a faltering claim for pos-session of the world's first ski lift, since the bucket line of the Plumas-Eureka Mine was used on winter Sundays to drag skiers to the top of the slope.

Thompson was a cross-country skier; he could hurtle down a mountainside, thread through a pine forest, and make leaps of fifty and sixty feet as he went, but the weekend skiers of the Sierra mining camps were strictly specialists in the downhill dash. With organized clubs and scheduled competitions, with cash prizes and excited side betting, the downhill racers began experimenting to increase their speeds. John Madden of Gib-sonville emerged as the leading ski maker in the region, offering his custom-made products at $10 for a pair of ten-footers and $15 a pair for anything longer. Madden's skis were the first in North America to sport grooved bottoms, and he also provided such accessories as moccasins to cover the after ends of the skis for easier climbing.

Since each ski racer used the same technique — five or six quick, powerful thrusts with the single pole at the start, then a low crouch over the boards with the pole extended directly forward to "split the air" — the best skis could determine the outcome of a race. Further sophistications appeared, the most spectacular of which was "dope," a preparation which pre-vented snow from sticking to the bottoms of the skis. When "Jackson the Racer" won the 1863 Howland Flat races by the use of a secret dope formula which he mixed right on the slopes to suit the conditions of each heat, the *Mountain Messenger* went mad with enthusiasm: "Great is Dope, and Jackson is its prophet — by whom we all swear."

All but Snowshoe Thompson. He thought all that tinkering with secret preparations was twaddle, and in February, 1869, at the third annual meeting of the Alturas Club at La Porte, he accepted the challenge to race downhill. Top prize from the total purse of $600 was $125, and Thompson planned to take it home with him. The course was a simple straight descent, the kind of thing he had done a thousand times.

But by rigid specialization, the use of dope, and incessant practice, the Plumas County contestants were masters of their one specialty, the downhill dash. Thompson was skunked. He left the meet in disgrace after only two races. Actually, he needn't have felt too humiliated. In the spring of 1873 a downhill racer named Todd swept down an icy 55 percent gradient at a measured speed fractions under eighty-eight miles an hour, a speed seldom equalled even today.

Thompson never entered another race (no one would accept his challenge to race on his own terms), but by the time of his death in 1876 skiing was so popular and well-established a sport in the mountains that special contests were arranged for ladies, children, and Chinamen. With so vigorous a beginning, it might seem that skiing would become a widely popular sport, but it did not. Skiing remained as exotic a recreation as ju-jitsu. When mining slowed and the mountain populations dwindled, the sport became even more a local curiosity. Annual races continued at La Porte until 1911, but they went unnoticed beyond the immediate locality.

During the Winter of 1894—95 an editor and entrepreneur named C. F. McGlashan opened a much-ballyhooed winter recreation complex at Truckee. A full acre of skating ice, long slick toboggan chutes, and carefully marked ski slopes were touted to leisured residents along the railroad to the west. Special trains brought thousands from San Francisco, Oakland, and Sacramento to execute intricate figures on the ice and to shriek with delicious terror on the rabbit-fast toboggans. But the ski slopes were ignored. Skiing was not for refined gentlemen and ladies. Skiing was for hillbillies.

Not until the Lake Placid Winter Olympics of 1932 did America's attitude toward skiing show any inclination to change. A slope near Tahoe Tavern was used for Olympic tryouts in 1931, and remained open to the public afterward. Enough foreigners and eccentrics used the facility to justify the expense. Even so, the biggest attraction in the Sierra that winter was Alaskan sled-dog driver Scotty Allen and the cross-country dog team races.

After World War II, demand for developed ski areas began to increase dramatically. Nevada skiers had been schussing in short takes near the eastern base of the Sierra at Galena Creek for years before the first rope tow was installed at Sky Tavern in 1938. Tannenbaum, just below Sky Tavern, opened shortly after the war's end. Slide Mountain, higher up Route 27, opened in 1953. The Mount Rose runs on the north slope of Slide Mountain were opened in 1965, and Ski Incline greeted its first skiers in 1966. Farther to the south, Heavenly Valley opened its Nevada side slopes in late 1967, at about the same time Sky Tavern was being purchased for the exclusive use of the Junior Ski programs operated for youngsters in Carson City and Reno.

The present variety of skiing opportunities on Nevada's Sierra slopes would gratify both Snowshoe Thompson and Jackson the Racer. Here are the details:

Tannenbaum

18 miles southwest of Reno via U.S. 395 and Nevada Route 27. Lacking advanced or expert slopes, Tannenbaum is nevertheless a delightful area catering largely to family groups who throng the T-bar and rope tow throughout the full season (Tannenbaum has snow-making equipment). Easiest and quickest access of all the Sierra slopes from Reno or Carson City.

Slide Mountain Ski Bowl

20 miles southwest of Reno via U.S. 395 and Nevada Route 27. Slide Mountain is closer to jet airliner service than any other major ski resort in the U.S. and was the alternate site selected for the 1960 Winter Olympics. Lodge and lift terminus are at 8,250 feet, and the ski summit is at about 9,700, from which, when conditions are right, it is possible to ski a mile in vertical drop to the valley below. From the top of the Overland lift, the view encompasses the thickly forested shores of Tahoe to the west and the rumpled procession of desert mountain ranges to the east, a panorama of staggering beauty and diversity. Largely a "local" ski area until its discovery by lift-line-weary skiers a few years ago, Slide Mountain offers slopes for every class of skier from beginner to expert. Gold Run, accessible from the top of the Pioneer lift, has been ranked among the ten toughest runs in the nation. A bunny lift serves a twenty-acre bowl devoted to beginning skiers, and a variety of excellent runs fall between Gold Run and the bunny bowl in difficulty. The day lodge packs in a cafeteria, bar, sales and rental shops, and ski school headquarters. No overnight accommodations are available.

Mount Rose

24 miles southwest of Reno, 36 miles northwest of Carson City via U.S. 395 and Nevada Route 27. Bunny slope acreage is adjacent to the lodge, served by the Ponderosa double-chair lift, and one of the most famous advanced slopes, Northwest Passage, 4,500 feet of constant challenge, begins at the 9,600-foot summit. The Chutes presents an even richer challenge, as it drops fifteen hundred feet through the pines — quite suddenly. The lodge provides overnight accommodations for folks forethoughtful enough to make reservations in advance, and features a cook-your-own-steak dinner house as well as a bar and coffee shop. Entertainment and music for dancing is presented in the evenings.

Sierra Nevada skiing

Ski Incline

35 miles southwest of Reno via U.S. 395 and Nevada Route 27; about 25 miles northwest of Carson City via U.S. 50 and Nevada Routes 28 and 27. Overlooking Lake Tahoe from the west slopes of the Carson Range, the trails at Ski Incline thread through some twelve hundred acres of steep, pine-forested mountain terrain. Incline had, at last report, the largest snow-making system (eighty acres) in the entire West, and lifts with the capacity to carry a total of 3,600 skiers per hour. The lodge at Incline is at the upper terminus of the Orange lift, and contains dining facilities, cocktail lounge, and a quarter-acre sundeck facing south down the last undeveloped lakeshore remaining at Tahoe. The lodge is also accessible by car and by bus; a regular schedule is maintained from Incline Village. Because it is so convenient to Tahoe locals, Ski Incline is as strong in beginner skiing as it is in advanced and expert; Blue lift for beginners, Red and Gold lifts for advanced and expert skiers.

Heavenly Valley

5 miles northeast of Stateline via U.S. 50 and Nevada Route 19; 19 miles west of Minden-Gardnerville, 30 miles southwest of Carson City via U.S. 395 and Nevada Route 19. Opened strictly as a California area with access from South Tahoe, Heavenly Valley opened its Nevada runs in the 1967-68 season. Lifts and trails connect the California area on the western slope of Monument Peak with the Nevada area on the eastern side of East Peak. Boulder Chair, which departs from the parking lot at the summit of Kingsbury Grade (Nevada Route 19), soars to 1,700 feet above the summit as it glides a mile and a half to East Peak Lake. Big Dipper lift continues southward over a mile farther, and rises another 1,250 feet to the ten thousand-foot summit of Heavenly Valley Peak. The Nevada slopes are sheltered from both sun and prevailing winds, providing skiing on a par with the best in the Sierra.

Many other excellent ski areas are available to the devotee just short drives from the Nevada line at both the north and the south ends of Lake Tahoe.

ORSON HYDE'S CURSE

When the Mormon faithful returned to Zion at the call of
Brigham Young, many were required to abandon the fruits of
their labors in the shadow of the Sierra Nevada. One such was
Orson Hyde, the magistrate sent west to arrange the affairs of
Carson County, who had constructed a sawmill in Washoe
Valley (between the present sites of Reno and Carson City).
Hyde had sold the mill before returning to Utah, but had
managed to get only "one span of small indifferent mules, an old
worn-out harness, two yokes of oxen, and an old wagon," as
part payment on the $10,000 sale price. The rest was never
forthcoming, despite Hyde's best efforts to collect.

By early 1862 Hyde had despaired of ever collecting, and
planted his suit "in the Chancery of Heaven" by reading, in the
Utah legislature of which he was a member, an open letter to the
people of Carson and Washoe valleys. The letter read in part:

"The Lord has signified to me, his unworthy servant, that
as we have been under circumstances that compelled us to
submit to your terms, that He will place you under
circumstances that will compel you to submit to ours, or do
worse.

"That mill and those land claims were worth $10,000 when
we left them; the use of that property, or its increased value
since, is $10,000 more, making our present demand $20,000.

"Now if the above sum be sent to me in Great Salt Lake
City, in cash, you shall have a clean receipt therefor, in the
shape of honorable quitclaim deeds to all the property that
Orson Hyde, William Price, and Richard Bentley owned in
Washoe Valley. The mill, I understand, is now in the hands of
R. D. Sides, and has been for a long time. But if you shall think
best to repudiate our demand or any part of it, all right. We shall
not take it up again in this world in any shape of any of you; but

the said R. D. Sides and Jacob Rose shall be living and dying advertisements of God's displeasure, in their persons, in their families, and in their substances; and this demand of ours, remaining uncanceled, shall be to the people of Carson and Washoe valleys as was the ark of God among the Philistines. (See 1st Sam. fifth chapter.) You shall be visited of the Lord of Hosts with thunder and with earthquake and with floods, with pestilence and with famine until your names are not known amongst men, for you have rejected the authority of God, trampled upon his laws and his ordinances, and given yourselves up to serve the god of this world; to rioting in debauchery, in abominations, drunkenness and corruption. . . .

"I have no sordid desire for gold, and have manifested it by my long silence and manifest indifference; and should not say anything now had not the visions of the Almighty stirred up my mind. . . .

"I care not what our mill and land claims are, or were considered worth — whether five hundred thousand dollars, or five cents — twenty thousand dollars is our demand; and you can pay it to us, as I have said, and find mercy, if you will thenceforth do right, or despise the demand and perish. . . .

Orson Hyde

GUIDE TO THE
NEVADA STATE PARK SYSTEM

The Nevada State Park System is a small and highly individualistic one, in contrast to the systems operated by neighboring states. A brief history of the system may be helpful in explaining why a state so rich in physical attractions has done relatively little to develop them into parks.

It wasn't until 1923 that the state concerned itself with the idea of parks at all. It was then that the Lost City area in Clark County's Moapa Valley was first brought under systematic excavation and began to yield significant information about the Anasazi (popularly thought of as "cliff dweller") culture which had been established there until about the fifteenth century. The finds there coincided in many respects with the famous digs at Pecos and other Arizona and New Mexico Anasazi sites, and the newly-inaugurated Governor James Scrugham caused the region to be declared a state reservation. As a result of his encouragement, too, several parcels of land were donated for use as parks and recreation areas. Most of them are located in the southeastern part of the state.

It wasn't until the 1930s, though — by which time Scrugham had been elected Nevada's lone congressman — that any form of systematic development began to take place. Scrugham managed to have a number of Depression inspired Civilian Conservation Corps companies assigned to Nevada, where they built the present Lost City Museum, built roads and campground facilities in the Valley of Fire, and developed facilities in Cathedral Gorge and the small Lincoln County parks. In 1935 the state legislature designated these areas state parks and simultaneously created a four-member Park Commission. The state highway engineer was named ex-officio superintendent and given $500 per year to manage and maintain the system. In 1939 no appropriation at all was made.

Inevitably, the CCC-built facilities began to fall into disrepair, except at Kershaw-Ryan, where the Lincoln County commission stepped in and hired its own caretaker, and at Lost City, where other agencies performed maintenance and development work. With these exceptions, Nevada's park system was abandoned to neglect, and the commission lapsed into torpor. The prevailing attitude in the legislature was simply that a state with so much public land, so few fences, and so little tax revenues couldn't afford parks and didn't need them anyway. In 1941, in fact, the legislature decided that because the

Valley of Fire was so remote and difficult of access, and because the federal government was developing the Lake Mead Recreation Area adjoining it, the park lands could be traded to the federal government for other lands elsewhere. By the 1950s about two thousand acres of the Valley of Fire had been signed over to the federal government, and another two thousand were waiting for final transfer approval.

In 1952 the Park Commission was reactivated, but without any appropriation of funds by the legislature. In 1955 the legislature made its first appropriation in sixteen years: $40,000 to operate the park system for two years. The commission at once hired a director, a ranger, and a stenographer so that mail which had been piling up since before the war could be answered and some cleanup and maintenance construction could be done. By the end of the decade the park system had been reorganized and had received into its control a number of existing parks and properties which had been in the care of other agencies. The governor was given the power to proclaim state parks, and the parks appropriation was increased to permit development.

Thus the Nevada State Park Department, though its beginnings can be traced back some fifty years, has had an effective existence of scarcely more than a dozen years. Its achievements within that span of time are considerable, and a bond issue recently passed by the voters, authorizing a $5 million budget for the acquisition of new park properties, indicates that more progress is in store.

A complete list of Nevada's state parks follows. Details on a majority of these areas may be found in appropriate sections of this book (see index), and the remainder are discussed here:

Beaver Dam State Park.

Berlin-Ichthyosaur State Park.

Cathedral Gorge State Park.

Cave Lake State Recreation Area. 8 miles south of Ely via U.S. 93, then east about 6 miles via the Success Summit Road. A seven-acre reservoir provides excellent trout fishing, and although the area is undeveloped, primitive camping is allowed. Access may be restricted during the winter months.

Echo Canyon State Recreation Area. 14 miles southeast of Pioche via Nevada Highways 85 and 86. Featured is a sixty-five-acre reservoir with adjacent day-use and camping facilities. A boat-launching ramp is available and fishing and hiking are popular at this year-round facility.

Fort Churchill Historic State Monument.

Kershaw-Ryan State Park.

Lahontan State Recreation Area.

Lake Tahoe—Nevada State Park.

Mormon Station Historic State Monument.

Red Rock Canyon Recreation Lands. 15 miles west of Las Vegas via West Charleston Boulevard. The beauty and grandeur of the multicolored formations are the primary attractions of this area. The towering features of the Red Rock escarpment, the rugged La Madre Mountains, and the red and white hues of the Chinle and Aztec sandstones that make up the Calico Hills are major features. Picnicking, hiking, and exploring; limited camping facilities. Managed in cooperation with the Bureau of Land Management.

Rye Patch State Recreation Area.

Spring Valley State Park. 18 miles east of Pioche via Nevada Highway 85, offering a variety of water-oriented recreation at the sixty-five-acre Eagle Valley Reservoir. Adjacent pioneer ranchlands are being preserved for hiking and exploring pleasure. Boat launching, picnicking, and camping facilities; open year round, although weather conditions may restrict winter access.

Valley of Fire State Park.

Ward Charcoal Ovens Historical State Monument.

Washoe Lake. A recently acquired area off U.S. 395 about midway between Reno and Carson City. The area is as yet undeveloped, but public access for limited day-use activity is provided.

NEVADA HIGHWAY PATROL

The Nevada Highway Patrol is one of the finest units of its kind in the nation. Nevada is still small enough in population and (despite millions of visitors) in traffic to permit high standards of selection for patrolmen, and to allow these patrolmen to retain their humanity on the job without sacrificing high professional standards. But it is a small force (about 150 uniformed personnel) to patrol more than thirty-eight thousand miles of primary and secondary federal and state highways.

The small size of the unit contributes, certainly, to its characteristically high morale and *esprit*, but it may also present problems to motorists in the state. There are twenty-seven Highway Patrol duty stations in Nevada, and about 130 troopers assigned to them. However, taking vacations, sick leave, court time, and other factors into account, the effective patrol strength is reduced to an average of about fifty men, or about sixteen men per eight-hour shift covering the highways. Clearly, despite every effort of the patrolmen, many miles of Nevada highway are only occasionally covered, and an accident or other mishap on an infrequently traveled route may go undiscovered by the patrol for many hours, perhaps even days. Even when an accident is reported by a passerby, the nearest patrolman may be more than a hundred miles away. In a case like that all anyone can do is hope that the accident victim is not seriously injured. Or that they have had the foresight to equip their cars with a first aid kit, drinking water, blankets or sleeping bags — anything and everything that might serve a useful purpose in an emergency until a patrolman can reach the scene.

That is the principal disadvantage to the Highway Patrol in Nevada: that it is spread so very thin. On the other hand, the patrol is famous within the state for rendering assistance to motorists in trouble. A patrol car will *always* stop where a disabled motorist is pulled over at the edge of the highway. All patrol cars are equipped with gasoline pumps so that gas may be transferred to an empty tank in the middle of the desert without delay. Patrolmen carry first aid kits and are thoroughly trained in their use. They are usually willing — as long as they are not needed at an emergency elsewhere — to help get a disabled car running again if they can recognize and correct the problem. They cannot be everywhere at once, but where they are, they can help reduce a potential disaster to an inconvenience.

At the same time, patrolmen will not hesitate to remove a dangerous driver or a dangerous vehicle from the road.

Nevada Highway Patrol duty stations are located in the communities listed below. In an emergency, a motorist may contact the nearest Highway Patrol unit by asking the telephone operator for ZENITH 1-2000. The call will be directed to the appropriate communications center and the patrol car nearest to the emergency will be located and dispatched at once.

Alamo	Fallon	Oasis-Wendover
Austin	Fernley	Overton
Battle Mountain	Glendale (Clark Co.)	Reno
Beatty	Hawthorne	Searchlight
Caliente	Incline Village	So. Lake Tahoe
Carson City	Indian Springs	Tonopah
Elko	Las Vegas	Wells
Ely	Lovelock	Winnemucca
Eureka	Minden-Gardnerville	Yerington

CATTLE COUNTRY

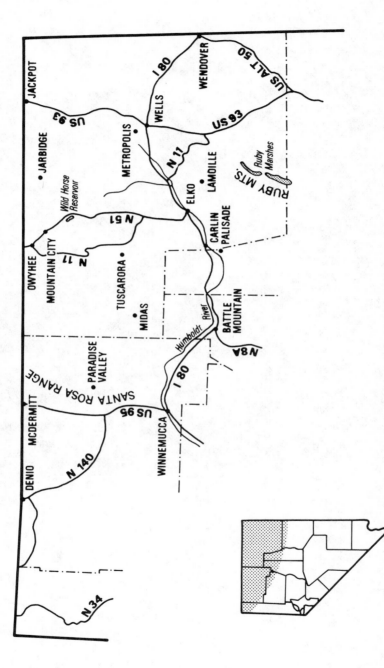

The Humboldt River runs through Nevada's cattle country like a strip of gristle through a cheap cut of beefsteak. It is a sluggish stream of no discernible distinction that slithers westward about three hundred miles past the nub-ends of scuffed and ribby mountain ranges. It courses languidly through broad, alkaline valleys in which only sagebrush grows.

The Humboldt lay too far east, beyond the Sierra Nevada, and too far north, beyond the Colorado, for the Spaniards to discover from California or Arizona. It lay too far west, beyond the Rockies, for the French or the Americans to discover from the Dakotas or the plains. And it was too far south, beyond the Columbia and the Snake, for the Astorians or their British successors to discover from the Oregon country. And so the Humboldt was the last major American river to be found.

To most of the travelers who bullet in either direction along Interstate 80 between the Utah border and the north end of the Humboldt Range, the river is a minor element in a monotonous landscape, and they scarcely notice it at all. Yet this Humboldt River was for twenty years one of the best-known and most important rivers in America.

It was 1828 when Peter Skene Ogden led a party of Hudson's Bay Company trappers south out of the Nez Percé country of Idaho and followed one of the Humboldt's tributaries down to the river's big bend, about where the town of Winnemucca is today located. Ogden trapped beaver there briefly, then went east into Utah for the winter before returning in the spring to what he had first named the Unknown River, and then Paul's River after one of the trappers who had died along its shore in the snows of late autumn. Ogden led his party slowly downriver, trapping as they went, until they reached the marshy bog in the shadow of the Stillwater Range where the river spread out into the desert sand and disappeared.

For ten years British and American trappers worked the river, which they called Mary's River then, or St. Mary's. By 1838 the beaver had been trapped out, but silk hats were already replacing beaver on the heads of fashionable eastern men, and the economy of the Far West was already going through drastic change. Only three years later the first party of American immigrants to California hazarded the grueling overland desert journey.

On the advice of the mountain men, they followed the Humboldt west from near its source at Humboldt Wells to its sink, then crossed the Forty-Mile Desert without water to the banks of the Carson and with great hardship scaled the Sierra. They had been forced to abandon their wagons early, and they survived the ordeal of the mountain crossing by eating their oxen and most of their horses. But they reached California, and established the Humboldt Trail as a feasible overland route for those who would follow.

In 1845 Frémont began his explorations and — more important — his publicizing of the desert country between the Rockies and the Sierra Nevada. It was he who named the river Humboldt. In 1846 the Donner party followed the Humboldt west to a rendezvous with horror. No traveler used the trail without learning to hate the river it followed, for except for providing a source of bitter, sometimes nearly undrinkable water, the Humboldt did little to alleviate the exhausting difficulties of the trail.

After 1849 those difficulties were multiplied out of all expectation by the California gold rush. Within the space of a single season the scant forage along the river's course was grazed away. Reeds and willows were devoured by hungry animals, and parties that made the journey late in the season were horrified to find the river barren of grass for their oxen and horses, and destitute of game for themselves. More than that, the Indians, infuriated by the ceaseless intrusion of heedless strangers, began to resist the westward march. Outrage motivated their attacks at first, but avarice became a factor, too, when they learned what treasure the settlers carried with them: guns and tools and clothing and food as well as the animals. The emigrants were weak, exhausted, and confused as they plodded west day after blistering day beside the sullen, naked banks of the Humboldt: easy prey to a carefully thought out attack. So the Humboldt meant adventure, hardship, despair, and death.

> Meanest and muddiest, filthiest stream,
>   most cordially I hate you;
> Meaner and muddier still you seem
>   since the first day I met you. . . .

> What mean these graves so fresh and new
>   along your banks on either side?
> They've all been dug and filled by you,
>   thou guilty wretch, thou homicide.

> Now fare thee well, we here shake hands
>   and part (I hope) to meet no more,
> I'd rather die in happier lands than
>   longer live upon your shore.

The Iowa man who wrote the poem about the river in 1850 was the only one to express his loathing in meter and at leisure; most of the survivors of the Humboldt Trail shouted their hatred out at the tops of their lungs as their wagons mired down in mud, as their animals fell down dead from starvation, as their exhausted children screamed with hysteria and hunger.

In 1850 a group of enterprising Mormons from Salt Lake City established the first settlement along the Humboldt Trail, at Mormon Station (now Genoa) at the eastern base of the

White water, northern Nevada

Sierra, and for a few years after that, while the wagon traffic along the river continued strong, a few trading posts appeared on its banks. These were crude, rough-built shanties offering a limited supply of staples at staggeringly high prices, and most of them were temporary. A trader stayed just long enough in that desperate country, and no longer.

The grandest of these outposts was located on a tributary of the Humboldt, near the west foot of the Ruby Mountains, and was established in 1852 by Peter Haws, an apostate Mormon slung out of Salt Lake City for manufacturing whiskey there. Haws farmed, and husbanded a few cattle, and bartered with the emigrants. He also traded with the Indians, providing them with a market for the goods they stole from the wagon trains and had no use for. He even organized attacks on the wagon trains himself, attacks resulting in massacres, looting, and the driving off of livestock. He himself was driven out after two years, following the shooting of one of his Indian accomplices.

But even before Haws had taken over the south fork of the Humboldt, the Jackass Mail was using the Humboldt Trail to haul the U.S. mail between Salt Lake City and Sacramento. And the trail was used in trade. In 1852 Kit Carson herded thirteen thousand merino sheep from New Mexico to Wyoming, and then west to the California gold fields by way of the Humboldt. The sheep contributed to the devastation of the fragile desert ecology, but Carson realized $15,000 for himself at the mines and went home rich to Santa Fe.

Through the 1850s, wagon trains of every description trundled painfully along the meandering course of the Humboldt, their metal-rimmed wheels cutting tracks so deep into the rock at some places that they can still be seen today. Horace Greeley came west along the Humboldt in 1859, and was horrified by the river.

"The Humboldt," he wrote, ". . . is the meanest river of its length on earth. . . . Though three hundred and fifty miles in length, it is never more than a decent millstream; I presume it is the only river of equal length that never even had a canoe launched upon its bosom. . . . I thought I had seen barrenness before. . . . Here, on the Humboldt, famine sits enthroned, and waves his scepter over a dominion made expressly for him. . . . The sage-brush and grease-wood, which cover the high, parched plain on either side of the river's bottom, seems thinly set, with broad spaces of naked, shining, glaring, blinding clay between them; the hills beyond . . . seem even more naked. Not a tree, and hardly a shrub, anywhere relieves their sterility."

This repellent picture of the Humboldt was not Greeley's alone; since the early 1850s attempts had been made to find a more direct southerly route to the Sierra Nevada, and in 1858 a route surveyed by Captain Simpson through the Ruby Valley was adopted for the mail service, which was now making weekly departures between Salt Lake City and Sacramento, and covering the route in the fast time of sixteen days.

The new route was also selected for use by the Pony Express when it galloped into operation in 1860. The Overland Telegraph Company selected the new route also, because of the lack of timber for stringing its lines along the Humboldt, and the Overland Stagecoach Company used it as well. In 1862 Fort Ruby was established in Ruby Valley to police the trail; both it and Fort Churchill became Pony Express stops. In the Ruby Valley the Overland Stagecoach Company and the Fort Ruby soldiers farmed to provide feed for their animals. Colonel Jeremiah Moore, who commanded Fort Ruby for a while, used soldiers under his command to develop a ranch for himself, and when they had finished, he resigned his commission and rode away to Texas, returning a few months later with a herd of eight hundred longhorns.

Longhorn cattle were selling cheap in Texas after the Civil War. Hundreds of Texas ranchers were bankrupted by the collapse of the Confederacy. Their herds were largely intact, but their markets were destroyed and their cash was worthless. Many sold out for whatever their animals would bring and started from scratch; others trailed their herds out of Texas for the grazing lands of Wyoming, Montana, Utah, and Nevada.

Other herds migrated into Nevada from the droughted,

overgrazed, and increasingly fenced ranch lands of California and Oregon. Ranches were established everywhere in Nevada — everywhere there was water. But northeastern Nevada was the prime grazing land, and by the middle 1860s most of it had been appropriated to the use of the cattle ranchers, usually on the basis of a small freehold and unrestricted use of the adjacent public lands. The Indians were increasingly confined to reservations. Still there were few settlements, and those that existed were no better than way stations on the single stagecoach line that bisected the great empty spaces south of the Humboldt.

Then came the railroad. Surveyors followed the course of the Humboldt from west to east in the fall of 1868. Grade-building crews followed their markers early the following year, and rails were spiked to ties before winter was gone. When the intercontinental railroad was linked at Promontory, Utah, in May, 1869, the Overland stage line and the Army posts that guarded it became superfluous and the Humboldt River once again became the line of development in Nevada's cattle country.

The railroad brought towns. Wells, Elko, Carlin, Winnemucca: odd desert hybrids combining the antique, handmade qualities of the outlying ranches with the up-to-date, mechanized character of the railroad. The towns prospered. In January of 1869 Elko was four sun-bleached, leaky canvas tents. Six months later, after silver strikes at Bullion to the south and Aura to the north, Elko was a thriving shipping center with a population of nearly two thousand, and more than a dozen permanent buildings of planed lumber. Ranchers continued to drive herds into the country. The Garat family sold out the San Joaquin Valley property they had ranched in California since 1852 and drove one thousand head of cattle into Elko County; the Altube brothers, Basques who had built large dairy herds on the San Francisco peninsula since the early 1850s, brought a thousand animals to the Independence Valley and founded the Spanish Ranch.

Scottish herders had brought bands of sheep into western

Nevada from California and Oregon in the 1860s. They were succeeded by the Chinese who had worked in the construction gangs that built the railroad, and the Chinese were replaced in their turn by Basques from the Pyrenees Mountain provinces of Spain and France. In the late 1880s and early 1890s, when the cattlemen of northeastern Nevada were staggering under the impact of the disastrous Winter of 1889-90, the sheepmen invaded.

They pushed in from the north and west, driving their bands into the public grazing lands the cattlemen had come to think of as their own. The ranchers responded by posting armed guards at watering places, by scattering the bands of sheep, and by sniping at the herders. But the sheepmen were as tough as the ranchers, and they stayed.

By the turn of the century Elko and Winnemucca were bustling provincial capitals for about half of Nevada's cattle and perhaps two-thirds of its sheep. Headquarters for huge cattle and sheep outfits and railheads for the mines still producing in the far mountain ranges, the towns — county seats now — represented a much greater concentration of wealth and influence than their unprepossessing appearance suggested.

The same is true today; there is nothing about Nevada's cattle country to indicate its importance to the casual glance. Interstate 80 follows the course of the Humboldt. The towns along its length are only now beginning to concern themselves about the good opinion of travelers. Yet these towns are the rarest kinds of place. They are about the closest thing to the "classic" western town that yet remains. And once out of the barren trough which funnels the Humboldt west, the scenery and outdoor recreation opportunities — ranging from simple touring to backpacking into isolated mountain lakes of stunning beauty — are unutterably delightful.

Here in Nevada's cattle country the trappings of the twentieth century are only lightly, and awkwardly, laid over the very present past. And because that past encompasses the mountain men, the wagon trains, the U.S. Cavalry, renegade Indians,

Lamoille Canyon in the Ruby Mountains

cattlemen vs. sheepmen, the railroads, and the miners, it is a unique present indeed.

TOWNS

Wendover

On the Utah line, 59 miles southeast of Wells on Interstate 80. This small settlement on the Utah-Nevada border is the community nearest to the famous Bonneville Salt Flats which begin almost precisely at the state line. Two small but modern and complete casinos do a brisk weekend business, and a handful of cafes and service stations round out the business district which extends across the state line.

Wells

59 miles northwest of the Utah line and 50 miles east of Elko via Interstate 80; 68 miles south of the Idaho state line; 137 miles north of Ely via U.S. 93. Established in September, 1869; by the end of the year Humboldt Wells (as it was originally called because of the headwater springs of the Humboldt River nearby) boasted a Wells Fargo office, a single log shanty saloon, and a railroad station housed in a box car.

By 1872 stores and hotels had been added to the single business street paralleling the south side of the railroad tracks, and stagecoaches ran south into White Pine County three times a week. Severe fires in 1877 and 1881 slowed development, and lacking any business beyond that provided by the railroad and the ranches, growth was very slow. Since the turn of the century Wells, like many old railroad towns, has been shifting its center away from the railroad tracks toward the highway, and many of the buildings in its original business blocks now stand empty. It is well worth the brief detour to see the old main street. It is a life-sized, utterly authentic diorama of a nineteenth century western cowtown, with no concessions to the Hollywood myth, and only a light veneer of the twentieth century stuck on here and there.

The new main street on Interstate 80 is no traveler's dream, but it offers a good assortment of service stations, motels, cafes, and gambling houses. Wells has not prospered much from gambling since Wendover to the east, Jackpot to the north, and Elko to the west siphon most of the out-of-town business from the highway before they reach Wells, and there is only the local trade to sustain the action.

Elko

109 miles west of the Utah line, 125 miles east of Winnemucca, via Interstate 80; 101 miles south of the Idaho border via Nevada Route 51. Elko County seat. Founded as a railroad-promoted townsite and railhead for the White Pine mines in 1869, Elko prospered rapidly. By the following year townsite lot prices had multiplied three and four times, the population had risen to two thousand or more, and the place had begun taking on its character as the leading settlement of Nevada's great northeastern cattle country. By 1873 Elko was in so soaring and optimistic a municipal mood, largely on account of the success of the mining discoveries in the districts to the north and south, that it had bid for and won the state university. The university opened with seven students in 1874, and closed with fifteen ten years later, to be moved to Reno. Elko followed the mining towns she served as a freight center into decline, and population fell to less than a thousand.

Despite the steady growth in size and importance of the livestock business in the valleys around Elko, the town's affairs did not brighten up considerably until 1907. In that year not only did the Western Pacific Railroad extend its rails to Elko, but mining activity revived in half a dozen camps that relied on Elko for freight and services. The price of beef went from three and a half to eight cents a pound, and wool from four to sixty cents a pound. In ten years Elko's population had nudged up toward three thousand.

Prosperity continued until the devastating one-two of the failure of the Wingfield banking chain and the national Depression which followed immediately after. Caught in the machinery activated to sort out the bank failure and bled by the decline in livestock prices, many of the ranches around Elko were foreclosed.

But around the time that beef and wool economies fell into chaos, gambling was made legal by the state legislature. Elko, like towns everywhere in Nevada, had a new industry. And unlike most, it had an entrepreneur to make the most of it.

Newton Crumley had operated saloons and hotels in Tonopah, Goldfield, and Jarbidge before he settled in Elko in 1925 and bought the Commercial Hotel. He and his son, Newton Jr., operated the hotel with an eye toward the future. By 1937 they had added a two-hundred-seat cocktail lounge to the Commercial, and by 1941 they hired Ted Lewis, the "High-Hatted Tragedian of Jazz," his orchestra, and his twenty-one-person Rhythm Rhapsody Review for an eight-day engagement. After Lewis came Sophie Tucker, then Skinnay Ennis and his band. For drowsy little Elko, more than 250 miles from the nearest radio station, the situation was stunning. Even more impressive was the effect on traffic along U.S. 40: little of it passed through Elko without a detour into the Commercial. By 1946, when they began "remodeling" an eighty-eight by ten-foot rootbeer stand into the sixty-eight room Ranchinn Motel-Casino (at that materials-short time remodeling was permitted, new construction prohibited), the Crumleys had the largest non-ranching payroll in Elko County after the railroads, and in 1948 they sold an accumulation of ranching properties north of town to Bing Crosby.

With ranching restored to prosperity, with gambling and big-name entertainment adding to the municipal vigor, and with newcoming ranchers like Bing Crosby, Joel McRae, and Jimmy Stewart providing glamor and sophistication, Elko entered its golden age at the end of the 1940s.

Crosby and his Hollywood colleagues have sold their Elko County ranches now, and the Crumleys are gone. There is entertainment at the Commercial and at the Stockmen's, but nothing so ambitious as in the 1940s. Yet the town retains its air of awkward splendor. It is the marvelous diversity of its population that is responsible. In Elko there are cowboys and Indians, sheepherders, miners and railroad men, gamblers and whores, schoolmarms and ribbon clerks.

It also has a liberal sprinkling of tourists, truck drivers, and other travelers, both because Elko is at the approximate mid-point of the drive between Reno and Salt Lake City, and because of the number and variety of Elko's attractions.

The two large hotel-casinos, the Commercial and the Stockmen's, still face each other across the railroad tracks around which Elko grew up. Elko's three Basque hotels are along the south side of Silver Street (behind the Stockmen's). They cater to a regular lodging clientele of Basque sheepmen but open their dining rooms to the public for supper. All offer similar menus of hearty food and plenty of it served family style. The atmosphere is at once homey and foreign, a most pleasantly provocative combination.

Compared to most Nevada communities, Elko is a big city.

At the east end of town, alongside the highway that ribbons out across the desert to Salt Lake City, a large green park, a complex of pools, the chamber of commerce building, and an uncommonly good museum are all neighbors. The park, grassy and shaded, is the site of the annual National Basque Festival in July, and is furnished with a multitude of children's climbables, swings, and picnic tables. The swimming pools — there are three of them, one indoors, one outdoors, and one for wading small fry — are open to the public. Outside the small chamber of commerce building is the old Pony Express station from Ruby Valley, moved to town when it seemed that weather and vandals would finally bring it down. Letters and cards deposited here bear a special Pony Express cancellation.

A few steps closer to town is the Northeastern Nevada Museum, a small but professionally managed museum displaying exhibits of history, natural history, and Indian lore of Elko County and the surrounding region. All exhibit materials were donated by local people, with one exception — the old bar from the Halleck Saloon. For this relic the museum is required to pay a bottle of Beefeater's gin each year — to be served over the bar to its former owner. The museum exhibits art continuously and in wide variety, as well as sponsoring art festivals in the spring and fall and a flower show in the spring. The small selection of modestly priced Nevada Indian bead and buckskin work at the museum desk is one of the few places it can be purchased off the reservations. Also available for purchase: books and booklets which supplement the museum exhibits, and pottery.

Lowell Thomas called Elko the only real cowtown left in the West, and he was right. But he hardly went far enough. The vigor and variety that make up Elko's municipal character, and the magnificence of its scenic surroundings north and south, make Elko one of the three great towns in the American West.

Carlin

23 miles west of Elko, 102 miles east of Winnemucca via Interstate 80; 89 miles north of Eurkea via Nevada Route 51. Founded late in 1868 as the eastern terminus of the Central Pacific Railroad's Humboldt Division, Carlin was known briefly as Chinese Gardens. Carlin grew quickly to accommodate housing for the railroaders employed at the round house and machine shops, and the crews of the trains that rattled through town daily. The business district at the south side of the tracks grew rapidly to encompass a hotel, telegraph office, and express office as well as a number of saloons, two cafes, and four grocery and merchandise stores. The railroad built and furnished an eleven-hundred-volume library, and the county built a jail. By the turn of the century Carlin was a noisy, dirty, barren little goiter of prosperity along the iron rails through the desert, wholly the railroad's child.

During five succeeding decades Carlin was subject to gentle, slow alternations of rise and decline in municipal fortunes. In the early 1950s, however, those fortunes were cast violently down when steam engines were replaced by diesel power. Carlin's maintenance shops were no longer required. Introduction of refrigerated cars brought the abandonment of an icing station. Families moved away. Carlin's business district began inching toward the highway and away from the railroad tracks. Even the opening of the Carlin Gold Mine by the Newmont Mining Company in 1965 did relatively little to restore Carlin's old vitality, since many of the workers employed at the mine and mill made their homes in Elko. Consequently, there has been little change along the town's old main street on the other side of the tracks from the highway.

It is a street of gaunt, dilapidated old buildings. A few of the old facades attempt a spurious youthfulness, about as persuasive as grandma's rouged cheeks. The Overland, the State, the Humboldt Club, and other places without any names at all, as if the paint had faded away and never been missed — the dim and homely buildings lean glumly against one another in a single row. It is an unromantic monument to all the railroad towns that fronted the Central Pacific across a thousand miles of western landscape. A stop here for lunch, or just for a cup of coffee, makes a fascinating detour from Interstate 80.

To get across the railroad tracks drive south on 4th Street. Once across the tracks turn left. A pedestrian walkway also crosses the switching yard from one side of town to another, and provides an excellent view of the railroad activities that still account for most of Carlin's enterprise.

An odd, homely little town, lacking in any appearance of romance. Yet in January, 1889, the Carlin correspondent to the Elko *Free Press* wrote amiably about a ghost that shared the house into which she and her husband had just moved: "Sometimes he taps on the headboard of the bed. Other times he stalks across the kitchen floor, and he hammers away at the door but nobody is there. But the gayest capers of all are cut up in the cellar. There he holds high revels, and upsets the pickles and carries on generally." When the ghost persisted, the lady's husband went into the cellar and probed the earthen floor and walls. Behind the pickle shelves he found the partially burned and dismembered corpse of a man. The husband and wife who had formerly occupied the house were eventually tried and convicted for murder and hanged behind the Elko courthouse. The hanging was the first legal execution of a woman in the Pacific region, and the only one in the history of Nevada.

Lodgings and meals of adequate character and automotive services are available in Carlin.

Winnemucca

125 miles west of Elko, 164 miles east of Reno via Interstate 80; 73 miles south of the Oregon line via U.S. 95. Humboldt County seat. A trading post established here in 1850 to serve the westward-bound wagon trains that crossed the Humboldt River at this point was called French Ford. Renamed by an Army mapmaker in honor of the principal Paiute chief at the time, and developed as a townsite by the Central Pacific, Winnemucca grew rapidly.

It was a railroad center of some importance, and the shipping point for numerous ranches north and south and for the mines of several districts. It was also the natural stagecoach and freighting junction for Idaho traffic. By 1872 the bustling young railroad town had snatched the county seat away from faltering Unionville beyond the Humboldt Mountains. By 1874 its population had reached sixteen hundred and a historian wrote in 1880 that Winnemucca "in consequence of being situated on a line of extensive travel, where persons of all nations and character come in contact, has an extensive record of homicides."

Like Elko, which it somewhat resembles, Winnemucca is largely a livestock center, its fortunes rising and falling with the markets for beef and wool for more than a hundred years. Until 1873 and the passage of the national act demonetizing silver, the mines of half a dozen surrounding districts played a major part in the town's economic life. Today only a few mines in the region are in production, and one of them, the Cordero Mine to the north of Winnemucca, is one of the world's leading mercury producers.

Since the end of World War II, the tourist trade has assumed increasingly greater importance in the economic life of the community. The Winnemucca-to-the-Sea Highway (Nevada Route 140, which continues through Klamath Falls and Grant's Pass to end at Crescent City, California) is attracting growing traffic, and the presence of Interstate 80 has generated a new local awareness of the tourist trade. This awareness has manifested itself in the form of a handful of small but flossy casinos. The Star was the first, in the center of town, and for some years it had the gambling business pretty much to itself. There are newer casinos now, with plenty of lights and modern decor — but Winnemucca hasn't made the transition wholeheartedly to being a tourist town as yet, and these gaudy plastic palaces stand awkwardly in the narrow streets, flashing their too-eager fluorescent smiles. Winnemucca is largely green, placid, and friendly. It is well furnished with modern overnight accommodations and can offer all services required by travelers.

DEVELOPED CAMPGROUNDS

(Season of use for all below: June 1 to October 31,
unless otherwise noted)

Winnemucca Area

Lye Creek Campground. 55 miles northeast of Winnemucca via U.S. 95, Nevada Route 88, and Hinkey Summit road. At about eight thousand feet in the Santa Rosa Range, the campground has developed camping units and a large group unit for as many as seventy persons. Water is piped to all units. June 1 to September 30. Administered by the Humboldt National Forest (HNF).

Elko Area

Jack Creek Campground. 63 miles northwest of Elko via Nevada Routes 51 and 11 and marked dirt road. Developed camping units and picnicking; water provided. HNF.

Wildhorse Reservoir, near Elko

North Fork Campground. 71 miles northwest of Elko via Nevada Routes 51 and 11 and marked dirt road. Developed camp sites and picnicking on the flank of the Independence Range and the north fork of the Humboldt River. Water provided. HNF.

Wild Horse Crossing Campground. 74 miles north of Elko, 10 miles south of Mountain City via Nevada Route 51. A large number of developed camping and picnic units, including some group units, all with water available. HNF.

Gold Creek Picnic Area. 73 miles north of Elko, east of State Route 51; 11 miles northeast of the northeastern shore of Wild Horse Reservoir; 16 miles east of Mountain City by marked dirt roads. This facility has tables, fireplaces, privies, and water. Gold Creek Ranger Station is a few hundred yards away. This facility shows on some maps as *Martin Creek*. HNF.

Big Bend Campground. 2 miles northwest of the Gold Creek Ranger Station via Forest Service Road 037. Fully-developed family camping units and a single group unit; picnicking, water. HNF.

North Wild Horse Campground. On the north shore of Wild Horse Reservoir 68 miles north of Elko via Nevada Route 51. Family camping units and picnic units overlook the three-thousand-acre reservoir. A free boat launching ramp has been installed, and hand-pumped well water is provided.

Pine Creek Campground. 100 miles northeast of Elko via Nevada Route 51, Rochester-Jarbidge road, and marked dirt road. This campground, just below the western boundary of the Jarbidge Wilderness Area, contains family campsites; water is provided. Because of late-lying snow, this campground usually is not accessible before July. HNF.

Jarbidge Campground. 2 miles north of Pine Creek Campground via Jarbidge road, about 1 mile south of Jarbidge. Family camping units, water provided. HNF.

Ruby Marshes, northern Nevada

Lower Lamoille Campground. 22 miles southeast of Elko via Nevada Route 46, Lamoille Road, and marked access road. Family camping units near the eastern base of the marvelously beautiful Ruby Mountain Range. Water provided; picnicking. Usually accessible by mid-May. Fourteen-day camping limit. HNF.

Thomas Canyon Campground. 7 miles beyond Lower Lamoille Campground into the Rubies. Family camping units, picnicking, and trailer spaces in the magnificent surroundings of the Ruby Mountain Scenic Area. Water provided. June 1 to September 30. HNF.

Ruby Marsh Campground. 50 miles south of Elko via Nevada Route 46 and the Harrison Pass road 3 miles south of Jiggs; or some 70 miles on Interstate 80 and State Route 11, via Secret Pass. Family camping units nestled against the east side of the Ruby Mountains overlooking the Ruby Lake National Wildlife Refuge. This is one of the few Golden Eagle Passport fee campgrounds in Nevada. Water is provided. April 1 to December 1. BLM.

Wells Area

Angel Creek Campground. 8 miles southwest of Wells via paved access road. Family camping units, trailer spaces, water, picnicking. HNF.

Angel Lake Campground. 4 miles beyond Angel Creek Campground. Family camping units, trailer units at lakeside. Good (but chilly) swimming during the heat of a summer day at this exceptionally beautiful recreation site in the shadow of Hole in the Mountain Peak. Water provided; group areas. HNF.

GHOST TOWNS

Metropolis

11 miles northwest of Wells via graded dirt road. Built and financed by the Pacific Reclamation Company beginning in 1911, Metropolis was to be a planned community of 7,500 resi-

dents in the center of more than forty thousand acres of intensively cultivated fields. A Salt Lake City sales office sold farm land at prices of from $10 to $75 an acre, and city lots for as much as $300. The Metropolis *Chronicle* began publication that year, and the Southern Pacific built a spur line, complete with ornate depot and tree-shaded park. In 1912 a dam was completed across Bishop Creek and canals were dug to distribute the water. A four-block business district with cement sidewalks and streetlights contained an elaborate three-story hotel and a wagon factory, as well as the usual collection of enterprises serving a farm community. But in 1913 an unfavorable court decision regarding water rights resulted in the failure of the parent company, and Metropolis remained a hamlet. Even the reduced level of activity could not be sustained, however. In 1925 the railroad spur was abandoned; in 1936 the hotel burned; in 1942 the post office closed, and the schoolhouse closed in 1947. Ranching continues in the region, but Metropolis itself is untenanted. Empty-windowed ruins of the mammoth hotel, once the grandest between Ogden and Reno, dominate the town site.

Jarbidge

102 miles north of Elko via Nevada Route 51 and the graded dirt road leading east 4 miles north of North Fork. A gold strike in 1909 prompted a rush the following spring when reports of the region's spectacular richness appeared in the press. Some fifteen hundred miners reached the deep canyon to stake claims on the snowdrifts covering the ground to a depth of as much as eighteen feet, but when the snow melted it exposed the exaggeration of the newspaper reports, and most of the prospectors melted away. Further discoveries were made in 1910, however, and by the end of the year Jarbidge was a long, narrow community of several hundred residents connected by stagecoach with its nearest neighbor, Rogerson, Idaho, some 65 miles away. The population rose to about twelve hundred the following year and then began a fluctuating decline which continued despite the

Jarbidge

large-scale mining which commenced in 1918, when the Guggenheim interests acquired the Jarbidge mines, and lasted until 1932. Perhaps a dozen permanent residents remain at Jarbidge, which has a store, a gas pump, two bars, and a post office.

The last stagecoach robbery in the West took place at the outskirts of Jarbidge during a December blizzard in 1916. The bandit leaped onto the empty stage from a place of concealment, killed the driver, and continued on almost into town before he could turn the frightened horses off the road. Town authorities found the stagecoach abandoned, the driver dead in his seat, and the U.S. mail bags rifled. A $3,000 cash shipment was missing. A trail of circumstantial evidence led to the conviction of a mine cook and town rounder whose eleventh-hour confession resulted in commutation of his death sentence to life imprisonment. He was released in 1944.

Jarbidge is the most isolated of all Nevada's prominent mining camps, and the most beautiful. The Jarbidge River, running down the canyon in which the town is wedged, is a busy stream which squirms its way to the Snake, and the wilderness area to the east is magnificent. One July visitor counted more than sixty varieties of wild flower in bloom on the way to Jarbidge and in the tightly-woven maze of canyons around the town.

Tuscarora

52 miles northwest of Elko via Nevada Routes 51, 11, and 18. Discovered in 1867 and named for the Civil War gunboat on which one of the locators had served, Tuscarora was at first only a placer camp. Three hundred miners staked out diggings around the adobe fort they built for protection against the Indians.

After completion of the Central Pacific in 1869, a large number of Chinese miners drifted to Tuscarora to sift through worked-over claims and work as laborers on the ditch projects aimed at supplying water to the placer mines. When silver lodes were discovered nearby in 1871, most of the placers were abandoned to the Chinese altogether, and a rush developed. By 1877 Tuscarora had a permanent population of nearly four thousand, not counting the Chinese who continued to work the placers and cut the sagebrush used for fuel in the mills. They inhabited one of the largest Chinatowns east of San Francisco.

The citizens of Tuscarora were tireless joiners, and the social season was full with the doings of every conceivable organization from a National Guard company to a ballet society. In 1878 alone more than a million dollars in bullion was hauled south to the railroad, but in the 1880s the mines began to falter. Production continued more or less regularly until 1900, then surged up again briefly in 1907. Activity has been practically nil since World War I.

Many of Tuscarora's old buildings remain, but they are overshadowed, as in Manhattan, by the bright aluminum trailers and campers moored in empty lots all over town. There are perhaps two dozen permanent residents, enough to support a small post office and a single business house; the museum, a labor of love, is well worth a visit. A nominal charge is made.

Midas

42 miles west of Tuscarora via Nevada Route 18, or 60 miles northeast of Winnemucca via Interstate 80 and Nevada Route 18. The original discoverers wanted to call their town Gold Circle in the summer of 1907, but post office officials refused to allow another Nevada postmark with "Gold" in it, so they settled for Midas. Two thousand people had crowded into camp by the following year, which turned out to be about 1,750 more than the mines could actually support; the supernumeraries were gone by winter. Production was small until 1915 when a new cyanide mill was built and Midas prospered. Production ended suddenly when the mill burned in 1922, resuming spasmodically until 1942 when it ended for good.

Eighteen buildings still stand in Midas, including Ann & Andy's Saloon, the single business. There is a cafe in through the saloon that is open sometimes, and an old Armstrong gasoline pump out at the porch. Early photographs of Midas show a ragged line of tents on a naked slope; the camp's remains are pleasantly shaded by mature cottonwoods. Except in deer season, there is nothing much to do in Midas but have a drink or a cup of coffee at the saloon and contemplate. A lollygagger's paradise.

Palisade

11 miles southwest of Carlin via Nevada Route 51 and marked, graded dirt road. Established in 1868 as a station on the Central Pacific, Palisade thrived as the shipping point for mining districts centered at Mineral Hill, Hamilton, and Eureka. After 1874 it was the northern terminal of the Eureka & Palisade Railroad. At its peak, Palisade had a population of about six hundred, mostly employed by one or the other of the railroads. Decline began as the Eureka mining output diminished, choking

off activity on the E&P during the middle 1880s. It is said that idle railroad workers sometimes amused themselves by staging enormous fake gunfights on the station platform as the westbound transcontinental passenger trains drew in. Many of the easterners aboard the train gave up their suppers rather than risk the dangers outside.

In 1908 the Western Pacific laid tracks through the narrow canyon and Palisade's prospects improved. But in 1910 heavy flooding swept much of the town downriver. The collapse of the Eureka & Palisade Railroad in 1938 effectively ended Palisade's career, and it has not a single resident left. It is not among the most impressive of Nevada's ghosts to look at, but the Southern Pacific trains still thunder through the place with little warning, and make a night time visit there quite sensational.

Paradise Valley
40 miles north of Winnemucca via U.S. 95 and Nevada Route 8B. Established in 1864 by W. M. Gregg, who had entered the valley to prospect the surrounding mountains. He turned around and traded his mining gear for farmer's tools, and returned to build a hay ranch. Others soon joined him, but many of the settlers were driven out again by hostile Indians in 1865, only returning after the establishment in late 1866 of Camp Winfield Scott in the northern part of the valley. Paradise City (as it was then known) grew up in the late 1860s as a hybrid town. Its immediate surrounds were crop and grazing lands, but early in the 1870s a number of mining discoveries were made a few miles to the northeast. While Paradise Valley never became a mining town, it prospered greatly from the traffic of the mines and grew to substantially larger size than it would have done otherwise. The failure of the mines reduced the town's population again, and today many of its buildings stand empty. A store, a saloon, and a gasoline pump are manned in Paradise Valley; the churches, hotels, and most of the other buildings along the two wide, pleasantly cottonwood-shaded streets are not. Perhaps the only community in Nevada which can be called "quaint" with a straight face.

Humboldt City ruins

ROAD AND PARK INFORMATION

Throughout this book an attempt-has been made to locate for the traveler the major camping and recreational areas. In addition, an effort has been made to indicate which state or federal agency has jurisdiction over a particular area.

Motorists are urged to check with the proper agency concerning up-to-date information on the types of facilities afforded by each area, and particularly on whether the area is currently accessible.

Winters are severe in the high mountains of Nevada, and while this may not pose the obvious problem during the spring and summer months, flash flooding may completely wash away a service road leading to one or another of the remote camping areas.

You may check with the following, with local chambers of commerce, or with local offices of the Nevada Department of Highways when traveling through the state:

Nevada State Parks, Room 221, Nye Building, Carson City, Nevada 89701.

Humboldt National Forest, 976 Mountain City Highway, Elko, Nevada 89801.

Toiyabe National Forest, 111 North Virginia Street, Room 601, Reno, Nevada 89501.

Lake Mead National Recreation Area, 601 Nevada Highway, Boulder City, Nevada 89005.

Washoe County Parks and Recreation Department, 2601 Plumas Street, Reno, Nevada 89509.

Bureau of Land Management, Room 3008, Federal Building, 300 Booth Street, Reno, Nevada 89502, or one of the branch offices as follows:
2002 Idaho Street, Elko, Nevada 89801.

801 North Plaza Street, Carson City, Nevada 89701.
Pioche Star Route, Ely, Nevada 89301.
Second and Scott Streets, Battle Mountain, Nevada 89820.
1859 North Decatur Boulevard, Las Vegas, Nevada 89108.
Highway Interstate 80 East, P.O. Box 71, Winnemucca,
    Nevada, 89445.

SPEED LIMITS

Until only recently, many miles of Nevada highways had no assigned maximum speed limits. Thanks to federal government demands, however, the state now enjoys a 55-mile-per-hour posted maximum speed — a questionable blessing considering the miles of wide open space where your vehicle may be potentially hazardous to nothing more than an occasional jackrabbit or two. Or to yourself, of course.

Driving at speeds which are consistent with the safe and reasonable operation of your vehicle are still urged, nonetheless. In stormy weather, for example, 20 mph might be too fast for certain stretches of road in the state which can safely be driven at maximum allowable speeds when conditions are ideal.

In spite of the temptations, watch your speed since determining precisely what it is no longer presents any great difficulty to the Nevada Highway Patrol. All patrol cars have been equipped with VASCAR. This is an electronic system related to radar, but of far more sophistication. It permits a patrolman to determine your exact speed whether he be traveling in the same direction you are, approaching you from the opposite direction, or even if he is sitting at an intersection and your line of travel cuts his path.

Bubble and fume all you like; if VASCAR says you were doing 59 mph, you were doing 59 mph.

Maximum-speed-limit signs are posted periodically on all major highways, while lesser limits are posted where there is increased hazard to traffic or to pedestrians. Limits are firmly enforced, but there are no "speed traps" in Nevada.

IMPLIED CONSENT LAW

In 1969 the Nevada legislature adopted an "implied consent" law. It provides that anyone operating a vehicle on the public highways of the state is deemed to have consented in advance to a chemical test of blood, breath, or urine if arrested on a charge of driving while intoxicated. A refusal to submit to such tests results in a mandatory suspension of driving privileges in Nevada for a period of six months.

The law stipulates that anyone whose blood contains one tenth of a percent (.10%) of alcohol is legally intoxicated. As an aid to drivers who want to avoid not only the possibility of arrest but the prospect of mayhem or death, the state's Office of Traffic Safety has devised the following table. It shows the approximate relationship between a person's body weight, the number of drinks he has had in a two-hour period, and his blood alcohol concentration (BAC).

Body Weight	Number of drinks in a two-hour period							
100	1	2	3	4	5	6	7	8
120	1	2	3	4	5	6	7	8
140	1	2	3	4	5	6	7	8
160	1	2	3	4	5	6	7	8
180	1	2	3	4	5	6	7	8
200	1	2	3	4	5	6	7	8
220	1	2	3	4	5	6	7	8
240	1	2	3	4	5	6	7	8

Caution
BAC under .05%

Driving impaired
BAC .05% to .09%

Legally drunk
BAC .10% or more

Hot coffee, fresh air, and cold showers won't make a drunk driver safe — only time will "burn up" alcohol. One reliable estimate indicates that a 150-pound man who has had eight drinks in three hours will still be legally drunk two hours after he stops, and that his driving will be seriously impaired for at least three more hours. Thus he shouldn't drive for at least five hours after his last drink (until his BAC falls below .05%). You should know, however, that the presence of any alcohol whatsoever may be considered with other competent evidence in determining the guilt or innocence of a defendant. Individual reactions to alcohol vary substantially, and those who gamble with a jail sentence or death on the basis of the above example are foolhardy, to say the least.

MORMON COUNTRY

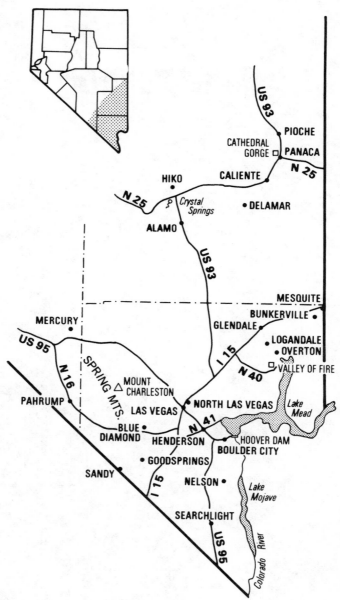

reat undulating valleys separate gaunt mountain ranges. The soil is often alkaline, and on the broad playas, trees are unknown. Even the brush grows sparsely. The mountains are timbered in the heights, but the runoff from springs and snowmelt seldom trickles far into the flats before the fierce heat evaporates it. Dry washes, some of them nearly a hundred miles long, scar the empty landscape. So inhospitable is this desert land that astronauts were brought here to stump about in space suits in order that they might get a feeling for walking on the moon. In summer the temperature regularly rises to 115 degrees and more. In winter there is a brief frost. To the east, across the Colorado, the badlands are as fierce and forbidding as any on the continent. Here the sweep of mountains and valleys is a little gentler, a little less shocking to the eye, but it is a bleak and desolate landscape.

The Mormons came out of the Middle West like the Jews out of Egypt, despised and harassed by their Gentile neighbors who had slaughtered the prophet Joseph Smith in Illinois. They trekked west more than a thousand miles into the wilderness behind the "Lion of the Lord," Brigham Young, and built a raw-boned, rough-hewn city on the shore of the Great Salt Lake. And no sooner had the beginnings of their Zion begun to take shape along the broad boulevards of Salt Lake City than they began sending small parties of colonists out into the farther reaches of their arid kingdom to settle the land and make it fruitful.

The first party of Mormons to reach Nevada did so in 1849, a small body of men struggling with difficulty across the grain of the landscape in search of an easy route to the seaports of Southern California. They lost themselves in the valleys and mountains of what is now southern Nevada, abandoned their wagons, and pressed on. At Death Valley they perished of starvation and thirst.

But they persisted. By 1851 they had established a number of scattered outposts, including a colony of some five hundred at San Bernardino, in California. In the following year the Mormons were awarded the contract to carry mail between San Bernardino and Salt Lake City, and three years later a few families were dispatched to a tiny spring-watered green patch on the Old Spanish Trail a few miles west of the Colorado River. They were to protect the mail route, harvest hay, and work the Potosi lead mine recently discovered in the desert hills to the southwest.

In two years they had managed to construct a small adobe building to house the mission, had planted trees, and developed the artesian springs into a true desert oasis on the broad sweep of gray sand between Frenchman Mountain and the Spring Mountains. But in 1857 they and other far-flung Mormon settlers were recalled to Salt Lake City by Brigham Young to meet the threat of an invasion by federal troops. The tiny settlement at Las Vegas was abandoned to the Gentiles.

At the same time, Mormons from the southern Utah settlements were sent west into the virtually unexplored lands north of Las Vegas to scout out places of refuge in case the invasion actually took place. In some of the most promising locations, corrals were built of native stone, the sagebrush was grubbed out, and corn was planted. Eventually Brigham Young abandoned the concept of an independent and sovereign Mormon state and made peace with the U.S. The refugee centers were thereupon left to the mountain lions and big horned sheep.

But they were not forgotten, and when colonists again went out from Zion in the middle 1860s, many of the centers were permanently occupied. One party of settlers, consisting of seventeen men, women, and children, reached Meadow Valley in the spring of 1864 with five wagons, some cattle, sheep, and hogs. In February of the following year, fifteen settlers reached the valley of the Muddy River, having passed in their journey "a family of three that had died of thirst in the desert. Their faces were all swollen and black, tongues exceedingly large and black, protruding from their mouths most horribly." There were no roads to the Pacific Coast through this fierce and unforgiving country except the route through Las Vegas, and the missionary-farmers lost precious equipment getting to their new assignments.

Despite the almost indescribable difficulties, more settlers followed at the command of Brigham Young to establish farming settlements at Panaca, Eagle Valley, Saint Thomas, Saint Joseph, Rioville, Moapa, and the Pahranagat Valley: isolated, crude, uncultivated in any intellectual sense, deprived of most of the advantages of civilization, entirely dependent on their own labors and capacities for the overwhelming majority of their needs, harrassed by Indians who were hostile at worst and unsympathetic at best. And they succeeded.

They succeeded because they worked themselves as ruthlessly as they worked their livestock, and because they had come not for fortune or adventure but to establish homes for themselves and to build a fortress of the faith. They expected hardship because they were acting in opposition to "the adversary." They survived in canvas-, brush-, or sod-roofed dugouts, often for years, while they planted crops and worked to develop their livestock holdings. They cleared acre after acre of sagebrush, and plowed the ground to hay and grain. If their animals gave out, they hitched themselves to the plows and lurched and staggered hour after hour under the blazing sun.

The discoveries of rich ore bodies at the Comstock Lode, at Aurora, Austin, Unionville, and other places farther west were drawing prospectors into eastern Nevada, and friction developed between these Gentiles and the Mormons.

Part of the problem was the Mormon elitist attitude: they were the Saints; others were Gentiles. Part of the problem was Mormon clannishness: they preferred their own company to that of people who had not shared their difficulties and their persecutions. Part of the problem was the reputation given them by their detractors for more than a generation. Part of the problem lay in the religious differences between their faith and the more orthodox systems. But the principal cause of strife was not present in Nevada to the same degree it had existed in Illinois and Missouri. Here the Mormons were not so successful or so numerous that they could dominate the region economically or politically. For this reason, despite resentment and harrassment, they were spared the pogroms which had erupted in the Middle West in the 1840s.

Mining activity began in the region in 1859, at Eldorado Canyon on the Colorado, and was confined to the banks of the canyons entering the river.

Indians had previously related stories about the heavy rocks in the hillsides to the west of Eagle Valley, and the Mormons had staked claims to the richest silver outcrops — not to work them, but to prevent the Gentiles from working them. Word of these claims fired the interest of prospectors, however, and soon there were Gentiles prowling the hills and locating other rich ore bodies. In 1865 a strike was made in the Irish Mountains. Logan City became the first mining town in the Mormon country, though its population never exceeded two hundred. The miners and the Mormon farmers were too useful to each other — and too busy — to engage in hostilities. A second town, Hiko, grew up around the mill site in the Pahranagat Valley and became the Lincoln County seat.

The miners diverted water without apology from the Mormon springs and creeks, and hard feeling between the two groups might have broken into violence except for the Indians. Alarmed at the increasing intrusion into their lands, the Indians became a growing threat to Mormons and Gentiles alike. Small-scale pilfering became large-scale theft, and a fort was built at the newly organized town of Panaca by the combined labor of the Mormon farmers and the Gentile miners. A twenty-man force of Mormon Militia was sent out from Utah to aid in the defense of the region. When the troop departed a short time later, more than half of the Mormon settlers returned to Utah with it.

Shortly afterward the Gentiles succeeded in invalidating the Mormon mineral claims, and the rich deposits prompted heavy investments of outside capital and the building of two important cities: Pioche, in the box canyon beneath the mines themselves, and Bullionville, to the south and east, where the reduction mills were located close to springs near the Mormon townsite at Panaca. With the influx of a large Gentile population to work the mines and operate businesses at Pioche and Bullionville, anti-Mormon antagonism increased despite the fact that both cities depended in large measure on the produce of the Mormon farms. This resentment focused on the issue of taxes.

The Mormons, with no evidence to the contrary, had always assumed that their lands lay within the borders of Arizona and Utah. They had paid their taxes in those states, and had even sent delegates to the legislatures. Officials of Nevada's newly-formed Lincoln County, however, insisted that the valleys farmed by the Mormons were included within their jurisdiction, and they levied taxes against them at a rate appreciably higher than that charged by either Arizona or Utah. Having already paid their taxes to the other states, the Mormons refused to pay again and a series of court actions was initiated against them. When a survey was at last completed in 1871, the settlements were shown to be inside the Nevada border, and many of the Mormon pioneers deserted their lands in disgust.

As the fortunes of the Pioche mines waxed and waned, the farmers who remained perfected their properties and improved their sleepy towns through blistering summers and mild winters. They planted tens of thousands of trees, built irrigation ditches to reclaim thousands of unproductive desert acres, grazed ever larger herds and, in a quiet, unspectacular way, they prospered.

They financed schools and organized relief societies, and they kept to themselves. Pioche, meanwhile, became one of the roughest mining towns in the West, with a reputation for sudden, violent death rivaling Tombstone's and Bodie's. When the mines began the long, slow, petering out, Mormons acceded to many of the key county offices.

In 1903 the ranch property at Las Vegas, long in Gentile hands, was purchased by the San Pedro, Los Angeles, and Salt Lake Railroad for a division point and townsite. This occurred just as the gold and silver strikes at Tonopah and Goldfield were raising two major mining cities on the desert to the north and west, and the Searchlight mines to the south, active since 1898, were approaching peak production. In May, 1905, the railroad conducted a two-day lot auction, disposing of twelve hundred town lots at Las Vegas for a total purchase price of $265,000.

Caliente, some 150 miles to the northeast of Las Vegas and about 25 miles south of Panaca, came into existence at about the same time as another division point, and was settled equally by railroad families and second- and third-generation Mormons. In June, 1906, the rail connection between Salt Lake City and Los Angeles via Caliente and Las Vegas was complete, and in 1907 the Las Vegas and Tonopah Railroad linked up with the booming mining cities to the north. Las Vegas became so important a shipping center that in 1909 the Nevada legislature lopped off the southern portion of Lincoln County and created Clark County, with Las Vegas as its seat.

But in 1910 the railroad was ripped up by unexpectedly heavy flooding in Meadow Valley Wash, and rail traffic was suspended for five months. The effect of the panic of 1907 was now heavily felt in the mines, and Las Vegas reverted to a near-subsistence economy. There was a pleasantly raffish air about the place, but no glamor. Las Vegas lay quietly in the board-warping desert heat, fly-blown, thin-walled, and dry-mouthed: a hick town. Caliente was no more vivacious. One Mormon who grew up there recalls that when he was a good boy, his dad would take him down to the station to listen to the railroad men eat.

Southern Nevada fortunes took a sudden turn for the better when Congress approved the U.S. Bureau of Reclamation's recommendation for a huge dam on the Colorado. The site of construction was at Black Canyon, thirty-one miles from Las Vegas and only a short distance downstream from the Mormon settlements on the Muddy and Virgin rivers. Las Vegas began at once to swell with arriving engineers, government officials of every weight and stripe, truck drivers, hardrock miners, heavy equipment operators, scalers, and laborers.

Construction commenced officially on September 17, 1930, and peak employment on the project reached 5,218. The impact on Las Vegas was tremendous, since the population there was only 5,165 before the dam was begun. Even when the government built the model town of Boulder City to house the project headquarters and the bulk of the workers, Las Vegas thrived. Legalization of gambling by the 1931 legislature prompted the opening of six small casinos on Fremont Street, all within a short walk of the railroad station, and Las Vegas began to jump in a small-time way.

Even so, remainders of the Old West hung on. The renegade Cocopah Quejo, who had been murdering and pillaging at isolated households in the desert southeast of Las Vegas since 1910, was still somewhere out beyond the shimmering horizon. He had been spotted buying a can of peaches in a Fremont Street grocery store in 1930 while a posse was clattering through the fantastic grottoes of the Valley of Fire searching for his tracks. It wasn't until 1940 that his body was found in a cave near the Colorado, partially mummified and apparently the victim of a natural death.

In 1940 Richard Lillard was writing his excellent book about Nevada, *Desert Challenge*, and describing Las Vegas as "respectable, bumptious, and decadent," where culture consisted in the fact that Rex Bell and Clara Bow had a ranch south of town, and where "a new resident isn't a stranger long. Someone will clap him on the back. 'You're a stranger here, aren't you? come in and have a drink.' Anywhere else such a greeter might be a 'con man,' but not in Las Vegas. There he is just a citizen who has a town to share." That easy affability began to wane a little during the war when the development of war-related industry, notably the magnesium plants at Henderson between Las Vegas and Boulder City, brought thousands of newcomers. Nevertheless, at war's end Las Vegas was still largely a yokel town and still playing a decidedly second fiddle to Reno where some of the "first families" had already made it beyond the second generation, and where the state's economic and political power had been concentrated since the decline of Tonopah and Goldfield.

By 1945 the Las Vegas Strip existed in the embryonic form of two small casinos along the highway south of town. The Last Frontier was a kind of Knott's Berry Farm gambling parlor heavily flavored with old western atmosphere; the El Rancho Vegas was a flossy motel with a small casino and an even smaller cabaret lounge featuring relatively-unknown entertainers from the Hollywood nightclub circuit. When the management of the Last Frontier approached the gambling concessionaire to help with the expense of hiring better-known talent — stars, in fact — they were met with indignation. "You must be crazy!" he exploded. You get into that kind of thing, it could run you as much as five grand a week! I've been in the gambling business all my life and I can tell you there's not a casino in the world that can get by with a nut that big!" When the owners insisted, he walked out, thus earning a place in history with the people who laughed at Robert Fulton and latter-day prophets who bet on the Baltimore Colts against the New York Jets.

Because farther down the dusty valley toward Los Angeles a man named Benjamin "Bugsy" Siegel was building an enormous hotel, the Flamingo, as fast as he could lay his hands on hard-to-get building materials.

Some day Siegel will achieve his rightful place among Nevada pioneers. In terms of his impact on Nevada's fortunes, he ranks far above the trapper Ogden and makes John Frémont look like a dilletante. His achievement ranks with the discovery and development of the Comstock Lode. He is the man who invented Las Vegas, yet the school texts do not even mention him in a footnote.

When Siegel threw open the doors of the Flamingo, he revealed the future of Las Vegas inside: an enormous, luxuriously appointed, casino-resort-hotel, and two of the hottest properties in show business, Abbott & Costello and the Xavier Cugat Orchestra, entertaining the customers in a large theater-restaurant.

Seen from the surface, the *entente cordial* between an alleged Eastern gangster like Siegel and the strait-laced Mormons of southern Nevada was an incongruous alliance. But the underlying realities were like those in other states where a bootlegger-Baptist alliance keeps a county dry. For one thing, the Mormon population of southern Nevada had already been severely diluted with Gentiles. The mines at Searchlight had largely failed, and many of the residents there had moved to Las Vegas. So, too, had hundreds of railroad men and the business people catering to them. Some of the men who came to build Hoover Dam (or Boulder Dam as it was first known) stayed when the project was completed, as did many of the war workers who came later. Nevertheless, the Mormons represented the largest cohesive political force in Clark County.

Fortunately for Siegel and his colleagues, the Mormon faith is long on material achievement and short on broad social involvements outside the church membership. After Joseph Smith, the Mormons have brought forth no theologians or religious philosophers of impact, but they can point to scores of extremely successful businessmen. Confronted with Siegel, the Mormons in Clark County in 1945 adopted approximately the same attitudes their grandfathers had toward the miners at Hiko and Pioche. They saw the advantages in the presence of a large capital investment and a continuing payroll and need for supplies. If Siegel had an unsavory reputation, well, that was back east. Out here he wasn't proposing to do anything illegal at all. So why shouldn't he have his chance like anyone else. If he succeeded, everyone in the county would get some of the benefit. And if he didn't, that was no skin off their noses.

Siegel himself showed a certain perspicacity in arriving at a good working relationship with the Mormon community by hiring a public relations man who had good connections in Las Vegas, and having him quietly change his given name to Brigham. So the story goes.

Almost as soon as the Flamingo opened, Las Vegas joined the long list of Nevada boomtowns and set out rapidly on its way to becoming a major Western city. Unlike its hundreds of predecessors, Las Vegas was not built on a ledge of silver or an outcrop of gold. Its foundations rest on the deeper and more yielding soil of human nature, but the immense casino-hotels that began to line the Los Angeles highway to become "The Strip" took on the same unmistakable air of authority as the hulking mines and mills that dominated Gold Canyon on the Comstock Lode.

The Flamingo closed briefly when Siegel was murdered in Los Angeles, but the Thunderbird opened in 1948, and Wilbur Clark soon built his famous Desert Inn. To celebrate his opening, Clark went Siegel one better by headlining three major acts: Edgar Bergen, Vivian Blaine, and the Ray Noble Orchestra. The other hotel-keepers glumly watched the action from their own sparsely attended gaming rooms and reluctantly joined the bidding for top stars. Casino costs went up, but the association between Las Vegas gamblers and the aristocracy of international show business very quickly proved very rewarding.

For one thing, the gamblers found themselves with a commodity they could advertise beyond the state line. So energetic was promotion, and so eager the players who came to Las Vegas from all over the world, that the old-line gamblers could settle back in the counting rooms, turn the management of their table games and slot machines over to the accountants, and let the odds grind out their fortunes.

Nevertheless, risk had not been eliminated from gambling with the transition from a small shopkeeper's business to a volume industry. It had only been moved from the casino to the showroom. Because the principal casino-resort-hotels were furnished and appointed with equal opulence, the public displayed an annoying tendency to follow the most popular entertainers. A headliner of limited appeal became a real liability. The gamblers met this difficulty by raising the ante. When Jack Entratter at the Sands plunked down $20,000 a week to pay Tallulah Bankhead's salary (nearly thirty years ago, remember), Wilbur Clark reached deep into the Desert Inn's safe to drag out $100,000 for four weeks of Betty Hutton. This approach was successful in bringing the sure crowd-pleasers to the showrooms.

Unfortunately for the gamblers, it also created an inflationary spiral in entertainment costs, and in their uneasiness they began experimenting with alternatives to the high-priced stars. In the fall of 1955 the Royal Nevadan announced the signing of Sam Levine, Vivian Blaine, Stubby Kaye, and B. S. Pully to star in the first full-fledged Broadway musical ever to be staged for a nightclub audience: *Guys & Dolls*. It was a tremendous success in every way except as a means of saving the financially troubled Royal Nevadan, which soon collapsed into bankruptcy. Casino managers who had been intrigued with the idea of Broadway shows went hurriedly back into booking negotiations with the big stars.

It was two years before another Broadway show was attempted, but the unqualified success of *Pajama Game* at the Riviera prompted the long and profitable series of Broadway productions on Las Vegas stages which still continues. Such shows as *Flower Drum Song, Gypsy, Irma La Douce, Tenderloin, Sweet Charity, Fiddler On The Roof, Mame*, three different productions of *Hello, Dolly,* and many other top Broadway successes have played in the big showrooms of Las Vegas hotels.

In 1958 the Stardust tried yet another tack. Abandoning its big-name policy, it instead staged an extravaganza review made up of orderly Parisian naughtiness (in the shape of topless-costumed showgirls), train wrecks, chariot races, blizzards, and even an erupting volcano, a combination of apparently inexhaustible appeal which — many years and many editions later — is still playing to eager audiences as the *Lido de Paris*. In 1960 the Tropicana acquired the exclusive American franchise for the *Folies Bergeire*, and four years later the Dunes opened *Casino de Paris* on a stage — a complex machine, really — which requires highly trained specialists to operate and cost a quarter million dollars to construct.

Hotels continued to proliferate along the Strip, and Las Vegas continued to prosper and grow. Las Vegas's growth was not a smooth progression, however, but a series of bucks and bursts. The population doubled between 1950 and 1960, and doubled again between 1960 and 1964; and now more than half the population of the state resides in Clark County.

Only about a quarter of the city's population is employed directly in tourist-connected jobs, but there is no question in anyone's mind that the other three-quarters would be out of work in a minute if the tourist industry foundered and the fifteen million visitors a year stopped coming.

That had always been a worry when men like "Icepick" Willie Alderman, Ruby Kolod, Benny Goffstein, and others with unsavory pasts were running Las Vegas casinos. As legal as their Nevada operatons were, their past associations made everyone a little uneasy. In 1958 the state created a stringent apparatus of control over the gambling industry, aimed at policing it carefully. Incidents of cheating have been very few, for with close scrutiny it simply made no sense for a man with a multimillion dollar property to jeopardize it for a few extra dollars. The majority of cheating incidents exposed have been the result of private enterprise on the part of dealers, and they have been cheating the house as often as the customers.

The state's gaming control machinery did not eliminate the potential for scandal altogether, however. Federal investigators were pressing their probe of casino counting-room operations to determine whether or not cash was being skimmed off the top of the day's winnings and slipped out of the casino without being entered on the books. So spirited was the federal effort to obtain information that the executives of one major casino were reduced to holding conferences while walking in circles around the big splashing fountain in the parking lot so that their conversations could not be overheard with listening devices. A worry began to grow that with firm evidence of skimming, the federal government might take action which would severely damage or even destroy Nevada's principal industry.

That worry began to be dispelled by the arrival of Howard Hughes in early 1967. When he took up residence on the ninth floor of the Desert Inn for an extended stay, and dealt out the cash to buy seven Strip casino-hotels, everyone in Las Vegas breathed a sigh of relief. The departure of so many of the subjects of federal investigation eased the threat of government intervention into Nevada gambling. More than that, Hughes' own reputation for shrewdness and square dealing at once gave Las Vegas gambling a new air of respectability. As a result of his investment, several other Strip properties have been purchased by corporations which had previously held themselves aloof from the gambling business.

As Las Vegas has so rapidly and fantastically grown, the rest of Nevada's Mormon country has continued relatively unaffected. After sputtering along for years, mining finally petered out altogether in Pioche in 1957. A recent revival of the Number One Mine was short-lived. Searchlight has no working mines, drawing its threadbare prosperity instead from the weekend and vacation visitors who frequent nearby Lake Mohave.

Yet the effect of Las Vegas's booming presence is undeniable, even in the farthest reaches of the region. There are, for example, four state parks in sparsely-populated Lincoln County, more than in any other county in the state. They are there to serve the expanding Las Vegas population in its affluence and its hunger for recreation at a slower pace, outside the walls of the air-conditioned casinos where so many of them spend their working days and nights.

CITIES AND TOWNS

Las Vegas

Aside from being the "Entertainment Capital of the World," Las Vegas is also the largest city in Nevada and the principal shipping and marketing area for the southern part of the state and for adjacent desert areas of Arizona and California. Las Vegas is like Egypt in that its history is a series of clearly defined epochs, and just now the city is in transition from the waning epoch of individual entrepreneurs to that of corporation gambling. This change is having a profound effect on Las Vegas, as much for vacationers, tourists, and weekend visitors as for the "locals."

While the corporate casino owners have brought a new and desirable respectability to Las Vegas's chief industry, it has also resulted in a fading of personality in casino operation. Decisions which were once made by a single (and usually highly individualistic) boss and carried out by men directly loyal to him, are now made by boards of directors and their committees and put into practice by corporation employees. Corporation boards of directors have different ideas about how to run a business than "Banana Nose" Kleinman ever did.

Some Las Vegans are calling these modern days The Age of the Cost Accountant, because the casino-hotels are now operating on a policy which requires every part of the operation to show a profit: restaurants, showrooms, and hotel, as well as the gambling floor. This attitude has brought prices up, most noticeably in the showrooms where menu prices averaged from $6 to $10 not long ago and have now reached $15. From the visitor this takes away the delicious illusion of getting something for nothing (or almost nothing), which was always a big part of the Las Vegas lure. So conscious are the local citizens of this change in affairs that there is a certain nostalgia brewing for the bad old days. "Gee," one prominent Las Vegas attorney mused over lunch recently, "I wonder what it would take to get the mob back."

Despite the departure of some of Las Vegas's most extravagant and colorful management personalities, the new owners are far from being fools or prudes, and Las Vegas is still the sensational indoor playground it always was. If the precocious doll-baby of a few years ago has put on a little weight, she's still a lot of fun.

The Las Vegas Strip. No brief description in a book like this can do it justice. A few historical notes, however, may be of interest as you scan the neon horizons.

The Tropicana Hotel was built in 1957 and operated for years by a former mining engineer who turned gambler back in the twenties when he lost his job and his last paycheck simultaneously. The home of the *Folies Bergeire* since 1963.

The *Casino de Paris* has been the feature attraction at The Dunes since 1964 and will undoubtedly continue until every American tourist has seen his fill of ostrich plumes and bare breasts.

The Aladdin was originally built as a no-gambling hotel. It went into financial collapse almost as soon as it opened.

The Flamingo is still essentially the hotel that "Bugsy" Siegel built although it has been enlarged and remodeled several times since the old days. There should be a State Historical Marker out front, but there isn't.

Caesar's Palace has been a success since the day it opened. It is the epitome of The Strip: vulgar, vigorous, gaudy, and self-confident. Historically inclined gentlemen will appreciate the mini-toga costumes. The Bacchanal, the hotel's gourmet restaurant, is complete with bubbling pool and wine-bearing "slave" girls. After dessert: a neck and shoulder massage. Unforgettable.

Beside the pool at The Castaways is an elaborately carved wooden temple brought from some Asian jungle to contribute to the motif.

The Desert Inn is where Howard Hughes' historic casino-buying spree began. After slipping into town and checking into

Las Vegas Strip

his suite at the D.I. via the back stairs — or so the story goes — Hughes was asked to leave after he had stayed at the hotel for a while. Some high rollers were coming in from the East and owner Moe Dalitz needed the rooms. Miffed, Hughes bought the hotel. The Monte Carlo Room is the gourmet restaurant. Among the delicacies on its menu is Nevada quail. But not the kind you see in the chorus line.

The Stardust is a labyrinthine monster resulting from a series of compromises that began when its first owner — a former operator of gambling ships off the coast of California — dropped dead at a Desert Inn crap table during construction. This is where Paris first came to Las Vegas in the form of the *Lido de Paris*, which continues to be one of the most popular entertainment attractions in town.

History in Las Vegas is measured in months, but most of the enormous hotels on the "second strip" haven't been around long enough yet to cast a shadow. The Strip is glamorous and exciting, electric with excitement, wallpapered with money. Millions of dollars change hands every day and there is nothing like it in all the world.

Downtown Las Vegas is different. Here there is no concern with architecture, and no restraint on the pace of the action. It is like payday night in a joy factory, a constant whirring, clacking, holler of a place ("Howwwdy, Pardner!") where people bounce in and out of the clubs in the three blocks of Fremont Street like ball bearings in a pinball game. There has developed a tradition along this Glitter Gulch that any sign that can't be read with the naked eye from the surface of the moon is too small. At last count there were forty-three miles of neon tubing in the signs along these three blocks, and about two million light bulbs. Not bad for a town that didn't have two statistics to rub together thirty years ago.

In addition to the more ballyhooed hotels, there are more than three hundred motels in Las Vegas, all of them air-conditioned, most of them with swimming pools, and ranging in appointments from comfortable to elegant.

In fact, it is quite possible to spend an entire vacation in Las Vegas without once setting foot in any of the glamorous hotels and casinos at all. I'm not seriously suggesting it, and I can't imagine anyone wanting to, but theoretically it's possible. There are lakes, the Colorado River, state parks, ghost (and almost-ghost) towns, winter sports, water sports, and near-virgin wilderness, all of it easily accessible in the family car.

Desert north of Las Vegas

Henderson

13 miles southeast of Las Vegas via U.S. 93/95. A product of
World War II years when its magnesium plants worked at full
throttle to equip the war machine, Henderson rapidly became
one of Nevada's largest cities. The urgency with which it was
built, the heavily transient nature of its residents, and the domi-
nance of the heavy industry which gave it a reason for being
have given the town a number of advantages, but charm and
attractiveness are not among them. There are a pair of small
casinos in town similar to the gambling houses in downtown Las
Vegas. They rely for their prosperity primarily on local customers and the Las Vegas—Hoover Dam tour buses making lunch-
eon stops at Henderson. The community offers full services to
travelers. There is a municipal swimming pool and an excellent
golf course, the Black Canyon Country Club. Both are open to
the traveling public.

Boulder City

24 miles southeast of Las Vegas via U.S. 93/95. Boulder City was built in the 1930s by the government to house the workers who built Hoover Dam. It was the first planned community built in the U.S. and after almost forty years still stands in such pronounced contrast to the higgledy-piggledy aspect of most Nevada towns that it seems an exotic flower indeed to have grown from the gritty desert soil. For many years Boulder City was operated as a government reservation; homes could not be purchased, only leased; gambling was prohibited and no liquor licenses were issued. It is now possible to own property there, and to buy beer at the grocery store, but there is still no casino: Residents are content to make the twenty-minute drive to Las Vegas when overtaken with the urge to throw away the car payment. The highway is routed down Boulder City's main street, just as it always was, and things have moved at a generally slower pace than they have in Las Vegas and Henderson. It is an attractive town, offering all services to travelers, but with no particular attraction beyond the pleasant appearance of the community and its proximity to Hoover Dam (seven miles to the east) and the Lake Mead Recreation Area.

Searchlight

55 miles south of Las Vegas via U.S. 95. A mining town that grew up around a rich gold strike made in 1879, Searchlight succeeded Pioche as principal city in southern Nevada. In 1907, when Las Vegas was still a town of tents and shanties sprinkled along the railroad tracks, Searchlight's population was nudging five thousand. There were only a few less than fifty mines in production, several mills, two newspapers, a complete, if undistinguished, business district, a telephone exchange, a Chamber of Commerce, and a through rail connection with the Santa Fe at Needles. By 1910, though, Searchlight had grown dim with the simultaneous catastrophes of the Panic of 1907 and the depletion of high-grade ore. Mining continued, but at a much reduced pace. The townspeople who remained derived their livelihoods

as much from the highway traffic and the surrounding ranches as from the mines. The recent development of the Lake Mead Recreation Area resort at Cottonwood Cove, fourteen miles east, has improved the economic climate of the town, but in appearance Searchlight varies downward from unprepossessing. Some traces of its former high station remain, as do a number of mine ruins. All services are available, including a few gambling games in two tiny casinos.

Overton

63 miles northeast of Las Vegas via Interstate 15 and Nevada Route 12. One of the early Mormon settlements in the Muddy (now Moapa) Valley, and the site of the first store in the region, Overton received a heavy influx of population when the residents of St. Thomas were forced to relocate by the rising waters of Lake Mead. The farms in the vicinity are noted for the quality of their vegetables, melons, and fruit. So superior is this produce, in fact, that during the 1920s a local farmer sold vegetables by mail from Overton: four heads of lettuce, four bunches of radishes, four bunches of green onions, two bunches of spinach or beet greens, two bunches of asparagus, two bunches of carrots, one bunch of garden cress or parsley, and, as a graceful touch, a rose or a small bouquet of sweet peas. Price, post-paid as far as Salt Lake City or Los Angeles: one dollar.

Overton offers a small shopping center, a branch of the Bank of Las Vegas, and the Lost City Museum. The museum is devoted to displaying the relics salvaged from the Pueblo Grande de Nevada, another victim to the rise of progress (and the waters of Lake Mead). Ruins of a village with buildings of as many as twenty-one rooms had been noted as early as 1827 by Jed Smith. Archeologists have determined it to be one of the westernmost outposts of Anasazi culture, built perhaps as long as two thousand years ago by a people of sophisticated skills who manufactured pottery, wove textiles, mined salt, and farmed. The museum, built in the 1930s by the Civilian Conservation Corps, is the only one of its kind in the state.

Logandale

6 miles north of Overton via Nevada Route 12. Of little interest to travelers except, perhaps, for the thoroughbred stables located here. Logandale horses are big money winners on California tracks.

Glendale

At the intersection of Interstate 15 with Nevada Route 12. A junction settlement of the usual kind, notable only for the fact that it marks the intersection of the Old Spanish Trail from Santa Fe to Southern California with the old stagecoach road from Pioche to Prescott, Arizona.

Mesquite

80 miles east of Las Vegas via Interstate 15; 2 miles west of the Arizona border on the north bank of the Virgin River. A Mormon community which prospers better from the flow of traffic along the interstate highway than it ever did from the flow of water through the Virgin. An undistinguished town, except for its air conditioning.

Bunkerville

5 miles southwest of Mesquite via paved road. An agricultural community originally settled by Mormon members of the United Order. All lands were jointly owned and developed by the early colonists, so that the difficult job of bringing irrigation water from the river to the arable bench lands beside it could be carried out with effective cooperation. A commune, in other words. The Bunker family has been prominent in southern Nevada affairs since its arrival.

Alamo

95 miles north of Las Vegas via U.S. 93. The social and business center of the rich Pahranagat Valley. In the early 1860s this valley was prime range for horsethieves who stole stock in Utah and Arizona and drove it here to rest up for the long trail across

the desert to California. One old-timer reported counting 350 different brands in the valley at one time. The discovery of gold, the establishment of mining towns, and the creation of Lincoln County brought civilization too close to the valley for the comfort of the bandits, but before these unexpected events changed its character, the valley was described by one of the original settlers as "the toughest place I ever saw."

So peculiar was its society, and so remote, that in 1862 Dan De Quille, an editor of Virginia City's *Territorial Enterprise*, chose it as the locale of one of his elaborate hoaxes. It was a peculiarity of the valley, he wrote with an air of earnest astonishment, that the stones lying about the valley floor were pulled to its center by some mysterious power which then reversed and sent them rolling ponderously back to their original places. He advanced a deadpan theory of magnetism to explain the unique phenomenon, and the piece was enthusiastically reprinted in other papers throughout the country.

Eventually the story — in translation and undoubtedly garbled from passing through so many presses along the way — reached Germany where scientists working with electromagnetics wrote requesting more details. When De Quille demurred, the Germans furiously demanded that he cease withholding scientific knowledge. P. T. Barnum's reaction to the story was more succinct, if no more perceptive. He offered $10,000 if the stones could be made to perform for his audiences.

A cafe, several service stations, a grocery, and an air of small-town friendliness have not yet been corrupted by the passage of too many tourists.

Caliente

25 miles south of Pioche via U.S. 93. A pleasantly unassuming community, small, quiet, and shaded by immense cottonwood trees that forest the residential streets. Caliente offers a peculiar sight in that the main street is divided by a broad railroad switching yard, so that business houses face one another through lines of boxcars waiting shipment to Salt Lake City or

the coast. This unexpected scene is presided over by an immense railroad station, large enough to serve, say, Los Angeles. Its presence in Caliente is enough to make the town memorable. And that is just as well, for there is little else to interest the traveler since the hot-springs-fed swimming pool began to leak and had to be emptied. The motel at the hot springs still pipes naturally heated water into the showers in all the rooms, but that isn't the same thing, somehow. Caliente offers all services without pretense to elegance.

Panaca

12 miles south of Pioche via U.S. 93 and Nevada Route 25. Another of the early Mormon communities and perhaps the classic example of the genre in Nevada. A historical marker on one of the principal thoroughfares in the town notes that its sleepy appearance has changed only imperceptibly since its establishment in the 1860s. As many business houses in Panaca are boarded up or in ruins as are open for business, and these cater principally to local needs. There is a service station and cafe intended for the convenience of travelers at the junction of U.S. 93 and Nevada 25 a mile west of town. So little has Panaca been affected by the passage of time that when the Panaca Centennial Book Committee published *A Century In Meadow Valley* in 1946, the biography of virtually every individual who ever resided in the vicinity, and details of virtually every event of note or interest in the history of the region was contained in fewer than three hundred pages. This interesting volume also effectively dismisses the notion that the Mormon pioneers were dour and humorless folk. One day, the authors inform us, a stranger stopped in front of a group of men sitting on the porch of the N. J. Wadsworth store. Impressed, perhaps, by the lavish display of greenery in the fields, he asked the group what the precipitation was in the area. One of the natives who was "unlearned but friendly" replied: "I think it's potatoes."

Another gathering of Panaca philosophers has been immortalized in the book for their discussion on the porch of the

Panaca Co-op regarding wagons. The question was, which kind of wagon would run the longest without grease. "Each man seemed to have his favorite brand of wagon, which he defended vehemently. Bert Price ended the argument by saying, 'The kind of wagon that will run the longest without grease is a borrowed one.' "

The sidewalks at Panaca roll up at dark, except when there is a Little League game, or a dance at the Mormon church.

Pioche

175 miles northeast of Las Vegas and 109 miles south of Ely via U.S. 93. Named for the San Francisco mining promoter who financed development of the ore body, Pioche was at once the richest, roughest, and most remote mining boomcamp of its day. It is still a source of considerable municipal pride that seventy-five (more or less, the figure varies with the source) men were buried in the cemetery before anyone in Pioche had the opportunity to die a natural death. The shootings and knifings were not only the products of quarrels between violent and reckless men, but also between private warring "armies" defending mining claims against encroachment. According to one reputable source, nearly 60 percent of the killings reported in Nevada during 1871–72 took place in and around Pioche.

A favorite example of the town's bloody character recalls the arrival, in 1871 (when the population had reached two thousand and Pioche had become the seat of one of the largest counties in the United States), of a young Illinois lawyer and his bride. As the pair collected their baggage, a flurry of shooting broke out, and before they could sprint into the hotel, three men sprawled dead, still twitching in the dirt street. The bride didn't even bother to unpack; she was headed back to mother within minutes of her arrival.

In 1871 the town was pulverized by the explosion of three hundred kegs of powder in a Main Street business house during an exuberant celebration of Mexican Independence. Beams, splinters, and debris mowed through the crowded street like grapeshot, killing thirteen and injuring forty-seven. The accompanying fire left virtually the entire population homeless.

By 1876, despite construction of a narrow-gauge railroad to the mills at Bullionville, low-grade ore and strangling litigation combined to force suspension of operations at all but the smallest mines. Until 1890 activity was minor. A brief flurry in that year subsided until 1907, when activity picked up again with the completion of a spur line from the Union Pacific at Caliente. Mining continued intermittently until 1958, when all production ceased.

Pioche today is an uncomfortable mixture of the old and the older. The continuing trickle of prosperity from the mines after 1907 permitted the remodeling of the old buildings along Main Street, but the result is that whatever Victorian charm the town might have had is lost under coats of stucco or a facing of tile.

But Pioche makes a rewarding stop aside from the gasoline, food, and lodging that represent the principal attractions for travelers. The old Lincoln County courthouse still stands, brooding, no doubt, over the facts of its remarkable history. Contracted for at $26,400 in 1871, the cost amounted to $88,000 by the time the two-story building was completed in 1872. Declining tax revenues and corrupt officials forced refinancing of the building several times, and every year interest accumulated. In the 1880s the unpaid balance, plus interest, amounted to $181,000. By 1907 the debt had reached $670,000. By the time the obligations were finally paid off, in 1937, the total had grown to nearly a million dollars. The building itself had been condemned since 1933. In 1958 it, together with the four lots it stands on, was sold at auction. For $150.

There is only one attraction in Pioche especially provided for travelers, the museum on the south side of Main Street. In the building it shares with the library, a varied collection of early materials has been gathered. Antiques (especially organs), photographs (including a series depicting an outdoor leg amputation, caption reading in part: "Note the leg propped up against the box — 2nd picture"), documents, and other memorabilia make an interesting stop, and the library itself is an excellent one for its size.

The old Thompson's Opera House, a two-story frame building, stands shuttered and boarded up on Main Street. Next door is the Gem movie house — the frosted glass marquee of which is in shards, and the doors padlocked. Pioche has had hard times. But in the fall of 1969 the old Number One Mine at the head of Main Street went back into production at the twelve-hundred-foot level. Thirty miners working two shifts a day were retimbering the old shaft and tunnels, and blasting toward an ore body estimated to contain ten thousand tons of $100 ore. It didn't pan out.

Pioche and Panaca represent the classic Nevada contrast: the rough, roistering mining city in the mountains above, and the slow, steady Mormon farming town in the valley below, communities as different in character as can be imagined, yet as closely dependent on one another as two boys in a three-legged race.

STATE PARKS AND RECREATION AREAS

Hoover Dam

31 miles southeast of Las Vegas via U.S. 93/95. When built, Hoover Dam was the largest dam ever created by man. The structure rises more than 725 feet from bedrock to plug Black Canyon. The section of two-lane highway along the crest of the dam which connects Nevada and Arizona is 1,244 feet long. The dam is 660 feet thick at its base, tapering to 45 feet at the top. Three and a quarter million cubic yards of concrete were required for construction. These and other facts are amplified and illuminated by the guides who lead thirty-minute tours through the dam, its hydroelectric power generating facilities, and the spillways and penstocks of the water distribution system. Tours begin at the Nevada side of the dam at 8 A.M. and accommodate twenty-eight visitors every four minutes until 5 P.M.; or until 8 P.M. during the peak visitor season beginning Memorial Day and ending Labor Day. There is a modest charge.

Hoover Dam

It is more comfortable to take the tour early in the day, especially during the summer months, since temperatures regularly climb to around 110 degrees during the afternoons, resulting in seats and steering wheels too hot to touch after a few minutes in the parking areas. The guides, too, are weary by late afternoon. It is not only the heat, but the fact that they have answered every conceivable question about the dam about eight million times already, and they are pretty sure you are going to ask one of them again. Early in the morning they are fresher. This is no criticism of the guides, by the way; they do a marvelous job.

A good bet here is to visit the free museum located on the Nevada side of the dam before taking the tour itself. There is a large model of the entire complex of dams along the length of the Colorado from its headwaters (and that of the Green River, its principal tributary) to Yuma and the Sea of Cortez. An illuminated lecture details the function of this complex network of waterways and generating facilities. Hoover Dam received its seventeen millionth visitor in January, 1976, and peak tourist load is nearly one hundred thousand a month in July and August. There is a snack bar and souvenir stand on the Nevada side, and a limited amount of shaded parking reserved for people with pets on the Arizona side. Other points of interest at the dam site are enumerated and explained in the tour.

Lake Mead

One hundred fifteen miles long at its farthest reach from Hoover Dam, Lake Mead is 589 feet deep at its deepest point, has a 550-mile shore line and a surface area of 229 square miles. The lake offers every variety of watersports, including exotic ones like drinking martinis on a floating saloon. The National Park Service manages the lake and has overseen the development of a large complex of concessions, campsites, picnic areas, and other recreation facilities.

Visitor Center. Located on U.S. 93/466 between Boulder City and Hoover Dam, National Park Service personnel offer maps, advice, and information about all recreation facilities on Lake Mead. Exhibits, narrated slide presentations, and a short movie provide the first-time visitor with a good introduction to the lake and its recreation opportunities.

Boulder Beach. 2 miles northwest of the Visitor Center, at the lake shore, Boulder Beach is almost urban in its concentration of services. There are campgrounds affording a vast number of individual campsites, rather densely developed but separated by a luxurious growth of oleander bushes for privacy. Tables and fire grates are provided at each campsite, with water and restrooms in abundance. A swimming beach is roped off and supervised during the hot summer months, and the water is pleasantly warm. There is a boat launching ramp and dock available for free use, picnic shelters, and a ranger station.

There is also a large marina where boats may be rented or chartered for cruising, by the hour or for overnight sightseeing, and fishing; waterskis and equipment are also available. Scheduled lake tours and excursions depart the marina daily; the *Seacraft* offers a two-hour tour of the lake, including Hoover Dam, and a cruise along the scenic shoreline. The *Echo* makes a daily run from Boulder Beach to Echo Bay and return. Passengers may arrange to take a combination boat and bus tour including one-way passage on the *Echo* and one-way bus tour of the Valley of Fire. Arrangements are easiest through the bell captain of your hotel in Las Vegas.

Boulder Beach also offers a small country grocery store, moderately-priced accommodations in a modern fifty-unit motel, a coffee shop, cocktail lounge, and dining room afloat on the marina.

Las Vegas Bay. 10 miles northwest of the Visitor Center; 9 miles northeast of Henderson via State Route 41. Facilities as at Boulder Beach, except no trailer court or overnight accommodations. A large number of campsites, a small grocery store and cafe, boat launching ramp, and marine supplies.

Callville Bay. 27 miles from the Visitor Center; 23 miles from Henderson via State Route 41. No developed campsites, but there is a boat launching ramp and marine supplies are available. The Mormon community of Callville, established in 1864 as a freighting center for Colorado River traffic, lies submerged in the warm waters of Lake Mead near here. Steamboats made the difficult and dangerous ascent of the rapids in Black Canyon by winching to ring bolts driven into the bedrock along the banks during the few months of the year when there was enough flow through the canyon to allow passage at all. Down-river terminus for the stern-wheelers *Esmeralda* and *Nina Tilden* was Yuma.

Echo Bay. 49 miles from the Visitor Center; about 46 miles northeast of Las Vegas, beyond Callville Bay. All boating and fishing needs are provided for, as well as a large number of campsites, a privately operated trailer park with complete hookup facilities, and a modern resort hotel with restaurant and

Lake Mead recreation area

bar. This is the terminus for the *Echo* excursions from the Lake Mead Marina near Boulder Beach.

Rogers Spring. 5 miles north of Echo Bay. A developed picnic site.

Overton Beach. 14 miles beyond Echo Bay; 9 miles south of Overton. No developed campsites, but a full range of boating and fishing services including a small store and overnight accommodations. The Mormon farming settlement of St. Thomas, once a thriving community of six hundred, lies offshore, another victim of the rising waters of Lake Mead. At stages of low water, a single chimney and a few rock walls can be seen poking up above the surface of the lake.

Temple Bar. This resort-and-boating center is the principal development on the Arizona side of Lake Mead. Temple Bar is accessible from U.S. 93 some 20 miles east of Hoover Dam by a well-marked, paved road to the north and east, a total of approximately 50 miles from the Visitor Center. This is the terminal point for many of the commercial companies running the rapids of the Colorado River through the Grand Canyon, and the facilities are as complete as any explorer could ask: all boating and fishing requirements, a lodge with overnight accommodations, a small store, trailer hookups — even a three-thousand-foot landing strip.

NOTE: Fishing licenses are available at each of the locations listed above except Rogers Spring.

Lake Mohave

Below Hoover Dam the Colorado River resumes its flow — the water released after funneling through the system of penstocks, tunnels, and tubes to spin the immense turbine generators. This new lease on life is only temporary, however. A few miles downriver the current slows and stops as the Colorado flows into Lake Mohave, a long, slender body of water bulging out over the old riverbed upriver from Davis Dam. Lake Mohave is a part of the Lake Mead Recreation Area and, like Mead, has been developed under the supervision of the National Park

Service. Immediately below Hoover Dam, where the water current is a factor, rainbow trout are large and willing, particularly in the five months beginning in October. In the warmer lake waters, farther downchannel, bass, channel catfish, and crappie are the principal game fish, especially active from March through May. Fishing remains good through the summer and peaks again in the autumn months. The following are the developed areas on the shores of Lake Mohave.

Willow Beach. 17 miles southeast of Hoover Dam via U.S. 93, then 5 miles west by a well-marked, paved road to the Arizona shore of the Colorado. All boating and fishing services and facilities; restaurant, motel, small grocery, trailer village with full hookup capacity, campground, picnic sites. The fish hatchery located here welcomes visitors and provides a fascinating tour.

El Dorado Canyon. 34 miles southeast of Boulder City, via U.S. 95 and Nevada Route 60, on the Nevada shore of Lake Mohave. All boating and fishing services, trailer hookups, a small store, and cafe. No developed campsites. This canyon was the scene of intensive mining operations beginning in 1857 when soldiers from Fort Mohave discovered placer gold. Rich silver deposits were uncovered in 1861, and lode mines were active despite the incredible isolation which required six months to freight supplies from the Pacific Coast.

Remote from even the rough camps at Hiko and Pioche, El Dorado Canyon was so lawless a place that not even a killing provided sufficient inducement for law officers to make the difficult journey there. Mining continued with erratic momentum until 1890, revived again in 1905, lurched on through the early decades of the century, and bottomed out for good in 1941 after producing a total of some $10 million, principally from the Techatticup Mine.

Legends of previous Indian and Spanish mining in the region are plentiful; the camp was a busy port of call for the stern-wheeled steamers on the Yuma-Callville run. The townsite and mills of El Dorado are submerged beneath Lake

Mohave, though mining ruins, including aging structures housing a population of about fifty, remain at Nelson.

Cottonwood Cove. 14 miles east of Searchlight, on the
Nevada shore of Lake Mohave. All boating and fishing services
and facilities, trailer hookups, cafe, grocery. Cabins and house-
keeping trailers for rent; campground.

Lake Mohave Resort. 32 miles west of Kingman, Arizona,
via Arizona Route 68; 35 miles southwest of Searchlight,
Nevada, via U.S. 95 and Nevada Route 77, on the Arizona shore
of Lake Mohave at Davis Dam. All boating and fishing services
and facilities. Trailer village, cabin and motel accommodations,
grocery, cafe.

Katherine Landing. Adjacent to Lake Mohave Resort. Boat
launching facilities, mooring slips, dock, and rentals.
Campground, swimming beach, and picnic area. There are additional campsites and a launch ramp on the Nevada shore as well.
The Arizona resort community of Bullhead City, four miles
downriver from Davis Dam, provides all services and facilities
for travelers.

Valley of Fire

12 miles south and west of Overton, Nevada, via Nevada
Routes 12 and 40; 50 miles northeast of Las Vegas via Interstate
15 and Nevada Route 40. Twenty-six thousand acres of brilliantly colored sandstone contorted into a maze of spectacular
spires, domes, beehives, and more fanciful forms, the valley
undergoes a subtle transformation with each moment that the
sun moves across the metallic blue sky above. Stare at any given
point for a minute and you will see no change. Glance away for a
sudden moment and back again, and the landscape has shifted:
it is a different shade of red; shadows have slithered like snakes
out from hidden crevices; shapes have been imperceptibly al-
tered by the changing angle of the sun's rays. It is as if the
landscape were in surreptitious molten movement. That, and
the unutterable silence, make this an unforgettable place.

Gregarious folk may find themselves uneasy here, and

chatterers might hear their gabble gulped up by the ancient redrock walls: this is no place for "touring" in the usual sense, despite the remarkable scenery. You might as well "see" the Grand Canyon from an airliner as try to take in the Valley of Fire from a moving car. Stop. Get out. Sit for a while, and don't talk. Look. Feel the heat, gaze through the shimmering air. Listen.

Men came into this valley more than two thousand years ago and have left plentiful evidence of their presence. They built no permanent villages, only rough rock shelters at temporary campsties. Anasazi ventured here from their village at Lost City; hunters and gatherers from Utah; Mogollon people. None of them stayed.

The only natural sources of water in the valley are the natural tanks scoured into the rock by the action of centuries of wind and water, in which water collects during infrequent rains. One of these, called Mouse's Tank, is now accessible by self-guided tour from the roadside. Mouse, a Paiute renegade whose principal occupation was murder and plunder at isolated home-

Red Rock Desert

sites in the region at the turn of the century, kept himself alive
between forays with the water collected in this stone bowl.
There are numerous petroglyphs in the valley and many of them
are marked for visitors.

The park is open throughout the year, and there is a
ranger-staffed visitor center where complete information is
available regarding all park facilities. Bring all supplies you'll
need with you, including drinking water. The developed
campsites, and most of the picnic areas, have water available,
but there is virtually no water elsewhere in the park. Automotive breakdown, while not likely to prove fatal with 350,000
people a year visiting the park, could provide some very uncomfortable hours without a little water to sip.

Development of the park has been aimed toward promoting
ecological and esthetic values. There is nothing to buy. No soda
pop, no sno-cones, nothing. Merely the opportunity to observe
the majestic unconcern of the centuries in the solitude of remarkable scenic surroundings.

Kershaw-Ryan
3 miles south of Caliente via U.S. 93 and well-marked, graded
road leading east. The recreation area has only a handful of
developed campsites, and because of crowding the park is
chained shut from 10 P.M. to 7 A.M. Located in 240 acres of cliff
and canyon country, liberally shaded and laced with hiking
trials, the park gets heavy day use from travelers and from
residents of nearby communities. It is an extremely attractive
place, especially for travelers arriving from the heat and scenic
desolation of areas to the south.

Beaver Dam
35 miles east of Caliente via graded and graveled dirt road. This
is probably the loveliest — and the most remote — of Nevada's
State Parks. It hasn't the profound impact of Valley of Fire, but
it is so irrepressibly cheerful a place that the long dusty drive is a
small price to pay for a visit. The 1,713-acre park is set high in

Beaver Dam recreation site

mountain pine forests. Hiking trails wind under the trees and
breezes brush between the branches above. Beaver Dam Reservoir is stocked with fish but no boating services or facilities
have been developed. There are picnic sites and developed
campsites in the park, though both picnicking and camping are
permitted anywhere a visitor finds a spot he likes. No visitor
center here, and no concessions.

Cathedral Gorge

16 miles north of Caliente via U.S. 93 and the park road; 5 miles
northwest of Panaca via U.S. 93. Like Valley of Fire, Cathedral
Gorge is more a place for the exercise of the imagination than
legs and lungs. It is simply a wash, a cut in the earth's skin. But
what separates it from countless other washes and gulches in
this country is the fact that its walls are made of a chalky-soft,
suede-colored bentonite clay which has weathered and eroded

Cathedral Gorge

into a fantasy-land of intricate shapes. Cathedrals, yes, and wedding cakes; fortresses and hunchbacked men; pillars and dragons; palaces and melting elephants; baroque architectural creations and structures yet undreamed of — lacy, filigreed, fluted, and feathered. There are shaded picnic areas located at strategic viewing points, developed campsites, and a few scenic walking trails. The park comprises 1,608 acres in all, but outside the gorge itself, the country is relatively unremarkable. No visitor center, no concessions; nothing but drinking water, restrooms, and magic.

OTHER DEVELOPED CAMPGROUNDS

The Las Vegas Ranger District of the Toiyabe National Forest comprises some sixty thousand acres of high mountain country in the Spring Mountain Range. Charleston Peak, the highest summit in the range, towers nearly twelve thousand feet above the level of the sea, and nearly ten thousand feet above the Las Vegas Valley below, and the Forest Service's recreation developments are centered on the eastern side of this mountain, which is Nevada's third highest.

The Mount Charleston recreation areas are something more than an hour's drive north and west from Las Vegas via U.S. 95 and either Nevada Route 39 (the Kyle Canyon road) or Nevada Route 52 (the Lee Canyon road). They are the only Forest Service recreation areas in Nevada's Mormon Country, but they represent a varied complex of outdoor opportunities. One of them is the drive itself, which passes through a variety of life zones. As they meander up from the desert floor toward the summits, the Lee Canyon and Kyle Canyon roads leave the scrub desert brush behind at about five thousand feet and enter the piñon-juniper woodlands which extend up the mountainsides to about 6,500 feet. There the lowest outposts of the ponderosa pine forest begin to appear and the ponderosa forest belt dominates the mountainside to an altitude of approximately eight thousand feet.

The forest canopy gives over to firs and aspens. Roads do not reach up much above eight thousand feet, but trails have been cleared higher into the summit country where subalpine firs and bristlecone pine cling precariously to the crags. No more compelling "oasis" in the harsh, dry desert of southern Nevada can be conceived.

Kyle Canyon Recreation Area. 25 miles northwest of Las Vegas via U.S. 95 and Nevada Route 39. Three campgrounds with family campsites, trailer hookups, and a large-group picnic site in ponderosa pine forested canyon. Extremely popular in the summer months because of the thirty-degree temperature differential between the forested recreation areas on Mount Charleston and the desert valley below. One and a quarter miles of trail leads up scenic Fletcher Canyon. The Kyle Canyon Ranger Station is located a few hundred yards west of the recreation area, and the Forest Service plans to construct a visitor center at the site.

Fletcher View Campground. 1 mile west of Kyle Canyon Campground via Nevada Route 39. Family campsites, trailer spaces.

Charleston Park. About 2 miles west of Fletcher View Campground. Site of a whipsaw mill constructed by Mormon settlers to supply their mission colonies with timber. Until fairly recently, the site of Charleston Lodge, and presently the forest-fire-fighting headquarters.

Cathedral Rock Picnic Ground. Less than one-half mile west, then one-half mile southeast of the fire station via Nevada Route 39 and paved access road. Large developed picnic site dominated by Cathedral Rock on the canyonside above. An easy three-quarter-mile hike over the cleared trail from the picnic ground leads to the top of the rock. The view it affords of Kyle Canyon is well worth the walk. A fifteen-mile skyline trail to Charleston Peak and the west face of Mummy Mountain terminates at the picnic ground, as does a one-half mile trail to the head of Little Fall.

Mary Jane Falls Campground. At the end of Nevada Route

39, less than 2 miles west of the fire station. Numerous campsites and trailer spaces. A one-half mile trail climbs to the head of the small falls.

Robber's Roost Caves. 3 miles north of the junction of Nevada Route 39 with Forest Road 22 via the latter. According to local legend, these limestone caverns were used as hideouts by Mexican bandits in the middle years of the nineteenth century between raids into southern Nevada, western Utah, and northern Arizona. A trail covers the quarter mile between the caves and Forest Road 22.

Hilltop Campground. Just over 1 mile north of Robber's Roost Caves via Forest Road 22. Family campsites, trailer spaces, and a hundred-mile view.

Mahogany Grove Group Picnic Area. One-half mile west of Hilltop Campground via Forest Road 22. Group picnic sites for use of which reservations must be made. No camping.

Deer Creek Picnic Area. Adjacent to Mahogany Grove. Family picnic sites; no reservation required. No camping. The Deer Creek Trail, which connects with the Charleston Peak Trail near the summit of Mummy Mountain, meets Forest Road 22 between the Hilltop Campground access road and the Deer Creek Picnic Area.

Desert View Point. About 2 miles north of Deer Creek Picnic area via Forest Road 22; just over a mile south of the junction of Forest Road 22 with Nevada Route 52. A short walk from the road provides stunning views of the desert sunrise; brilliant lighting effects at sunset as well, and even in the flat light of midday the landscape is impressive.

McWilliams Campground. 3 miles southwest of the junction of Forest Road 22 with Nevada Route 52, at the end of Nevada Route 52; 40 miles northwest of Las Vegas. Many family campsites, trailer spaces. At eight thousand feet, there are bristlecone pines within relatively easy walking distance from the campground. The bristlecone pine is among the oldest living things on earth, achieving ages of five thousand years and more. They are recognizable by their preference for rocky,

Mt. Charleston skiing

exposed locations, their weather-whipped, twisted trunks and limbs, and relatively short stature.

Lee Canyon Winter Sports Area. Immediately adjacent to McWilliams Campground at the end of Nevada Route 52. For years a relatively little-known local ski slope, the Lee Canyon area has blossomed in the last few years as it has dawned on out-of-town skiers that Las Vegas is as grand an après-ski environment as the world affords. Ever since this discovery, development has been steady.

Presently a three-thousand-foot double chairlift and a T-bar serve advanced, intermediate, and beginner's runs of from a thousand yards to a mile long. The day lodge offers hot food, coffee, and light meals. A pro shop sells and rents a full range of equipment, and private and group lessons are available. Snow-making equipment is on hand in case of clement weather. Frank Sennes, a long-time entertainment producer in Las Vegas, has developed his Mount Charleston Restaurant at the head of Lee Canyon. Essentially a dinner house in the usual urban sense, it is elevated to excellence by its high-mountain setting, and is open year around.

GHOST TOWNS

Goodsprings

37 miles southwest of Las Vegas via Interstate 15 and Nevada Route 53. Mining began here in 1868 with the discovery of silver-lead ore, but soon bottomed out. In the 1880s, lead mining was resumed, and in 1892 a gold strike was made, drawing a population of about two hundred. In 1906 the presence of valuable zinc deposits was discovered. From 1915 to 1918, the years of Goodsprings's highest productivity, approximately fifty mines were producing and supporting a population of some five hundred souls. Production ended in 1921, picked up again in 1922, and continued until the U.S. entered World War II. More than $31 million came out of the ground at Goodsprings in various forms, accounting for about 40 percent of all Clark

County mineral production. As in many western mining towns closed early in the war, a small population of hopefuls remains at Goodsprings, as do a handful of homes and a large number of mining structures.

Sandy

14 miles south of Goodsprings via graded road over Columbia Pass. Growing up around a mill erected in 1893, Sandy never achieved much in the way of size or importance, and was dead by 1910. Attempts to resurrect it have been fruitless. A few buildings, a cemetery, and the ruins of a mill remain to mark the place. Off to the southeast, within sight of the old Sandy townsite, a settlement called Platina survived for a few years after the discovery of platinum, but no trace of it remains today except a few shallow depressions in the desert sand. The mill two miles to the south was built in the 1930s.

Nelson

41 miles southeast of Las Vegas via U.S. 95 and Nevada Route 60. Established in 1905 seven miles to the west of the old settlement at the mouth of Eldorado Canyon, near the Techatticup mine, Nelson maintained production almost continuously until 1941. The fifty-ton smelter standing in ruins below town blew up in 1909. There is a combination bar and cafe at Nelson, and trailer hookups, but the principal attraction (admitting that the "ghostliness" of the place is less than classic) is in the concessions seven miles to the east on Lake Mohave (see prior listing for Eldorado Canyon in Lake Mead Recreation Area), and in the spectacular descent into town through a narrow squeeze of tipped and tumbled rock after the long climb over the gentle slope from U.S. 95. All reds and blacks toward sundown, it suggests the entrance to hell. Magnificent.

Crystal Spring

On the south side of Nevada Route 25 at its intersection with Nevada Route 38, some 100 miles north of Las Vegas. Originally the site of a Paiute village, Crystal Spring was settled in 1865 in consequence of the silver discoveries nearby, though it had been used for as long as a decade previously as a resting place for travelers bound for southern California. Designated as the seat of the newly proposed Lincoln County in 1866, Crystal Spring never had a population of more than a few dozen, and most of those were transient. Hiko got the county seat in 1867, and now nothing remains at Crystal Spring but the spring itself and a few cottonwoods.

Hiko

5 miles north of Crystal Spring via Nevada Route 38. Lincoln County seat from 1867 until 1871, Hiko's municipal history is without further distinction. The few remaining stone buildings are now being used by a Pahranagat Valley rancher. A post office remains open on a part-time schedule, and the old cemetery is preserved. Ask the postmistress for directions to Logan City if you have a vehicle rugged enough for the twelve-mile trip over rough country roads.

Delamar

47 miles southwest of Pioche via U.S. 93 and marked, graded dirt road leading south away from the highway. Discovered in 1890, the gold deposits at Delamar prompted the establishment of Golden City, adjacent to the Monkey Wrench Mine, and Helen, near the Magnolia. Both communities gave way to Delamar when ownership of several of the most productive mines was centralized. By 1897 Delamar was the principal gold mining center in Nevada, supporting a thriving business district of stores, saloons, theaters, and professional offices. As many as 120 mule-drawn freight wagons were ceaselessly employed in importing supplies from the railroad at Milford, Utah.

The Delamar cemetery is large. Miners were glad to get the three-dollar-a-day jobs there during the generally slack times elsewhere in the state despite the terrible reputation Delamar had for silicosis. Improper ventilation permitted silica dust to waft continuously through the mines and mills with fatal results for many of the workmen. Three months was enough to kill a man in Delamar, and the town became notorious as a widow-maker. The gravy days were over in 1909, though small-scale activity continued for many years after. The rock ruins, crowded as they are into the shallow canyon above the mine dumps, make a fascinating picnic site.

OTHER POINTS OF INTEREST

Bonnie Springs Ranch
About 30 miles west of Las Vegas toward Blue Diamond, via Charleston Boulevard. A dude ranch catering to day visitors and overnight guests with a bar, cafe, stables, and a pleasantly hokey rustic atmosphere. You'll get an idea of what to expect when you see the confiscated neckties hanging from the rafters in the saloon. Kids like it.

Williams & Sons Ranch
30 miles north and east of Pioche via U.S. 93 and marked and graded ranch road. Once a bankrupt cattle ranch, this thousand-acre property is now being successfully operated as a guest ranch, with stables, hunting guides, fishing ponds, restaurant, bar, trailer hookups, and motel accommodations available. A landing strip a mile and a quarter long accommodates relatively large aircraft. Travelers can stop for a meal or stay for a month, but in either case you may want to phone ahead, since the steaks are in the freezer and will take a while to thaw. On the other hand, if you are in too much of a hurry to stroll down by the barns and animal pens while the meat thaws, you probably won't enjoy stopping here anyhow.

A family operation, the ranch attracts youngsters from Las Vegas and the Pacific Coast who spend part of their summers here in supervised activities (such as horseback riding and trout fishing). Thus the sheep, goats, hog, quail, pheasants, and buggy pony. One of the most distinctively good places in Lincoln County.

Tule Springs

12 miles northwest of Las Vegas via U.S. 95 and marked road leading northeast away from the highways. Originally — aboriginally is a better word — the small spring-fed lake attracted settlement by prehistoric peoples, and the site was a favorite with Indians down to historic times. A horse-changing station was located here during the days when freight and passengers moved by wagon between the railroad at Las Vegas and the mining camps to the north. Now developed as a park, there are tennis courts, canoe rentals, a swimming beach, and picnic facilities in addition to a small children's zoo.

Gypsum Cave

12 miles northeast of Las Vegas. Exploited by early settlers for its gypsum deposits, the cave was later found to contain evidence of early man: stone javelin points, charcoal fragments, and painted dart shafts. The cavern extends back some three hundred feet, sloping down from the seventy-foot-wide, fifteen-foot-high entrance through six chambers.

BIG GAME HUNTING

DEER. Nevada's deer population is scattered throughout the state, with the heaviest concentrations in the northern regions. Only the Rock Mountain mule deer is found here, one of the largest of deer species. Dressed weights of mature bucks average something less than 150 pounds, though there are many taken exceeding 200 pounds and a few authenticated reports of bucks dressing out at over 300 pounds. Does, when dressed, average less than 100 pounds.

Most Nevada deer migrate between summer and winter range, either by simply roaming upward in summer and valleyward in winter, or by trekking considerable distances, in some cases as far as one hundred miles. They feed principally on bitterbrush, mountain mahogany, sagebrush, and similar plants.

The deer season in Nevada commonly begins in October, by which time fawns have been weaned, and continues into the breeding season, usually ending in mid-November. Bucks develop antlers during their second autumn (fawns are born in late May and early June), either spikes or forked horns. In their third autumn a sizeable percentage of young bucks will have grown four-point racks, and thereafter all but a few mature bucks will have at least four-point racks. The deer lose their antlers in winter and begin growing a new rack within a few days afterward. The new antlers mature by late August, and by early September most bucks will have rubbed the velvet covering away and polished the new rack.

Hunting licenses and deer tags are available to all Nevada residents, and to nonresidents on a quota basis (presently about four thousand tags are provided annually to nonresident hunters). These quotas are normally established in May, and vary by region. Thus some parts of the state may be closed to nonresident hunters. Complete and specific information regarding seasons, licenses, tag applications, and other matters should be sought from the Nevada Department of Fish and Game in June. The address is given at the end of this section.

ANTELOPE. Nevada's pronghorn antelope population is limited to several hundred animals, most of them located in northern Washoe and western Humboldt counties, with occasional small bands reported in other counties. Even with the establishment of a large tract of land in northern Washoe County as a refuge and study area devoted to the pronghorns, Nevada's herds have not significantly increased since study began. Consequently, antelope licenses are reserved for Nevada residents only, and then issued in limited numbers after a lottery drawing is held. The season is usually scheduled in August and then limited to trophy bucks, defined as having horns longer than their ears. In an effort to stimulate the growth of antelope herds, transplants of population have been attempted, but without significant results. Nevada's pronghorn habitat locales appear sharply limited.

DESERT BIGHORN SHEEP. As recently as a hundred years ago, mountain sheep were commonly seen across much of Nevada. Since settlement by the whites, however, numbers have declined to between 2,000 and 2,500 Nelson's desert bighorn, most of them in the 2.25-million-acre Desert Game Refuge in Clark County with a few small bands remaining in the wild southern mountains outside the refuge.

Rams average about 170 pounds and stand about three feet tall at the shoulder. Horns are not shed, but continue to grow, achieving in maturity a spectacular curl that may exceed 360 degrees. Ewes also are horned, but with slender prongs extending eight or ten inches above the skull.

Annual trophy hunts are scheduled, usually in November or December, with resident and nonresident hunters alike eligible for the limited number of tags (about one hundred)

Desert Bighorn sheep

issued, though nonresident tags seldom number more than seven, and nonresident applicants seldom number less than five hundred.

ELK. Only about three hundred elk exist in Nevada, all of them descendants of twenty-eight animals imported from Yellowstone National Park in 1932. One group inhabits the Schell Creek Range in White Pine County, the other the Spring Mountain Range in Clark County. Largest of the true deer family indigenous to North America, Schell Creek bulls average about seven hundred pounds, cows substantially less.

Elk hunts are held annually, usually in association with the deer season, but tags are severely limited and available only to Nevadans. A drawing is held to distribute the small number issued.

MOUNTAIN LION. The largest member of the cat family found in the United States, the mountain lions taken in Nevada average about 140 pounds in weight and from six to eight feet from nose to the tip of the tail. They are considered game animals in Nevada rather than predators, and a current license and tag are required to take one, though no specific season is set aside.

The Nevada Department of Fish and Game may be contacted by writing P.O. Box 10678, Reno, Nevada 89510. The headquarters office is located at 1100 Valley Road, Reno, and regional offices are staffed in Elko, Fallon, and Las Vegas.

According to the department, many big game hunters in Nevada each year ruin what might otherwise have been a fine trip by violating one or more of the state's hunting regulations. Most of these infractions, they tell me, are committed by "tennis shoe and bologna sandwich" hunters, and the most common of them is failure to puncture the tag after an animal has been taken. Minimum fine is $50 for that one, and the department fields more than a hundred wardens throughout the state during the season to ensure that the rules are being met. They've encountered every dodge in the book, and some that aren't in the book at all. Such as the hunter who shot an illegal antelope and then tried to make it "legal" by paring its ears with his hunting knife until they were shorter than the horns. Or the hunter who tried to make a forked-horn out of a spike with a file. Or the hunter who tied his doe tag to a goat.

All hunters are urged to inquire locally before setting out to hunt. More and more of the vast expanse of Nevada's public domain has access controlled by private property owners. Increasingly, these ranchers and farmers are limiting access by closing their roads; some refuse access altogether, others charge a fee for permission. A trespassing charge will stick, so it is good manners as well as good sense to check first.

MAPS

For traveling paved highways in Nevada, any up-to-date oil company map (if you can still find one) or the map produced by the Nevada Highway Department is entirely satisfactory. Some are more useful and informative than others, but all of them are generally accurate enough for highway travel purposes.

This is not the case where dirt road driving is concerned. Here these maps are almost entirely useless. Worse than useless, in fact, since they are likely to be misleading, and anyone driving unfamiliar desert roads with misleading maps can soon be in serious trouble in any season.

Equally valueless are the Bureau of Land Management maps devoted to Nevada. They are accurate as far as they go, but they leave out too much. A traveler may find himself far from a paved highway, jouncing along toward a turnoff shown on the map, only to find when he reaches it that two roads turn off where the map shows only one. The decision about which road to take, made perhaps with a quarter of a tank of gas remaining and storm clouds scudding darkly overhead, is likely to be harrowing. A wrong choice may be disastrous.

Forest Service maps are generally good, but limited in Nevada where Forest Service lands correspond with the mountain ranges separating the broad desert valleys: too many gaps to be consistently useful, but usually satisfactory for a given area. They may be obtained from the appropriate headquarters office.

There is a series of good Nevada county maps (@ $1) at a scale of about three and a half miles to the inch, which are readily available through sporting goods stores and newsstands throughout Nevada. In the event you cannot conveniently get a better map for your purposes, these (published by Harry Freese) will serve.

The best are the U.S. Geological Survey maps; they are at once well-designed, informative, and comprehensive. Get them from any U.S.G.S. office or through sporting goods and stationery stores.

The Nevada Bureau of Mines and Geology sells U.S.G.S. maps in addition to many others designed to meet the needs of rockhounds, geologists, and amateur climatologists. They can be obtained in person or by mail from the Publications Office in Room 310, Scrugham Engineering Building, on the Reno campus of the state university.

The Nevada Highway Department also makes available a series of maps encompassing the entire state, in scales of either one inch to two miles or one inch to four miles. For information, write the Nevada Highway Department, Carson City, NV 89710.

One piece of advice which will make driving the back roads a little safer even with an inadequate map: use your odometer. It is good for more than alerting you to change the oil. By keeping close track of distances traveled over unmarked roads, you will be far more likely to recognize landmarks and discriminate between turnoffs. If the map is truly a bad one, it may not help you much, but if you're out in the desert with a bad map, you'll need all the help you can get.

ROCKHOUNDING IN NEVADA

Because so much of Nevada's history and character is tied closely to its mineral wealth, and because minerals and gems occur in profusion in every part of the state, an attempt to guide rockhounds to the sources of agate, geodes, jasper, petrified wood, garnet, and other treasure would require a book of enormous size, and even then it could hardly be complete. And anyhow, there's a better way

Most Nevada communities — even tiny hamlets — are likely to have at least one rock shop. And the people who run these shops do it as much for the pleasure they get from it as for the money. As a rule, the shops are stocked with rocks and stones from a variety of sources, some of them exotic, others no farther away than the next range of hills. And if you are a serious devotee, you will have absolutely no difficulty learning where it is permissible to hunt for rocks and where rockhounding is either illegal or unwelcome. And if you are merely a dabbler at it, you probably won't much care whether the pretty stone you discover within a few feet of the highway is this kind or that — and attractively marked stones occur everywhere you look in the state.

Moreover, these little stores will usually have samples on hand of a more dramatic and spectacular nature than can be found in a casual prowl through a canyon; and like the fisherman who stops off at the fish store on his way home, you may want to stop in at the rock shop after a day's exploring in the hills to pick up a better chunk of turquoise or beryl or brucite than you were able to uncover for yourself.

In larger communities there are active rockhounding clubs with enthusiastic memberships ready to help visitors. They can be located by a telephone call to the local chamber of commerce.

The dedicated rockhound who wants a generalized map showing the most interesting localities for amateur rock and mineral collectors should see the section on maps in this book.

Rockhounds must observe etiquette regarding trespassing and littering, and observe the commonplaces of caution in an unfamiliar desert environment. In addition, they should be aware that there is a law on the books forbidding "destruction or removal of . . . natural specimens." No one is likely to nail you for gathering a few mineral samples in unposted areas — unless you get greedy.

PHOTO CREDITS

The photographs in this volume were provided by the following:

The Greater Reno Chamber of Commerce, Reno News Bureau, pages 91, 144; Adrian Atwater, pages 43, 53, 72, 73, 103, 151, 154, 193, 252; Las Vegas News Bureau, pages 58, 216, 217, 234, 245, 259; Bureau of Land Management, pages 14, 20, 36, 45, 202,203,267;Nevada Historical Society, pages 11, 151, 188, 206, 210, 255; Division of Parks, Nevada Department of Conservation and Natural Resources, pages 111, 158, 254; Nevada Department of Economic Development, pages 10, 63, 102, 173, 182, 183, 248, 273; Nevada State Highway Department, pages ii, xii, 1, 107, 124, 140, 162, 236; from the collection of Robert Laxalt, 57, 104; Harrah's Club, Reno, page 95.

INDEX

INDEX

275